PARTNERSHIPS FOR PROTECTION

PARTNERSHIPS FOR PROTECTION
NEW STRATEGIES FOR PLANNING AND
MANAGEMENT FOR PROTECTED AREAS

Edited by
Sue Stolton and Nigel Dudley

with
Biksham Gujja, Bill Jackson, Jean-Paul Jeanrenaud,
Gonzalo Oviedo, Pedro Rosabal, Adrian Phillips
and Sue Wells

Earthscan Publications Ltd, London

First published in the UK in 1999 by
Earthscan Publications Ltd

A catalogue record for this book is available from the British Library

ISBN: 1 85383 609 5 paperback
         1 85383 614 1 hardback

Typesetting by PCS Mapping & DTP, Newcastle upon Tyne
Printed and bound by Creative Print and Design Wales, Ebbw Vale
Cover design by John Burke

The views of the authors expressed in this book do not necessarily reflect those of
WWF or IUCN

For a full list of publications please contact:

Earthscan Publications Ltd
120 Pentonville Road
London, N1 9JN, UK
Tel: +44 (0)171 278 0433
Fax: +44 (0)171 278 1142
Email: earthinfo@earthscan.co.uk
http://www.earthscan.co.uk

Earthscan is an editorially independent subsidiary of Kogan Page Ltd and publishes in
association with WWF-UK and the International Institute for Environment and
Development

This book is printed on elemental chlorine free paper from sustainably managed
forests

CONTENTS

PART I INTRODUCTION

PART II ADOPTING NEW APPROACHES TO PROTECTED AREA SELECTION

ABOUT THE CONTRIBUTORS

Karin Beland-Lindahl is a biologist with long standing experience of the Swedish environmental movement and the Swedish forest debate. She was a founder of the Taiga Rescue Network – a network for environmental and indigenous people's organizations in the boreal region – and worked as its international coordinator for several years. Today, she runs her own consultancy, Taiga Consulting, which concentrates on information dissemination, education, research and consulting services on forest related issues, primarily, in the boreal region.

Grazia Borrini-Feyerabend was until recently Head of the Social Policy Programme of the World Conservation Union (IUCN). She developed the programme around equity and participatory considerations in natural resource management, and she is currently pursuing the same concerns as an independent consultant. Her books include *Collaborative Management of Protected Areas* (1996); *Our People, Our Resources* (1997); and *Beyond Fences: Seeking Social Sustainability in Conservation* (1997).

Peter Bridgewater is Chief Science Adviser to Environment Australia. He is a past Chair of the UNESCO Man and the Biosphere Intergovernmental Council, the International Whaling Commission, and a member of the Independent World Commission on the Oceans. His research interests are land/seascape ecology, biodiversity conservation and management, origins, dynamics and management of cultural landscapes, and conservation and management of mangrove and saltmarsh.

Jessica Brown is Vice President for International Programs at QLF/Atlantic Center for the Environment, an NGO working in rural areas of New England and eastern Canada. She is responsible for QLF's international training, technical assistance, policy research and peer exchange projects. Her work focuses on stewardship and the changing role of protected areas in society. Over the last 15 years she has worked in countries of the Caribbean, Latin America and Central Europe.

Sandra Charity has worked for WWF (UK and Brazil) for 9 years. The major focus of her work with WWF has been on the design, development, implementation and evaluation of integrated conservation-development projects in several countries in Latin America (LAC), but mainly in Brazil. She was project supervisor of the Mamirauá project on behalf of WWF for over 6 years.

Ian Cresswell graduated in Environmental Science at Murdoch University, Western Australia, with an Honours degree in Landscape Ecology. He has focused on landscape patterns and processes and has worked at local through continental scales. His current work focuses on bioregional planning, developing a national protected area database, and integrating science with policy.

Adrian G Davey is Senior Lecturer in Environment Policy & Resource Management at the Applied Ecology Research Centre in the School of Resource, Environmental & Heritage Sciences at the University of Canberra, Australia. He has extensive experience in regional land use planning, community planning, protected areas management, and land care, in a wide range of environmental and social settings. He has worked throughout Australia, but also in Africa, South and South-East Asia and the Americas. He has a background in ecology and geomorphology.

Eric Dinerstein is Chief Scientist at WWF-US and also directs its Conservation Science Program. He is leading efforts to develop effective ecoregion-based conservation strategies. Eric is also a specialist in large mammal conservation, particularly for Asian rhinoceroses and tigers.

Nigel Dudley is an ecologist and independent consultant, concentrating on issues relating to global forest conservation and management and the environmental impact of business interests. In 1991, he established Equilibrium consultancy in partnership with Sue Stolton. He is a member of the World Commission on Protected Areas and at present is working with WWF, IUCN, WCPA and WCMC to produce a system for assessing management effectiveness in protected areas.

Paul F J Eagles is a Professor in the Department of Recreation and Leisure Studies at the University of Waterloo in Canada. Professionally he is trained as a biologist and a planner. For the last 30 years he has worked in many aspects of parks and recreation planning and management. In recent years he has concentrated on the planning and management of tourism in national parks and other forms of protected areas. Professor Eagles is presently the co-chair of the Task Force on Tourism and Protected Areas, of the WCPA.

Ueta Fa'asili is the Assistant Director (Fisheries) of the Fisheries Division in Samoa and National Co-ordinator of the community-based fisheries extension project in Samoa.

Steve Gartlan, WWF Country Representative for Cameroon, is a psychologist by background, specializing in the ecology and behaviour of non-human primates. He is the author of many publications and his main interests are the philosophy of conservation, ecosystem evaluation and institutional analysis.

Meg Gawler is the Founder/Director of ARTEMIS Services, a consulting firm in France for nature conservation and human development, specializing in monitoring/evaluation, project design, and strategic planning. She began her career as a plankton ecologist in North America and Europe, and then worked for over ten years in the Africa and Madagascar Programme of WWF. She is the author of a number of conservation publications, including the *WWF Strategy for Marine and Coastal Conservation in Africa & Madagascar*.

Michael J B Green is a specialist in the design and management of protected areas. He was Head of the World Conservation Monitoring Centre (WCMC) Protected Areas Unit, Cambridge and is currently Chief Conservation Officer at the Broads Authority, Norwich.

Biksham Gujja has worked with WWF-International since 1993 and is currently the Head of the Freshwater Programme. His main areas of concern at present are issues related to dams and involving people in wetland management. Before joining WWF he was Director of Environmental programmes of the Deccan Development Society, India.

Jeremy Harrison is responsible for coordination of work on protected areas at the WCMC and also works on projects concerning the implementation of various international agreements. He joined what is now WCMC in 1981 and spent many years developing the Centre's protected areas programme before moving to lead the information services programme in 1993. Following three years in information services and a further year in capacity building and regional programmes, Jerry has returned to working more substantially on protected areas.

Will Hildesley has worked with WWF's Endangered Seas Campaign for three years, principally on the development of the Marine Stewardship Council and more recently to review WWF's work on marine protected areas, both in the US and internationally. Prior to WWF Will worked for a consultancy specializing in the resolution of international boundary conflicts. A social scientist, Will has a Masters degree in Tropical Coastal Zone Management.

Marc Hockings is Senior Lecturer at the University of Queensland, Australia, where he lectures on protected area management and environmental problem solving. Marc's research focuses on the evaluation of management programs for nature conservation. He is a member of the IUCN WCPA and Chair of the Commission's Management Effectiveness Task Force.

Tony Iacobelli is the Senior Manager of System Planning and Analysis at World Wildlife Fund Canada, working for the Endangered Spaces Campaign. His background is in biogeography and forest microclimatology. He is currently involved in protected areas planning as part of the conservation science team at WWF Canada and has completed a Canada-wide protected areas gap analysis.

Bill Jackson is the Forest Conservation Programme co-ordinator at IUCN in Switzerland. His postgraduate studies focused on collaborative management of forests in Nepal. He has extensive experience in community forestry in South and South-East Asia and in Africa and in the forest sector in Australia where he worked with State Forests of New South Wales.

Jean-Paul Jeanrenaud is head of WWF International's Forests for Life programme based in Gland, Switzerland. He has a degree in Development Studies and a Masters in Forestry and Land Management from Oxford. He has worked in Nepal, Rwanda and Cameroon, in the latter advising the government on the establishment of two rainforest reserves on the slopes of Mount Cameroon. Before moving to Switzerland he spent four years as joint head of the Forest Unit at WWF-UK.

Sally Jeanrenaud is a consultant on conservation and development issues and is based in Switzerland. She has worked on community forestry, conservation and development projects in Nepal, Rwanda and Cameroon since the beginning of the 1980s, and has recently completed a review of WWF's people-oriented forest conservation projects. She completed her doctorate at the University of East Anglia in the UK in 1998, which involved a political and institutional analysis of people-oriented conservation since the 1960s. She is currently conducting a regional profile on community involvement in forest management in Europe.

Kevin Kavanagh is currently the Director of the Endangered Spaces Campaign at WWF Canada. He formerly headed the conservation science team at WWF Canada. His background is in forest ecology and biogeography. Kevin Kavanagh has been involved in protected areas planning in Canada for the past 15 years and assisted in WWF's conservation assessment of the ecoregions of North America.

Michael King is a fisheries consultant based in Australia. He was the team leader of the Samoan community-based fishieres extension project.

Manoel Lima Feitosa is the technical advisor for the Amazon region of CNPT, Centro Nacional para o Desenvolvimento Sustentado das Populações Tradicionais (National Centre for the Sustainable Development of Traditional Communities) in Brasilia, Brazil.

Don Masterson is currently the Latin America & Caribbean Forest Coordinator for WWF-US. He worked on the development of the Mamirauá Management Plan first as a consultant (1994), and later (1996–97) on a Brazilian National Science Council scholarship. He has a BSc in Natural Resouce Management from the State University of New York Environmental Science and Forestry School (1978) and a Masters in Forestry from Yale University (1984).

Jeffrey A McNeely is Chief Scientist at IUCN in Gland, Switzerland, where he has worked since 1980. He worked in various parts of Asia from 1969 to 1980, including 7 years in Thailand, 3 years in Indonesia, and 2 years in Nepal working on a wide range of conservation topics. He has written or edited over 30 books and is on the editorial board of 8 international journals.

Kenton R Miller is Vice President, International Development and Conservation, at the World Resources Institute (WRI) in Washington DC. His studies include a Bachelor and Master of Science in Forestry, and PhD in Forest

Economics, with specialized work in tropical ecology and wildland management. His career has included research, graduate teaching, and technical assistance in wildland management through positions with FAO, the University of Michigan, and as Director General of IUCN. Presently he is Senior Advisor to the World Commission on Protected Areas, and evaluator for the Scientific and Technical Advisory Panel of the Global Environment Fund. He has published in the fields of national park and reserve management, training, biodiversity conservation, bioregional planning, and decentralization.

Brent Mitchell is Director, Stewardship at QLF/Atlantic Center for the Environment, where he has worked for the past 12 years. For five years prior to joining the staff of QLF he worked on conservation projects in five countries of Latin America and the Caribbean. His work in private land conservation in eastern Canada and northern New England now informs efforts to promote land stewardship in Central Europe, Latin America and the Caribbean.

David M Olson is a conservation biologist with the Conservation Science Program of WWF-US. This programme has undertaken extensive analyses of global patterns of biodiversity and threats to identify conservation priorities. Developing conservation strategies for entire ecoregions has been emphasized. Mapping the world's terrestrial, freshwater, and marine ecoregions has been an important part of this process.

Gonzalo Oviedo is the head of the People & Conservation Unit at WWF International, in charge of coordinating issues related to conservation with indigenous peoples and local communities for WWF. He is an anthropologist and protected areas specialist and is a member of the WCPA.

Adrian Phillips is currently Chair of IUCN's WCPA. He has been a staff member of UNEP and IUCN, and for 11 years headed up a UK official conservation agency, the Countryside Commission.

James Paine was Senior Research Officer at WCMC, specializing in protected areas. He now runs a plant nursery in Norfolk.

Rafael Pinzón Rueda is the director of CNPT, Centro Nacional para o Desenvolvimento Sustentado das Populações Tradicionais (National Centre for the Sustainable Development of Traditional Communities) in Brasilia, Brazil.

Pedro Rosabal is a Geographer and MSc in Landscape Ecology with 18 years of experience in the field of protected area planning and management. He was involved in a number of protected area projects in Cuba and from 1989 to 1994 he co-ordinated protected areas as part of the National Commission for the Environment of Cuba. From 1990 to 1993 he was a member of the Technical Advisory Committee for the Protocol concerning Specially Protected Areas and Wildlife (SPAW) of the Caribbean Environment Programme of UNEP. He is a WCPA member since 1991 and from 1986 to 1993 he was member of the FAO's Technical Network on Protected Areas for Latin America and the Caribbean. He joined IUCN in 1994 as Programme Officer of the Programme on Protected Areas/WCPA.

Jeffrey A Sayer is an ecologist who has worked throughout the tropics on issues related to nature conservation, mainly in tropical forests. From 1985 to 1992 he headed the Tropical Forest Conservation Programme of IUCN in Switzerland. For the last six years he has been Director General of the Center for International Forestry Research, based in Bogor, Indonesia; he also holds the Prince Bernhard Chair of International Nature Conservation at the University of Utrecht in the Netherlands. He has published extensively on nature conservation issues in developing tropical countries.

Paul Sochaczewski is an independent journalist and communications coach. He ran WWF International's global public awareness campaigns, and their faith and environment network, for 14 years. Prior to moving to Switzerland he lived for 12 years in Southeast Asia, where he co-authored *Soul of the Tiger: Searching for Nature's Answers in Southeast Asia*, with Jeff McNeely.

Sue Stolton established Equilibrium Consultants with Nigel Dudley in 1991. Her experience covers research, writing and editing. In the boreal region she works with the Taiga Rescue Network, editing their newsletter *Taiga News*. She is a member of the WCPA and is currently working on a project with WWF, IUCN, WCPA and WCMC to produce a system for assessing management effectiveness in protected areas.

Gustavo Suárez de Freitas is the director of the Fundación Pro Naturaleza – The Peruvian Foundation for the Conservation of Nature and the regional Vice Chair for WCPA in South America.

Steve Szabo is the Director of Indigenous Policy and Coordination Section in Environment Australia. He has worked in Aboriginal Education at primary, secondary and adult education levels in remote schools in the north-west of Western Australia. His professional interests include developing and delivering Aboriginal Ranger Training programs, and developing policy and program initiatives to increase the level of participation of indigenous Australians in protected areas management.

Richard Thackway is a scientific coordinator in the Environmental Resources Information Network in Environment Australia. His professional interests include landscape ecology, bioregional planning and developing protected area systems, and development of public policy for management of natural resources and conservation programs.

Sue Wells is currently the coordinator of the Marine Programme at WWF International. Before joining WWF, she worked in Belize for two years, assisting with the establishment of marine protected areas. Previously she worked with a variety of organizations on issues relating to marine conservation, with particular emphasis on coral reefs.

A Summary of the IUCN Protected Area Categories

Category Ia: Strict nature reserve/wilderness protection area managed mainly for science of wilderness protection – an area of land and/or sea possessing some outstanding or representative ecosystems, geological or physiological features and/or species, available primarily for scientific research and/or environmental monitoring.

Category Ib: Wilderness area: protected area managed mainly for wilderness protection – large area of unmodified or slightly modified land and/or sea, retaining its natural characterstics and influence, without permanent or significant habitation, which is protected and managed to preserve its natural condition.

Category II: National park: protected area managed mainly for ecosystem protection and recreation – natural area of land and/or sea designated to (a) protect the ecological integrity of one or more ecosystems for present and future generations, (b) exclude exploitation or occupation inimical to the purposes of designation of the area and (c) provide a foundation for spiritual, scientific, educational, recreational and visitor opportunities, all of which must be environmentally and culturally compatible.

Category III: Natural monument: protected area managed mainly for conservation of specific natural features – area containing specific natural or natural/cultural feature(s) of outstanding or unique value because of their inherent rarity, representativeness or aesthetic qualities or cultural significance.

Category IV: Habitat/species management area: protected area managed mainly for conservation through management intervention – area of land and/or sea subject to active intervention for management purposes so as to ensure the maintenance of habitats to meet the requirements of specific species.

Category V: Protected landscape/seascape: protected area managed mainly for landscape/seascape conservation or recreation – area of land, with coast or sea as appropriate, where the interaction of people and nature over time has produced an area of distinct character with significant aesthetic, ecological and/or cultural value, and often with high biological diversity. Safeguarding the integrity og this traditional interaction is vital to the protection, maintenance and evolution of such as area.

Category VI: Managed resource protected area: protected area managed mainly for the sustainable use of natural resources – area containing predominantly unmodified natural systems, managed to ensure long-term protection and maintenance of biological diversity, while also providing a sustainable flow of natural products and services to meet community needs.

See Appendix 1 for a more detailed discussion of the IUCN Protected Area Categories.

FIGURES, TABLES AND BOXES

FIGURES

TABLES

BOXES

PREFACE

On the cusp of a new millennium, humanity is experiencing a transformation in our relationship with the natural world. For the first time, virtually all human communities – ranging in size from villages to groups of nation states – are recognizing that it is essential to respect non-human values within the landscape and seascape.

This book charts the progress in one particular aspect of this 'revolution' – protected areas. In the past, protected areas were viewed as isolated islands of ecological integrity in a sea in which human (and often commercial) values were predominant. This model has not proved successful. Radical developments in our approach to protected areas, and in the way we perceive land *outside* proteced areas, involve a rewriting of our relationship with nature.

Today, protected areas are increasingly seen as one tool in a much broader approach to both the conservation of biodiversity and also to the protection of a wide range of human values. As the statement adopted by the IUCN/World Commission on Protected Areas (WCPA) Symposium on Protected Areas in the 21st Century: From Islands to Networks noted:

> *We need to place protected areas in their broader context so as to demonstrate that they [also] contribute to local economies and human welfare as integral components of a productive and secure environment.*[*]

This new book, the result of a collaborative project between IUCN – the World Conservation Union, its WCPA, and the World Wide Fund For Nature, and involving many of the world's leading conservation experts, examines future directions for protected area planning and management. Specifically, the writers explore ways of ensuring that all major ecosystems are safeguarded, and of developing innovative approaches to conservation involving individuals, all aspects of civil society and governments. A common theme running through the book is the need to build partnerships with all those who have a stake in the care of land and water resources.

WWF and IUCN support these new partnerships and will ensure that they are reflected in our policy and field programmes.

David McDowell, Director General, IUCN
Claude Martin, Director General, WWF
Adrian Phillips, Chair, WCPA, IUCN

---

* IUCN (forthcoming) *Protected Areas in the 21st Century: From Islands to Networks*, conference report, Albany, Western Australia, 24–29 November 1997, IUCN, Gland

ACKNOWLEDGEMENTS

We would like to thank all the authors for their time and patience in putting together the chapters of the book and for their comments on the structure and contents of the whole volume.

In addition, we would like to thank all those at IUCN, WCPA, WWF and beyond who have commented on and supported the production of this book, including José Márcio Ayers; Oswaldo Boez; Bob Buschbacher; Rosa Maria De Sa; Holly Dublin; Andréa Finger; Charlotte de Fontaubert; Janet Gibson; Mary Lou Higgins; Per Larsson; Bing Lucas; Miriam Marmantel; Olga Nicia Nieto; Cassandra Phillips; Simon Rietbergen; Tom Rotheram; Eric Sollander; Gordon Shepherd; David Sheppard; Lee Thomas; Hernan Verscheure; Joao Paulo Viana; John Waugh and Sonia Wiedmann.

Painted storks at Bharatpur Reserve, India

Although the number of protected areas continues to increase, there is little excuse for
complacency about their future. Many are increasingly isolated and threatened
by events both inside and outside their own borders. A critical challenge
for the 21st century is to ensure that well-managed protected areas are
regarded as integral parts of the landscape and seascape.

PART I

INTRODUCTION

1   CHALLENGES FOR PROTECTED AREAS IN THE 21ST CENTURY

Nigel Dudley, Biksham Gujja, Bill Jackson,
Jean-Paul Jeanrenaud, Gonzalo Oviedo,
Adrian Phillips, Pedro Rosabel, Sue Stolton
and Sue Wells[*]

INTRODUCTION

On the face of it, the outlook for protected areas is excellent. New protected areas are being designated all over the world. In the last few years, countries as diverse as Australia, Brazil, Canada, Chile, Gabon, Greece, Russia and Sweden have announced major expansions in their protected area networks. The need for protected areas has had important backing from many institutions – perhaps most notably from the Convention on Biological Diversity. WWF's Forests for Life campaign has received pledges from 22 countries promising to set aside at least 10 per cent of their forests into protected areas by the end of the century. IUCN's World Commission on Protected Areas (WCPA) has made major advances in winning acceptance for a series of more innovative approaches to protected areas. New opportunities presented by the expansion of private protected areas, the increase in marine protected areas and the growth of ecotourism are all encouraging an expanded protected areas network.

Unfortunately, there is a downside. At the end of the 20th century, there has been some backlash against protected areas. The degree of criticism has come as a shock to many professional conservationists. Actions that were taken with the best of intentions have on occasion resulted in criticism that has undermined the status and effectiveness of protected areas. Some of the problems have resulted from a more-or-less organized movement coordinated by those who have commercial or political reasons for preventing further protection (Rowell, 1995). However, other more measured criticism has emerged from people involved in the rights of indigenous people (Colchester, 1994) or local communities (Ghimire and Pimbert, 1996). It is clear that there have been genuine clashes between the needs of biodiversity conservation and

* This chapter has benefited greatly from comments by Simon Rietbergen and Will Hildesley.

the needs of people. Matching protection priorities more closely with human needs and aspirations is increasingly being seen as an important element in conservation strategies.

At the same time, many ecosystems and species remain unprotected or inadequately protected. In addition, too many protected areas exist as 'islands' in areas where land-use changes have been profound; these have severe limitations on the long-term ability to protect biodiversity. In some countries, protected areas do not overlap very effectively with ecosystems or with the ranges of endangered species; protected areas have been set up on the most convenient rather than the most ecologically important habitats. There is still, therefore, a great deal of room for expansion of the protected area network especially in the marine environment.

It is also becoming increasingly clear that many protected areas remain at risk and that designation is often only the first step in a continuing, and sometimes unsuccessful, process of protection. The phenomenon of 'paper parks', where protected areas are designated but never implemented, is increasingly recognized. Threats from illegal incursions, poaching and fire are being matched by more subtle impacts from transboundary air pollution and climate change; indeed, many serious threats to protected areas cannot by their very nature be stopped by fences or guards. Protected areas are also being affected more generally as a result of pervasive economic changes at a global level that are reducing state revenues and increasing pressures on natural resources. Several important protected areas have recently been undermined by their own governments in order to, for example, open up new areas to extractive industries. Changes in land-use tenure, particularly in the former Soviet Union and communist countries of Eastern Europe, present both threats and opportunities for the future. More generally, we might say that protected areas are fighting hard to keep afloat over ever rougher waters. Unless they can be seen as more relevant to countries' development plans and to the needs of local people, many protected areas will, sooner of later, be overwhelmed.

Such are the challenges of the coming century. Increasing pressures, as a result of growth of consumption by the rich minority, human population growth and sometimes human migration, will put additional strain on resources. Progressive abandonment of traditional lifestyles will increase pressure for conversion of land to industrial agriculture. Private reserves and ecotourism may suffer setbacks as a result of economic conditions or changing fashions. Pressures on the environment, particularly when they involve shared resources such as water, will start to impinge upon national security. Land tenure and future funding for protected areas are both important issues that will continue to cause problems for protected areas managers into the next century (Poff, 1996). Changes in technology, information and communication, and in the structure of national and international institutions, will also all have important impacts on protected area management (McNeely, 1997).

NEW APPROACHES

If we were to sum up the lessons learned from the case studies and the experience distilled in this book, it would be that *in the future protected areas will have to be linked more effectively to sustainable development*. Protected areas

– and the people responsible for protected areas – will have to be more flexible, more responsive and more adaptable than has sometimes been the case in the past. Protected areas need to continue to *expand* both physically and philosophically, and to *connect* with each other, the wider landscape and more generally with society and the economy. A key challenge is to find ways of expanding protected areas without, for example, increasing hardship for indigenous peoples or clashing with the legitimate aspirations of other human communities.

The Santa Marta Declaration, agreed in 1997 at the First Latin American Congress on National Parks and Other Protected Areas, sums up the challenges. 'We have a new vision of protected areas that comes from considering these as strategic spaces for countries, because not only are they essential to their growth, to their future development, and to the search for suitable living conditions within those territories, but they also represent one of the main ways to protect our natural heritage' (Anon, 1997). These changes will, inevitably, mean trade-offs between biodiversity conservation and issues as diverse as human needs, and the pressures from market economies.

This book gives an overview of some new thinking about protected areas. It looks at how protected areas can be best placed within the larger framework of sustainable resource management and how their relationship to human communities is rapidly changing. It is, of necessity, partial in its coverage and many key issues – and even more examples – have had to be left out. In total, the book draws a picture of a world in which protected area managers are facing profound changes in the way that they are required to operate. Many of these changes are analogous to those affecting other natural resources, such as commercial forestry and fishery operations or agricultural enterprises: greater involvement of local people, the need to address bad management, the problems of illegal land use and so on.

At the same time, protected areas in the 21st century look set to become very exciting places. Although we identify some substantial problems, there are also enormous opportunities. These will require new approaches; some of these are summarized in Box 1.1.

BOX 1.1 NEW APPROACHES TO PROTECTED AREAS

Protected areas need to:

Expand
in size
in concept
in the number of partners involved
in vision – from island to a system

and

Connect
to each other
to the wider landscape
to society and the economy
to other countries

Many parts of the world remain poorly represented within the protected areas system. Not surprisingly, this includes many of the places with the most concentrated human populations, where natural resources are at a premium. Other obvious gaps, according to analysis of the UN list of protected areas, are in fertile lowland habitats, freshwaters, temperate grasslands and in many marine and coastal ecosystems. Two-thirds of countries protect less than 10 per cent of their territory and 13 per cent protect less than 1 per cent. Even in countries where large areas of land are protected, there may still be gaps where particular ecosystems have been omitted or underrepresented. It is easier to agree protection for marginal land or water with low human population density and little human use than it is to protect areas with a high economic value.

Particular challenges include how protected area networks can be extended into more crowded landscapes and more heavily used waters and how individual protected areas can be linked to networks. As the majority of the world's population lives near the sea, this is especially relevant in coastal regions, which have been particularly badly neglected to date.

Gaps are not only physical. There are also serious gaps in information about the current status of protected areas and in information about area, status and importance. Filling the information gaps is another crucial challenge for the next few years.

Selection

In the past, selection of protected areas was often made on scenic grounds or because of ease of availability. As a result, protected areas were not necessarily optimal in terms of biodiversity protection. Several chapters focus on selection of protected areas through, for example, gap analysis (see Chapter 6), system plans (see Chapter 10) and the use of the concept of *ecoregions* (see Chapter 5). Such approaches offer important opportunities for maximizing the effectiveness of the protected area network, particularly if used with national land-use plans as recommended by IUCN. These techniques also have to be backed up by ground-truthing, through rapid biodiversity assessment methods, use of local knowledge and participatory techniques.

At the same time, ecosystem needs have to be balanced against human needs. Theoretical models that optimize biodiversity protection will be of little use if they clash too directly with social needs or political realities. The challenges, therefore, rest both in refining methodologies in a scientific sense and in developing social methodologies for selecting and agreeing protected area locations, boundaries and categories.

Moving from site to landscape

Earlier this century, protected areas were set up mainly on land to preserve key wildlife species, habitats and 'national monuments' such as particularly striking landscapes. Such ideas were revolutionary at the time in the Western world. However, greater understanding of ecology, ecosystems and biodiversity means that we now recognize that protecting habitats in isolation is seldom a long-term solution in terms of biodiversity protection; such 'islands' of protected habitat usually degrade over time. A more robust approach is to view the protected area as an integral part of a larger landscape or seascape.

In a model that is nowadays increasingly viewed as an ideal, biodiversity protection would be a central component of any sustainable resource management plan. Strictly protected areas would be created for some specialized or particularly vulnerable species, because any management interference would put them at risk. These protected areas would be connected via a network of *corridors*, '*stepping-stones*' (places where migratory species can stop off on journeys between their chosen habitats), *buffer zones* in which management is particular sensitive to species' needs, and areas undergoing *restoration*. Other species would continue to survive in the areas subject to human use such as managed forests, farm edges, commercially fished wetlands and marine areas, and even in urban and suburban spaces.

Many conservation organizations are now stressing the importance of tackling protection issues on a wide scale. The precise scale and boundaries differ slightly – landscapes, integrated coastal management areas, bioregions, ecoregions, etc – but although the vocabulary may vary the concepts are similar. However, it is far easier to state the intention of working at this broad scale than it is to put the ideas into practice, particularly in areas already heavily used by humans. Implementing this broader approach to protection is probably the single biggest challenge facing protected area management in the next few decades. This is especially so since the protected area manager becomes only one actor among many in any landscape approach to conservation.

BUILDING ALLIANCES WITH PEOPLE

Changing attitudes towards the role of people in protected areas lies at the heart of this book. Early conservationists tended to view people as a 'problem' for wildlife. Later, as a result of a changing political perspective within the environmental movement, and of pressure from human rights groups, attitudes began to change. People started to be viewed differently, first rather simplistically as a 'resource' and then, gradually, as 'partners' in a wider effort towards sustainable management (see Chapter 14). Today, there is a growing understanding that conservation objectives have to be addressed *alongside* human needs if either is to make significant progress.

Most large protected areas have people living inside their boundaries (see, for example, Amend and Amend, 1995) and many more have local populations just outside the protected area limits. A key challenge for protected area managers is to find ways in which human needs can be better integrated with the needs of wildlife, biodiversity and the wider environment. This includes both the needs of local or indigenous people and the needs of people living far away from a protected area in towns and cities, but who nonetheless have a stake in its future.

We do not start from a state of complete ignorance. There have already been many successful attempts to integrate human and non-human needs within the landscape. For example, the philosophy of national parks in many parts of Western Europe is based on mixing social and conservation values. Marine protected areas in many parts of the world are integrated very closely with the local needs of fishing communities and others. WWF and IUCN/WCPA are developing guidelines on protected areas establishment in indigenous peoples' territory, based on policies on indigenous peoples that both institutions have adopted (see Chapter 11). The rapid development of ecotourism is another manifestation of this approach. However, there are other examples where conflict and bitterness still remain. Engaging local people in protected area designation and management requires new skills, and sometimes also new attitudes, amongst managers and communities. Experience suggests that protected areas established in the face of fierce opposition from local communities are unlikely to survive intact.

These issues also have important implications for allocation of resources to protected areas and to their links with governments and other financing mechanisms. In situations where protected areas are competing for land and resources – which is the norm – they need to demonstrate their value to the wider community.

SEEKING NEW PARTNERS AND ACCOMMODATING NEW INSTITUTIONS

These changes are so profound that they cannot be tackled by protected area managers working in isolation – indeed, a big challenge is to break down the barriers that lead to the isolation of such places. New partnerships, with local people, private initiatives, industry, tourism operators, resource users such as fisherfolk and hunters, development agencies, human rights groups, religious organizations, local government and the general public are increasingly important. Even in the case of partners that have a clear link to protected areas, such as tourism operators, much work remains to be done to maximize benefits and minimize costs to protective functions (Bensted-Smith and Cobb, 1995).

Protected areas exist, as we all do, in a world where institutions and political structures are rapidly changing. The state is generally becoming politically weaker and assuming a regulatory role with less direct involvement in either land ownership or management. Private corporations are growing more powerful, as are international trade bodies, non-governmental organizations (NGOs), local government and to some extent the wider international community represented by treaties, conventions, multigovernment initiatives and UN agencies. State power is being increasingly ceded: *downwards* to municipal and local government, *upwards* to international organizations and *outwards* to private industry and NGOs. The government still has a key role to play in setting and implementing standards, in providing capacity and resources and in catalysing action. However, these changes have reduced the power of many governments to enact meaningful protected area legislation or to set aside larger areas for protection. On the other hand, they have opened up new possibilities, of private protected areas, new forms of protection or comanagement agreements and transboundary protected areas.

The involvement of industry in owning or contributing to protected areas is also a new and important option. Voluntary codes, certification systems and management agreements provide the start of a framework for bringing such areas into national planning. However, these changes also create considerable challenges. For example, the long-term future of private reserves is often uncertain.

DEVELOPING NEW MODELS AND FACING NEW CHALLENGES

Several of the contributions discuss the opportunities presented by wider definitions of protected areas, represented in particular by IUCN Categories V and VI. At the same time, deliberately promoting a looser definition of protected areas poses some new risks, giving the opportunity for deliberate misrepresentation and undermining of protected areas. During the preparation of this book, for example, the World Commission on Protected Areas decided to make it clear that commercial clearcutting of forests was not acceptable within any protected areas, following attempts to argue that this was an appropriate form of management in certain categories. A global system of classifying protected areas is necessary to reduce confusion about terminology, to provide international standards and to help global and regional accounting of conservation gains and needs. More fundamentally, it can help demonstrate the importance of wider approaches to protected areas and can encourage governments to adopt these within systems tailored to national and local circumstances (Phillips, 1998). However, it is fair to say that there is still debate within conservation organizations about the application of these broader definitions, although in general there is an increasing tendency to adopt the wider view of protected areas along the lines of the IUCN categories.

This poses two urgent challenges. Firstly, there is still some way to go in explaining the concepts of the IUCN protected area categories, both inside and outside the world of conservation. Simple explanatory material and presentations to key groups could help this process. Secondly, there is a need to clarify and amplify the definitions themselves. Current efforts to develop a set of guidelines on mining in and near protected areas are an important indication of the kind of refinement that is needed. So too are the efforts to increase the understanding about the range of functions that protected areas are expected to fulfil, such as watershed protection, the extractive reserves being developed in the Amazon and fisheries management in many regions.

Improving management and implementation

Selection and designation are only the start of a long process towards effective protection. Many protected areas are protected in name only – so-called 'paper parks' – and continue to be degraded by illegal use or because governments do not take the designations seriously. (Indeed, in some countries protected areas have clearly been set up to protect a resource such as timber or minerals rather than to protect wildlife, whatever the claims made by governments.) Perhaps even more important than adding to the protected area network is the question of *implementation*. In countries where money is scarce, implementation often relies on outside assistance, both to develop management plans and to build up capacity and infrastructure. However, even in the richest countries, protected areas sometimes fail badly as a result of official indifference or inability.

Lack of capacity and resources, and sometimes also lack of political will, means that many protected areas are suffering degradation. Sometimes this is because of poor planning or insufficient regard for human rights – for example, when local people are expelled from their traditional lands and have little option but to continue using protected areas illegally. In other cases, damage comes from encroachment by commercial timber extractors, bushmeat or trophy poachers, illegal fishing operations, uncontrolled fires, coral or turtle egg collectors, poorly designed tourist facilities, mining operations and oil drilling. Many illegal users deliberately target protected areas because they are easier to steal natural resources from than private lands. Governments sometimes change the rules to increase access to commercial operations such as mining or oil companies, in extreme circumstances eliminating the protected area designation altogether. For example, the Venezuelan government has been attempting to open up many protected areas to mining.

There is also a growing recognition that more effort needs to be put into measuring the *effectiveness of management* in protected areas, to protect against degradation and the paper park phenomenon. Some options are examined later in the book. They vary from national, government-run systems for monitoring how well protected areas are being run to regional or international systems of monitoring, verification or even certification (see Chapter 27). Some are linked to NGO targets for conservation. Some proposals aim to increase pressure on those governments that are failing to make adequate arrangements to manage their protected area systems. It is clear that addressing this issue will define the extent to which protected areas succeed in protecting biodiversity.

Restoration of what has been lost

So far, most protected areas have focused on saving existing habitats. However, in several parts of the world whole ecosystems have already declined to the extent that there are no longer large enough areas left to provide the basis of a comprehensive network. Here, some form of restoration becomes important, and there is increasing recognition of the need for protected areas to provide space for *recreation* of habitat. This can include, for example, reflooding of drained land, restoration of forests, protection of marine areas to allow fish stocks to recover, and sometimes also elimination of invasive species. This restoration function is likely to increase in importance. It is recognised in category IV of the IUCN protected area categories. Restoration within protected areas often, but not invariably, assumes a higher level of management intervention than in other protected areas.

Protecting against pollution problems

Degradation as a result of human activity can also come from distant sources. Air pollution now exceeds *critical loads* – the levels of pollution that the ecosystem can absorb without experiencing damage – in many of Europe's protected areas (Tickle et al, 1995). Pollution is damaging some marine protected areas. Climate change also threatens many other protected areas as a result of such impacts as temperature changes, sea-level rise and increased pest and disease attack (Malcolm and Markham, 1997). Addressing such changes relies ultimately on reducing pollution at source and on placing protected area management within a wider development framework. On the other hand, the threats increase the need for some of the other changes suggested above. If species have to migrate because of changing climatic conditions, such elements of protected areas network as corridors and stepping-stones become increasingly necessary. There is also good evidence that large, stable blocks of habitat are better able to withstand rapid environmental change than are small and fragmented relics, which adds new arguments for completing and managing viable protecting area networks. Protected areas can also act as buffers against rapidly changing climatic conditions, for example the use of mangroves to protected against sea-level rise and maintenance of forests to protect human communities against violent climatic events.

SETTING PROTECTED AREAS WITHIN THE CONTEXT OF SUSTAINABLE MANAGEMENT

Protected areas should be one part of a larger portfolio of sustainable resource use. Protection would therefore be graded from strictly protected core reserves, through a range of relatively 'soft' management uses to areas where human needs predominate and there is relatively little emphasis on protecting wildlife. Although the concept of buffer zones and support zones around protected areas has been recognized for some time (Sayer, 1991), a range of other soft options is now becoming available, such as sustainable forest management, leisure fishing, organic agriculture, low-level collection of non-timber forest products and ecotourism.

Most people instinctively expect some such combination of resource uses. Although we tend to think of protected areas as a relatively new phenomenon, this is a rather simplified view. Under IUCN's definition, protected areas include many uses, such as customary tenure, that have been accepted for centuries.

It is inevitable that in many places planning will continue in a fairly piece-meal fashion, as a result of individual choices. Here, protected areas have to be established through negotiation, purchase, leasing arrangements and so on. However, in other areas, communities are already stating a preference for working together to achieve sustainable use of their land and water resources, and in many cases this includes protected areas. This philosophy stresses the concept of wider *environmental quality* – which includes social, cultural and economic values alongside ecological ones. Experiments ranging in size from the Meso-American Biological Corridor, through comanagement of catchment areas in British Columbia, to small-scale community forest management initiatives in Scotland are all looking at ways of integrating protection with sustainable use. Although none of these attempts are perfect – protection will never equal utopia – in many ways they represent the ideal combination of the various elements described in this book.

REFERENCES

Amend, S and Amend, T (1995) *National Parks Without People? The South American experience*, IUCN, Gland

Anon (1997) *Santa Marta Declaration: First Latin American Congress on National Parks and Other Protected Areas: Santa Marta, Colombia, May 21–24 1997*, IUCN, FAO and others

Bensted-Smith, R and Cobb, S (1995) 'Reform of protected area institutions in Africa' *Parks* 5(3):3–19

Colchester, M (1994) *Salvaging Nature: Indigenous peoples, protected areas and biodiversity conservation*, UNRISD, World Rainforest Movement and WWF, Geneva

Ghimire, K B and Pimbert, M P (eds) (1996) *Social Change and Conservation: Environmental politics and impacts of national parks and protected areas*, Earthscan, London

IUCN (forthcoming) *Protected Areas in the 21st Century: From Islands to Networks*, conference report, Albany, Western Australia, 24–29 November 1997, IUCN, Gland

Malcolm, J and Markham, A (1997) *Climate Change Threats to the National Parks and Protected Areas of the United States and Canada*, WWF US, Washington DC

McNeely, J (1997) *Conservation and the Future: Trends and options towards the year 2025*, IUCN, Gland

Phillips, A (1998) 'The thinking behind the IUCN management categories for protected areas', paper given at the International IUCN Seminar on the Classification of Protected Areas, Helsinki, Finland, 11 September 1998

Poff, C (1996) *Protected Area Management Options for the Next Century*, unpublished working document for IUCN/WCPA

Rowell, A (1995) *Green Backlash*, Routledge, London

Sayer, J (1991) *Rainforest Buffer Zones: Guidelines for protected area managers*, IUCN, Gland

Tickle, A, Fergusson, M and Drucker, G (1995) *Acid Rain and Nature Conservation in Europe*, WWF International, Gland

2 THE FRAMEWORK FOR INTERNATIONAL STANDARDS IN ESTABLISHING NATIONAL PARKS AND OTHER PROTECTED AREAS*

Adrian Phillips and Jeremy Harrison

INTRODUCTION

Virtually every country in the world has legal or customary measures for conserving or protecting biodiversity through management control over defined areas of land or sea. However, the objectives for establishing and managing these areas range widely, and responsibility for management may rest with organizations as diverse as statutory authorities or non-governmental organizations. These protected areas are found in countries of every political, cultural, social, and economic background and with a vast range of physical circumstances, ranging from small and crowded to large and relatively unpopulated.

The data base on protected areas managed by the World Conservation Monitoring Centre (WCMC) includes tens of thousands of sites varying in size from a few hectares to millions of hectares (see Appendix 2). There are more than 200 different designations used to describe these areas, ranging from the familiar terms national park and wildlife sanctuary to the less familiar Muttonbird Reserve and *Zapovednik*. To add to this confusion, even familiar terms such as national park mean different things in different countries.

Some 20 years ago, protected area professionals working with the International Union for Conservation of Nature and Natural Resources (IUCN) developed a series of protected area categories defined by management objectives (IUCN, 1978). However, over the years, the role of protected areas in both biodiversity conservation and sustainable development has been widely appreciated (McNeely and Miller, 1984; McNeely, 1993), leading to some significant changes in protected area management. This resulted in a need to review the ways in which protected areas are categorized.

During the late 1980s and early 1990s protected area professionals working with the IUCN Commission on National Parks and Protected Areas

* Originally published in *The George Wright Forum* (1997, Vol14, No 2, pp 29–38), the quarterly journal of The George Wright Society. Used by permission.

(CNPPA), now known as the World Commission on Protected Areas (WCPA), thoroughly reviewed the issue, and at the Fourth World Congress on National Parks and Protected Areas, held in Caracas, Venezuela (1992), confirmed a number of changes to the system previously developed by IUCN. The results of the discussions in Caracas are reported on by McNeely (1993), in particular Recommendation 17 and the report of Workshop IV.1, 'Talking the same language: an international review system for protected areas'. The revised system was approved by the IUCN General Assembly at Buenos Aires in 1994, and details of revised categories were then published in the *IUCN Guidelines for Protected Area Management Categories* (IUCN, 1994). The six categories are summarized on pages xiv–xv and discussed in more detail in Appendix 1.

DEFINITION OF A PROTECTED AREA

In order to be able to categorize protected areas, one must first define what constitutes a protected area. The IUCN protected areas management category system is based on the following definition, agreed at the Fourth World Congress on National Parks and Protected Areas (IUCN, 1993). A protected area is:

> *An area of land and/or sea especially dedicated to the protection and maintenance of biological diversity, and of natural and associated cultural resources, and managed through legal or other effective means.*

Conceptually, this definition encompasses all protected areas and there should be no protected areas outside this definition. All protected areas within this definition should fall within one of the six defined categories. On the other hand, there may be sites that meet the criteria for a particular category, but which do not qualify as a protected area because they do not fall within the definition given above.

CATEGORIZATION BY MANAGEMENT OBJECTIVE

Definitions of protected area management categories represent a compromise between the needs and situations of countries around the world. Understandably, they are not a perfect fit for all areas, but serve as a guide for interpretation and application at the regional and national levels. Protected areas are categorized according to their management objectives. This type of classification system serves a number of valuable purposes in the international context since it:

- emphasizes the importance of protected areas;
- demonstrates the range of purposes which protected areas serve;
- promotes the idea of protected areas as systems rather than as units in isolation;
- reduces confusion of terminology;

- provides an agreed set of international standards;
- facilitates international comparison and accounting; and
- improves communication and understanding.

The basis of categorization is by primary management objective: this principle is the most important of all. There are, in fact, a wide variety of potential primary management objectives for protected areas, and many areas have multiple objectives. Categorization is made according to the priority assigned to relevant objectives, as demonstrated in the following matrix (Table 2.1). At least three-quarters of the area should be managed for the primary purpose.

Table 2.1 *Potential primary management objectives, by category of protected area*

Objectives	Ia	Ib	II	III	IV	V	VI
Scientific research	1	3	2	2	2	2	3
Wilderness protection	2	1	2	3	3	NA	2
Preserve species and genetic diversity	1	2	1	1	1	2	1
Maintain environmental services	2	1	1	NA	1	2	1
Protection of natural/ cultural features	NA	NA	2	1	3	1	3
Tourism and recreation	NA	2	1	1	3	1	3
Education	NA	NA	2	2	2	2	3
Sustainable use of natural ecosystems	NA	3	3	NA	2	2	1
Maintain cultural/ traditional attributes	NA	NA	NA	NA	NA	1	2

1 = Primary Objective
2 = Secondary Objective
3 = Acceptable Objective
NA = Objective Not Applicable

Assignment to a category is not a comment on management effectiveness: the distinction between the primary management objective and the effectiveness of management is often overlooked. For instance, where Category II areas are poorly managed, there is a temptation to reclassify them as Category V areas. This is not the intent of the IUCN guidelines, which categorize by management objective. There are, in fact, two separate questions involved. Firstly, 'what is the aim of management?', which leads to assignment of a category, and secondly, 'how well is the area managed?', which leads to an assessment of management effectiveness.

The categories system is international. The IUCN categories system has been designed for global use. The guidance is therefore broad and general rather than being prescriptive and specific. The system is intended to be interpreted flexibly. Because the IUCN classification system is based on broad guidelines, it is right that regions or countries should interpret them for their own applications. This flexibility allows national relevance to be built into the system through processes such as national and regional workshops, and the development of 'rules of thumb' for application in different areas.

National (or state) names may vary. Throughout the world there are hundreds of different national names for protected areas. The IUCN guidelines are not intended to result in the renaming of these reserves. National names will therefore continue to mean different things in different countries. It also follows that national names and titles of international categories will often differ.

All categories are important: all categories are equally important and equally relevant to conservation. The categories indicate the necessity of developing systems of protected areas which use all the relevant categories. It should be noted, however, that some countries may not contain the potential for using all categories; for example, England does not contain wilderness.

The categories imply a gradient of human intervention: The IUCN categories imply a gradation of human intervention (Figure 2.1), ranging from effectively none at all in the case of some Category I areas, to quite high levels of intervention in Category V areas. Since Category VI was added to the system later it does not fit neatly into the general pattern, but lies conceptually between III and IV.

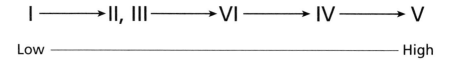

Figure 2.1 *Human intervention, by category*

CONCLUSIONS

No classification system is perfect, and its value really depends not so much on whether each protected area can be 'allocated' to one of the six categories without doubt or difficulty, but on whether the objectives of categorization are met. Experience since the publication of the new guidelines (IUCN, 1994) suggests that this process has certainly led to increased assessment of the roles of protected areas, and how protected areas with different roles and objects relate to one another.

For example, following publication of the guidelines, the Australian Nature Conservation Authority worked with state authorities in Australia to convene a workshop on application of the categories. This led to the development of guidelines and rules of thumb for applying the categories in Australia (ANCA, 1996). Perhaps more importantly it brought together the various state and federal authorities to review how the roles and objectives of protected areas varied throughout the country. Similar guidance is currently under development in Europe.

There is particular interest in Categories V and VI, the former because it is probably underused as a management category, and the latter because it is a new category and as such is resulting in increased controversy and debate. Some of the issues were discussed at a Global Biodiversity Forum in Montreal in 1996, and an attempt to focus attention on how these relate to forest conservation has been drafted by Dudley and Stolton (1998). However these debates resolve themselves, the primary purpose of categorization will have been achieved, as increased attention is given to the role of protected areas in helping to achieve conservation and development goals.

REFERENCES

ANCA (Australian Nature Conservation Agency) (1996) *Application of IUCN Protected Area Management Categories*, Draft Australian Handbook, Australian Nature Conservation Agency, Canberra

Dudley, N, and Stolton, S (1998) *Protected areas for a new millennium: The implications of IUCN's protected area categories for forest conservation*, WWF and IUCN, Gland

IUCN (1978) *Categories, objectives and criteria for protected areas*, IUCN, Gland

IUCN (1994) *Guidelines for Protected Area Management Categories*, CNPPA with the assistance of WCMC, IUCN, Gland and Cambridge

McNeely, J A, and Miller, K R (eds) (1984) *National Parks, Conservation and Development: The Role of Protected Areas in Sustaining Society*, Smithsonian Institution Press, Washington DC

McNeely, J A (1993) *Parks for Life: Report of the Fourth World Congress on National Parks and Protected Areas*, IUCN, Gland

3 STATE OF THE WORLD'S PROTECTED AREAS AT THE END OF THE 20TH CENTURY[*]

Michael J B Green and James Paine

INTRODUCTION

Protected areas are widely held to be among the most effective means of conserving biological diversity in situ. A considerable amount of resources has been invested in their establishment over the last century or more, with the result that most countries have established or, at least, planned national systems of protected areas. The purpose of this chapter is to examine the extent of the world's protected areas globally and regionally and to consider options for their further strengthening and development during the 21st century.

HOW ARE DATA ON THE WORLD'S PROTECTED AREAS MANAGED?

Historically, the collation of data on the world's protected areas was initiated by the IUCN Commission on National Parks and Protected Areas (CNPPA), partly in response to two resolutions of the United Nations which recognized the importance of protected areas in the wise use of natural resources and led to the compilation of the first *World List of National Parks and Equivalents*

---

[*] This chapter is an abridged version of a paper presented to the IUCN World Commission on Protected Areas Symposium on Protected Areas in the 21st Century: From Islands to Networks (Green and Paine, 1997). That paper benefited from input by Adrian Phillips, Pedro Rosabal, Graeme Kelleher and John Cooper.
The data set used is the same as that used for the 1997 *United Nations List of Protected Areas* (IUCN, 1998); it includes protected areas known to have been established up to the end of 1996. (As such it takes no account of the ratification of the Environmental Protection Protocol to the Antarctic Treaty in December 1997, whereby the entire continent and its dependent marine ecosystem have been designated as a natural reserve.) The only difference is that, whereas the analysis of protected areas for the 1997 UN list is restricted to listed sites greater than 1000 hectares, the present analysis includes all protected areas irrespective of their size. Nationally designated areas which do not qualify as protected areas *sensu* IUCN are excluded from the data set.

Reserves in 1961/1962. In 1981 the former CNPPA established the Protected Areas Data Unit to manage the ever increasing amount of data on protected areas. This unit subsequently became part of the World Conservation Monitoring Centre, which maintains a data base and geographic information system (GIS) on the world's protected areas.

The *WCMC Protected Areas Data Base* (see Appendix 2) currently holds some 30,350 records of protected areas, as well as 13,915 records of other designated areas which do not qualify as protected areas according to the IUCN definition, and a further 16,288 records of areas of uncertain status. Data are validated by comparing with existing records and other information held by WCMC, and entered into the data base as appropriate. The successor to CNPPA, the World Commission on Protected Areas (WCPA), is involved as necessary in the validation process, particularly with respect to the assignment of IUCN management categories to protected area designations for which it is ultimately responsible.

The entire database is regularly updated, in particular every three years, to facilitate production of new editions of the *United Nations List of Protected Areas* (see Appendix 2) in synchrony with each IUCN General Assembly (renamed in 1996 as the World Conservation Congress). In European countries, a different mechanism is now used to collect protected areas data. A collaborative partnership was formed in 1996 between the Council of Europe, the European Environment Agency (EEA) and WCMC whereby the three organizations agreed to integrate their existing protected areas data bases into a single *Common Data Base of Designated Areas in Europe*.

CONSTRAINTS IN USING THE DATA

The data set used in this analysis is subject to the following limitations:

- Inevitably the dataset is not entirely complete. Of the 512 management agencies contacted, only 180 responded, despite reminders sent to non-respondents.
- The size is unknown for 2942 protected areas, which means that the extent of regional and global protected areas networks are somewhat underrepresented.
- The date of establishment is unknown for 6446 protected areas.
- The new IUCN management categories have been applied for the first time. It is likely, therefore, that not all protected areas have been allocated to the most appropriate category. This is particularly true for national parks in European countries, for which additional time and resources are needed to review many of them on a site-by-site basis.
- The geographical coordinates or, more importantly, the boundaries of over 20,000 protected areas are unknown, limiting the extent to which terrestrial and marine protected areas can be treated separately or compared, and constraining analyses of the representativeness of protected areas.

It should also be recognized that the data set does not include privately owned or managed protected areas which, in some countries, are very extensive.

GLOBAL PROTECTED AREAS NETWORK

Growth in number and extent

The world's network of 30,350 protected areas extends over a total area of 13,232,275 km², which represents 8.83 per cent of total land area. However, this percentage needs to be treated judiciously because it is inflated perhaps one percentage point or more by the large number of marine protected areas or protected areas having a marine component. The network is extensive from a global perspective, but there are many gaps at the national level.

The number and extent of the global network of protected areas have grown steadily throughout the latter part of this century. The number of protected areas established declined somewhat in the most recent five-year period for which data are complete (1990–1994), compared to the previous decade. However, there is little or no evidence of any decline during the most recent five-year period, contradicting a widely held view that opportunities to expand the network are diminishing. This indicates that there are continuing efforts by governments to establish new protected areas. Moreover, there is a discrepancy between the slight decline in the number of new protected areas and the continued growth in the extent of the network, which suggests that increasing emphasis is being placed on establishing larger protected areas.

Size

Conservation biology theory advocates that protected areas should be as large as possible in order to:

* maximize the degree to which their contents retain their integrity;
* minimize risks of species' extinctions; and
* maximize representation of ecological communities and their constituent species (Soule, 1983; Wilcox, 1984).

Given that protected areas are often islands of natural or near-natural habitat in a sea of humanity, the larger they are, the better they are buffered from outside pressures. However, 17,892 (59 per cent) protected areas are less than 1000 hectares in size and they account for a total area of 28,713 km², which is only 0.2 per cent of the global protected areas network. Just 1673 (6 per cent) protected areas exceed 1000 km², but they comprise 11.56 million km² or 87 per cent of the global network.

In practice, many protected areas are effectively much larger because they lie adjacent to other protected areas. It is possible to assess the effective size of such protected area complexes using GIS techniques. The results of an analysis of 8055 protected areas whose boundaries have been digitized show that the mean size of adjacent protected areas is effectively increased almost three-fold, from 3765 hectares to 9368 hectares, through their juxtaposition. Many of these protected area complexes lie across international borders, highlighting the important role of transfrontier cooperation in increasing the effective size of conservation areas.

Marine and terrestrial protected areas

As noted above, it is not yet possible to quantify precisely the marine and terrestrial components of the global network of protected areas since digital boundary data are not available for all sites. The two largest marine protected areas are Greenland National Park (972,000 km^2). which is largely terrestrial, and Great Barrier Reef Marine Park (344,800 km^2), which is predominantly marine in character. With the inclusion of Great Barrier Reef Marine Park as marine and exclusion of Greenland National Park, the total area of marine protected areas is 1,580,609 km^2 and that of terrestrial protected areas is 11,65 1,666 km^2, the latter representing 7.78 per cent of the world's total land area.

Categories of management

Table 3.1 summarizes the distribution of protected areas with respect to management objectives, based on IUCN management categories. In general, it is evident that the wide spectrum of services provided by protected areas is fairly well represented within the global network. The exception is Category III which is least widely applied, a reflection of its more limited role in conserving specific natural features.

Most numerous is Category IV, comprising over one third of protected areas, indicating the importance of active management intervention in maintaining biodiversity. These tend to be among the smaller sites, established for habitat and species conservation.

Most extensive in terms of total area are Categories II and VI, reflecting their respective roles in protecting and providing for sustainable use of natural ecosystems. Although fewer in number, in total area they account for 57 per cent of the global network of protected areas due their often much larger size.

Table 3.1 *Global protected areas network classified by IUCN management Category*

IUCN management Category	Number	Per cent	Extent (km^2)	Per cent
Ia	4389	14%	978,698	7%
Ib	809	3%	940,360	7%
II	3384	11%	4,001,605	30%
III	2122	7%	193,021	1%
IV	11,171	37%	2,459,703	19%
V	5578	18%	1,057,448	8%
VI	2897	10%	3,601,440	27%
Total	30,350	100%	13,232,275	99%

Representation of biomes

Most biomes remain under-represented within the protected areas network, based on the 10 per cent target established for the protection of biomes at the

Fourth World Parks Congress (IUCN, 1993). Despite constraints with the data (see Table 3.2) it is fairly certain that evergreen sclerophyllous, temperate and needle-leaf forests are far short of the 10 per cent target, together with deserts. Least well represented are temperate grasslands and lake systems, with only 1 per cent of these biomes protected.

Table 3.2 *Extent of protection of the world's major biomes*

Biome	Total area (km²)	Number of protected areas	Extent of protected areas (km²)	% Biome protected
Tropical humid forest	10,513,210	1030	922,453	8.77%
Subtropical/temperate rainforest/woodlands	3,930,979	977	404,497	10.29%
Temperate needle-leaf forests/woodlands	15,682,817	1492	897,375	5.72%
Tropical dry forests/ woodlands	17,312,538	1290	1,224,566	7.07%
Temperate broadleaf forests	11,216,659	3905	403,298	3.60%
Evergreen sclerophyllous forests	3,757,144	1469	164,883	4.39%
Warm deserts/semi- deserts	24,279,843	605	1,173,025	4.83%
Cold-winter deserts	9,250,252	290	546,168	5.90%
Tundra communities	22,017,390	171	1,845,188	8.38%
Tropical grasslands/ savannas	4,264,832	100	316,465	7.42%
Temperate grasslands	8,976,591	495	88,127	0.98%
Mixed mountain systems	10,633,145	2766	967,130	9.10%
Mixed island systems	3,252,563	1980	530,676	16.32%
Lake systems	517,695	66	5814	1.12%
Total	145,605,658	16,636	9,489,665	6.52%

Source: adapted from Udvardy's biogeographical classification, Udvardy, 1975
Note: This analysis underrepresents the protection of biomes by about 30 per cent because only 16,636 (55 per cent) of the 30,350 protected areas have been classified. Their total area is nearly 9.5 million km², which represents just over 70 per cent of the global protected areas network.

REGIONAL PROTECTED AREAS NETWORKS

WCPA is divided into 15 regions for operational purposes (Antarctic, Australia/New Zealand, Caribbean, Central America, East Asia, Europe, North Africa/Middle East, North America, North Eurasia, Pacific, South America, South Asia, South East-Asia, Southern and Eastern Africa and Western and Central Africa), each region comprising a number of countries with their respective marine and terrestrial protected areas.

Growth in number and extent

There are many gaps in the extent of protected areas at the national level. An analysis of protected areas systems in 225 countries and dependent territories showed that while 77 (34 per cent) of such systems cover more than 10 per cent of total land area and 49 (22 per cent) exceed 5 per cent, 53 (24 per cent) of systems cover less than 5 per cent, a further 32 (14 per cent) are below 1 per cent of total land area, and a few countries have yet to establish protected area systems, namely Andorra, Comoros, Equatorial Guinea, Guinea-Bissau, Syria and Yemen, and the island territories of Cape Verde, Maldives, Marshall Islands, Micronesia, and São Tomé and Principe. Protected areas are also absent from the dependent territories of St Pierre and Miquelon (France), Macao (Portugal) and Anguilla (UK).

Size and categories of management

Political, socioeconomic, geographical and ecological differences between WCPA regions are reflected in the size and management objectives of protected areas. Fewer but larger protected areas tend to be found in the tropical developing regions of Africa and South America and in North Africa/Middle East and North Eurasia. Opportunities for establishing large protected areas are clearly much more limited in the islands of the Pacific and in Europe, with its much earlier history of industrial development.

From the distribution of protected areas with respect to IUCN management categories, some key observations include the following.

- Two-thirds of the protected areas network in North Africa/Middle East are represented by Category VI, although there are numerous smaller sites in Categories IV and V. Category Ib is poorly represented, with only three wilderness sites.
- Over half of Europe's protected areas network comprises Category V, reflecting the landscapes that have developed as a result of the interaction of people with nature over many centuries. More extensive representation of Categories Ib and VI is desirable but opportunities are limited in many countries.
- There is a very real and challenging opportunity to promote Category Ib in the Antarctic, following the recent ratification of the Environmental Protection Protocol to the Antarctic Treaty.
- Category VI is particularly applicable to the Pacific but many of the other categories are poorly represented. Not surprisingly, Category Ib is completely unrepresented. Application of a wider range of categories to this region needs careful consideration.
- By contrast to the Pacific, the categories are more widely applied in the Caribbean region.
- In North America, Australia/New Zealand and East Asia, the categories are fairly widely applied.
- However, in North Eurasia, South-East Asia, South Asia, Central and South America and tropical Africa there is very limited application of Category Ib and, in most cases, Category V.

Table 3.3 Number and percentage of protected areas within WCPA regions, classified by IUCN management category

WCPA region	Area of region (km²)	Ia		Ib		II		III		IV		V		VI	
		No	%	No	%	No	%	No	%	No	%	No	%	No	%
North Africa/Middle East	12,866,541	30	0.01	3	0.00	60	0.96	39	0.10	264	0.54	125	0.40	21	6.05
Europe	5,061,153	513	1.54	77	0.13	215	1.59	457	0.03	5333	1.66	2654	6.72	76	0.26
Antarctic	14,268,633	82	0.02	0	0.00	2	0.00	0	0.00	14	0.00	1	0.00	0	0.00
Pacific	566,922	27	0.15	0	0.00	11	0.05	19	0.05	50	0.19	11	0.01	34	1.91
Caribbean	238,627	20	0.45	3	0.01	67	5.07	22	0.01	231	33.10	59	6.21	177	0.67
North America	23,443,386	658	0.23	630	1.67	1286	6.97	342	0.25	1249	3.51	2085	1.05	461	3.74
Australia/New Zealand	7,947,450	2184	3.13	61	0.50	685	3.35	940	0.09	1636	0.14	65	0.75	311	5.99
North Eurasia	22,100,900	173	1.45	1	0.00	55	0.46	30	0.00	368	1.06	21	0.00	0	0.00
South-East Asia	4,498,111	293	0.62	0	0.00	150	4.23	62	0.09	151	2.04	109	0.46	759	4.10
South Asia	4,368,713	33	0.08	0	0.00	108	1.44	1	0.00	564	3.28	9	0.04	4	0.04
East Asia	11,790,494	57	0.77	24	4.23	56	0.63	73	0.10	306	0.54	159	0.51	403	0.71
South America	18,001,095	253	0.59	1	0.01	360	3.44	75	0.47	197	1.27	245	1.39	306	3.04
Central America	542,750	26	2.11	0	0.00	78	5.41	27	1.77	163	2.61	9	0.01	81	3.95
Africa (West/Centre)	13,352,849	33	0.21	5	0.00	82	2.29	3	0.03	166	2.69	1	0.00	53	0.44
Africa (East/South)	10,773,580	7	0.01	4	0.01	169	4.65	32	0.00	479	2.38	25	0.11	211	5.07
Totals	149,811,204	4389	0.65	809	0.63	3384	2.67	2122	0.13	11,171	1.64	5578	0.71	2897	2.40

Marine regions

There has been a major increase in the awareness of the need for establishing a global representative system of marine protected areas. One of the most important catalysts for this has been the explicit recognition in the Convention on Biological Diversity, and its explanatory documents, of the benefits conferred by marine protected areas.

Increasingly, it is recognized that, while the contributions of marine protected areas to biodiversity are vitally important, they can also increase the sustainable catch of fisheries and provide a foundation for sustainable tourism. The opportunity to enlist the support of the tourism and fishery sectors in establishing community support for marine protected areas is being taken in many parts of the world, with consequent reduction in conflict and acceleration of WCPA's programme for marine protected areas.

A WCPA working group has been set up to deal with the high seas. This reflects growing international recognition that there are resources outside exclusive economic zones that theoretically can be protected only through marine protected areas.

DISCUSSION AND CONCLUSIONS

Managing data and compiling information on the world's protected areas, in order to monitor their growth and assess their status, is a major challenge that requires resources, expertise and collaboration. Considerable progress has been made in managing such information since the 1992 World Parks Congress. The number of records of designated and proposed areas in WCMC's Protected Areas Data Base has doubled to some 60,000, of which approximately half meet the IUCN definition of a protected area.

Despite these improvements, however, there remain significant gaps in the data which constrain the present assessment of the world's protected areas. As has been demonstrated in this chapter, a crucial gap is the lack of spatial data for approximately 75 per cent of the 30,350 known protected areas. The available data on protected areas show that the global network is extensive and is continuing to grow. Only in a few regions (Eastern/Southern Africa, North America, the Caribbean and the Pacific) is there any sign of declining growth rates. Clearly, there remains considerable scope for expanding the network further, both through conservation of natural areas or traditionally maintained land and seascapes and through restoration of biologically degraded land and seascapes. Analysis of this data, however, reveals some major gaps, as has been discussed above, in the protected areas network at global, regional and national levels.

As the 21st century unfolds, the further development of the global network of protected areas will need to focus on four areas:

1   *The consolidation of the existing network by addressing major gaps (including those identified in this chapter and the more detailed paper by Green and Paine, 1997).*
2   *Physically linking protected areas to each other so that they may function effectively as a network.* Major initiatives are underway to establish corri-

dors to link protected areas. Examples include the 2400 kilometre long Meso-American Biological Corridor that is planned to run from Panama to Guatemala and Belize (CCAD, 1997). Within Europe, as part of the Pan-European Biological Diversity and Landscape Strategy, there are plans to establish an ecological network (ECONET) of core protected areas, corridors or stepping-stones, buffer zones and restoration areas (COE/UNEP/ECNC, 1996). As already discussed, transfrontier protected areas contribute significantly to linking protected areas across international borders. A recent global study shows that there are 136 known transfrontier protected areas complexes, comprising a total of 406 adjacent protected areas (Zbicz and Green, in press). While collaborative management has yet to be established in most of these complexes, the physical link between protected areas either side of international borders represents a vitally important contribution to globally networking protected areas.

3   *The expansion of the networks by forming or strengthening links with other sectors, notably the private sector.* A pilot study by WCMC indicates that private initiatives contribute significantly to in situ biodiversity conservation in many parts of the world (Watkins and Green, 1998). This particular study was limited to countries in Eastern/Southern Africa, where private protected areas in Kenya, Namibia, South Africa and Zimbabwe contribute from 1 per cent to 7 per cent of total land area, and are marginally more extensive than legally designated protected areas managed by government agencies. The extent of private protected areas in other parts of the world is presently unquantified, but it is likely to be significant, particularly in the Americas and Europe (see Chapter 19).

It is also timely to link up with the military sector, given the significant, often extensive, training and other areas of importance for biodiversity that are occupied by the military. Zones demilitarized following the end of the Cold War, for example, provide rare opportunities for extending protected areas networks in often environmentally sensitive or fragile areas (IUCN, 1996). A recent study by IUCN (Wolff, 1997) shows that, while biodiversity conservation is receiving increasing recognition within military circles, there is tremendous scope for creating or strengthening alliances between the two sectors.

4   *Improving the effectiveness with which protected areas are managed.* Many protected areas exist in law (on paper), but there may be little to show for them on the ground due to various forms of encroachment (for example, poaching, livestock grazing, cultivation, settlement, roads and urban development). As protected areas are established, and opportunities for national networks to expand further diminish, so it becomes increasingly important to focus resources on ensuring their effective management.

WCPA has established a task force on management effectiveness to address this issue, often referred to as the paper park syndrome (see Chapter 27). A framework for evaluating management effectiveness has been designed for different scales (site, agency, national and global) and for different levels of monitoring that depend on a site's or system's conservation value, use, threats and the potentially available resources (Hockings, 1997).

Monitoring the world's protected areas in the 21st century

Managing information on the world's protected areas is a continuous process that, in reality, has only just begun. Past practices of acquiring data and compiling them in centralized repositories, such as the WCMC Protected Areas Data Base, are labour intensive, limited to the ability or willingness of agencies to respond, and constrained in so far as direct access to that information is concerned.

With the revolution in information technology and the birth of the Internet, it is now possible to network databases, using common interfaces, and provide direct access to all who need such information. A major advantage of decentralizing information management, through a distributed network of national or agency-level databases, is that responsibility for maintaining the information is distributed among the data holders.

Clearly, WCMC's role will change increasingly towards facilitating information exchange. This will result in moving away from gathering data and focusing more on:

- establishing common standards for information exchange;
- promoting and facilitating the networking of data;
- strengthening or building the capacities of protected area agencies to manage their own information; and
- compiling policy-relevant information from networked data.

Steps are already underway to network protected areas information and make it readily accessible to all. For example, WCPA and WCMC are in the process of establishing Protected Area Resource Centres (PARCs) at international, regional and even national levels. This initiative is set to gain considerable momentum as the 21st century unfolds.

References

CCAD (1997) *Buscando respuestas: nuevos arreglors para la gestión de áreas protegidas y del corredor biológico en Centroamérica*, Comisión centroamericana de ambiente y desarollo

Council of Europe, UNEP and European Centre for Nature Conservation (1996) *The Pan-European Biological and Landscape Diversity Strategy*, Council of Europe, Strasbourg

Green, J B and Paine, J (1997) *State of the World's Protected Areas at the end of the Twentieth Century*, paper presented at the IUCN World Commission on Protected Areas Symposium on *Protected Areas in the 21st Century: From Islands to Networks*, Albany, Australia, 24–29 November

Hockings, M (1997) *Evaluating Management Effectiveness: A Framework for Evaluating Management of Protected Areas*, IUCN World Commission on Protected Areas, Working Group on Management Effectiveness, IUCN, Gland

IUCN (1993) *Parks for Life. Report of the IVth World Congress on National Parks and Protected Areas*, IUCN, Gland

IUCN (1996) *Tanks and Thyme – Biodiversity in Former Soviet Military Areas in Central Europe*, IUCN, Gland and Cambridge

IUCN (1998) 1997 *United Nations List of Protected Areas*, prepared by WCMC and WCPA, IUCN, Gland and Cambridge

Soule, M E (1983) 'Applications of genetics and population biology: the what, where and how of nature reserves' in *Conservation, science and society*, UNESCO–UNEP, Paris and Nairobi

Udvardy, M O F (1975) *A classification of the biogeographical provinces of the World*, IUCN Occasional Paper No 18, IUCN, Morges, Switzerland

Watkins, C W and Green, M J B (in press) 'The contribution of private initiatives in conserving biological diversity: a pilot study', *Environments*

Wilcox, B A (1984) 'In situ conservation of genetic resources: determinants of minimum area requirements' in *National parks, conservation and development: the role of protected areas in sustaining society*, (eds) McNeely, J A and Miller, K A, Smithsonian Institution Press, Washington DC

Wolff, E (1997) *Study on Military Lands in Europe: Rehabilitation and Use for Conservation*, Report for the Meeting of IUCN's World Commission on Protected Areas, Rügen

Zbicz, D C and Green, M J B (in press) *Status of the World's Transfrontier Protected Areas*, paper presented at the International Conference on Transboundary Protected Areas as a Vehicle for International Cooperation, 16–18 September 1997, Somerset West, South Africa

4 GLOBALIZATION, LOCALIZATION AND PROTECTED AREAS*

Jeffrey A Sayer

INTRODUCTION

Processes of economic integration and the growing economic influence of corporations are creating new challenges for people in all countries to protect the lifestyles and habitats that they value. For conservation organizations, the first challenge is clearly defining objectives and priorities on what to conserve. There follows a need to mobilize the best available science and new techniques for working with local human communities to find ways of achieving conservation goals at the least social cost. For conservationists, the critical task is to determine the optimal extent, location and management of areas needed to achieve an acceptable balance between the development needs of local people and global biodiversity conservation needs. The inevitable trade-offs between biodiversity conservation and other uses of natural areas are more likely to be widely accepted if they are made in a transparent manner with the full participation of all people concerned, with related economic costs and benefits allocated in an equitable manner. IUCN and WWF need to play a leadership role in helping people protect their resources against global pressures and in enabling them to be fairly compensated for any costs they may incur when they live in areas where biodiversity values are primarily global rather than local.

WHERE ARE WE HEADED?

We live in a rapidly changing world. Current economic orthodoxy is pushing us inexorably in the direction of globalization. Capital, goods, information and, increasingly, people move freely between countries. The power of sovereign governments is being eroded, and multinational corporations are acquiring more and more power (Korten, 1995). Some people fear that market forces will inevitably lead us to a world that is less diverse and less driven by

---

* This chapter was originally presented at IUCN's 50th Anniversary Conference at Fountainbleau, France, 1998.

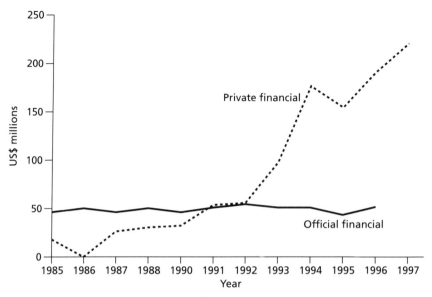

Figure 4.1 *Private and official financial flows, 1985–1997*

human values – a world that may be more efficient but perhaps less pleasant to live in, and certainly less sustainable. Market forces will be the primary determinants of patterns of resource use in the future; managers of protected areas ignore this reality at their peril (Sayer and Byron, 1996).

In the market-driven world, resources and power will no longer be in the hands of elected governments and the international bodies they have established. For example, the Turner Broadcasting System now has a budget almost three times that of the United Nations. At the same time, WWF now has resources that dwarf those of the United Nations Environment Programme (UNEP) (over US$350 million per year as opposed to less than US$50 million per year) and will inevitably have a greater capacity to influence environmental outcomes.

In this new market-driven world, international aid agencies will play a lesser role than the private sector in determining the financial health of poorer countries (see Figure 4.1). We may reach a point where only a handful of multinationals will determine what we eat and where it is grown, and what we consume and where it is produced. They will undoubtedly respond more to the purchasing potential of the rich than to the subsistence needs of the poor.

What does this mean for protected areas? Globalization challenges managers of protected areas in two ways. Firstly, it forces us to realistically confront the trade-offs between global conservation values and local development needs, and to decide how we might address these tensions. Secondly, it requires us to look more carefully at the widely accepted paradigm of achieving conservation objectives through ecologically based local-area management. As information, markets and corporate economic expansion increasingly penetrate even the remotest parts of the world, we cannot expect local populations who live in or near areas that are valued for their rich biodiversity and overall environmental importance to remain in the slow lane when the rest of humanity is travelling in the fast lane.

Historically, the conservation community has fought primarily on two fronts. Firstly, we have struggled to defend many biologically valuable *local areas* around the world from the threat of corporate encroachment. The forests of Amazonia have been threatened by cattle ranchers. Subsistence gardens in Indonesia have been expropriated to plant industrial estate crops. Wetlands throughout the world have been drained and flooded in the name of progress. For many local communities, especially those that are too small or weak to defend the areas they cherish for spiritual and material needs, economic progress has often come at a heavy cost. Secondly, increased awareness of the importance of preserving biodiversity has led us to recognize the global value of a number of areas that have high species richness, high levels of endemism and unusual assemblages of fauna and flora. But often, efforts to conserve these *global priority areas* have been challenged by local communities who fiercely protect access to the land and resources that they deem important in satisfying their own immediate well-being.

As a result, we can see that just as the pressures and opportunities from globalization are increasing, the tension between local and global needs and influences is also growing. The purpose of this chapter is to consider the new challenges that this development poses for conservation, and to speculate on the implications that this may have for conservationists.

COUNTERCURRENTS ARE UNDERWAY

The erosion of local cultural and environmental diversity as a result of corporate economic expansion and national government policies is already provoking a backlash. People in rich and poor countries alike are organizing themselves to protect the lifestyles and habitats that they value, and to strengthen their defences against the impersonal uniformization that is spreading throughout the world.

Rubber tappers in the Amazon have organized to defend themselves against loggers. Dayaks in Borneo have banded together to resist the expropriation of their land by government-sponsored colonization schemes. And many local communities throughout the industrialized world have mounted campaigns to resist the development of airports, power stations and waste disposal operations in their midst.

The tensions surrounding the establishment of protected areas do not arise only from pressures for development. Groups of local people who value natural land and seascapes for subsistence or spiritual reasons often band together to resist what they see as the 'expropriation' of their resources by distant bureaucracies for conversion to protected areas. Given these competing demands, is it possible to arrive at a worldwide system of protected areas that represents a happy medium between local and global conservation objectives? I believe that the answer is yes.

Firstly, we must define exactly what it is we want to conserve. Then, we must combine the best knowledge about conservation biology with social sensitivity to define a network of areas that will enable us to achieve our conservation goals at the least social cost. It is a question of efficiency and prioritization. It requires us to acknowledge that we cannot conserve everything, and to recognize that we must introduce greater transparency, objectivity and fairness into the process of allocating resources for biodiversity and other environmental goals.

For too long, conservationists have been pretending that most biodiversity conservation problems have win–win solutions. In reality, however, there are always trade-offs. Most conservation projects attempt to reconcile conflicts between global and local views of conservation and development. The critical task we conservationists are faced with is to determine the optimal extent, location and management of areas that are needed to achieve an acceptable balance between local people's development needs and global biodiversity conservation needs.

Trade-offs between biodiversity conservation and economic uses of natural areas are inevitable. Decisions about protection are more likely to be widely accepted – and the areas at issue to remain more sustainable – if they are made in a transparent manner with the full participation of all people concerned, with related economic costs and benefits allocated equitably. Past experience offers countless examples in which decisions about the extent and location of protected areas have been made at a national, or even international, level with the intention that local social and economic issues will be addressed later. Regrettably, there are many examples, especially from developing countries, in which international pressures have led to the establishment of unrealistic conservation objectives, with the result that managers of protected areas have been condemned to never-ending and irreconcilable conflicts with local people.

An important lesson for us in hindsight is that protected areas should not be designated until a wider range of biophysical, economic and social issues have been considered, and compromises achieved that maximize the probability of outcomes that will support both local and national and global values.

SUBSIDIARITY, OR AT WHAT LEVEL SHOULD DECISIONS BE MADE?

Greater globalization and corporate dominance are occurring at a time when many communities around the world are renegotiating their relations with government. More and more national governments are devolving decision-making about many aspects of life to regional and local levels – a trend that has been influenced, in part, by a Catholic dogma known as 'subsidiarity', which says that it is unjust to centralize power at levels higher than those needed for functional efficiency.

In line with this, the legitimacy of central governments' authority is being widely contested. People are indicating they will no longer tolerate the primacy of central dictates. This is likely to have far-reaching consequences for protected areas. It is likely to mean, for example, that the targets set by international conservation organizations of having 10 per cent of the world's terrestrial biomes allocated as totally protected areas is likely to be contested, especially in countries with large populations of poor people.

The implications of this decentralization and localization of authority for resource management are not yet fully understood. Studies by Kaimowitz et al, (1997) in Bolivia suggest that decentralization of authority for natural resource management may be good for the sustainability of certain types of forestry activities, but less good for protected areas. Total protection for esoteric biodiversity objectives does not usually represent a good economic option for poor farmers or people dependent upon natural products. A large body of opinion would like to see even more devolution of management decisions about natural resources to local levels. However, most protected area systems exist in locations where there are conflicting and overlapping sets of values that range from local to global. Such situations need some form of shared management responsibility.

Good models of collaborative management of protected areas already exist in some countries; unfortunately, they are often complex, have high associated transaction costs and take time to develop. Nature conservation agreements between government agencies and private landowners in the United States and several European countries are good examples. Successful models of resource comanagement in tropical developing countries are scarce, although they do exist in the case of some marine protected areas. At least part of the reason for this is that government agencies and even international conservation organizations have been reluctant to genuinely recognize the legitimacy of local claims on land.

For many areas targeted for protection, maintaining global values incurs local costs. In these situations, it will be necessary to retain management authority at the level of central governments, and to base conservation programmes on regulation and compensation. Most countries have institutions whose aim is to conserve nature at the national level. And for the conservation of resources of global value, we need global institutions. A number of these already exist for biodiversity. The Convention on Biological Diversity (CBD) is the leading example, but the Convention on International Trade in Endangered Species (CITES) and other instruments related to particular habitats or groups of species also operate at this level.

Most sovereign states are reluctant to alienate control of conservation areas to multinational bodies. But conservation organizations often transcend

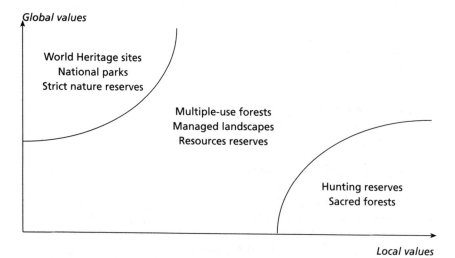

Figure 4.2 *A conceptual framework for determining governance models for protected areas*

national boundaries in their action and influence. The conservation community must therefore help local people to protect their resources against global pressures and, at the same time, develop mechanisms that will enable local stakeholders to be fairly compensated for the costs they incur when they live in areas whose values are global and not local. Every case must be assessed on its own merits, but Figure 4.2 provides a conceptual framework that could help managers of protected areas determine appropriate strategies for different situations.

WHAT WILL A SYSTEM OF PROTECTED AREAS LOOK LIKE?

Keeping in mind that any choice entails opportunity costs, we have to ask ourselves: how many totally protected areas will a world of ten billion people be able to afford (Waggoner, 1996)? And what should they look like?

Natural areas may be managed to maintain their biodiversity, to provide physical environmental protection, or because they constitute scenic features that have high amenity value. In many countries, protected areas serve all three of these functions, and management measures do not tend to favour one function over the others. In many cultures, however, amenity values are not particularly associated with natural, undisturbed habitats; indeed, many of the world's most treasured landscapes have been drastically modified by human activities. Similarly, functions of environmental protection (associated with soil cover, hydrological properties and so on) can be provided by a wide variety of modified natural and non-natural vegetation types.

Furthermore, it is beyond dispute that much biodiversity can be conserved in habitats that have been modified. Almost all habitats have been subject to significant human use over long periods of time and, in fact, it could be argued that the very quantity and quality of biodiversity in a specific area has been influenced by long-time patterns of use (Sayer et al, 1995).

It is very difficult to reach consensus about the nature and intensity of disturbance to which an area can be subjected and still be described as 'natural'. Nonetheless, there can be agreement on management systems that either seek to minimize human interference or that seek to maintain the genes, species and communities that are present in an area at a given point in time. It is essential, given the lack of knowledge of the response of biodiversity to modification and the fact that many important components of biodiversity are best conserved in habitats subject to minimal human interference, that extensive networks of minimally disturbed areas should remain the basis for biodiversity conservation efforts (Zuidema et al, 1997).

Ideally, the future worldwide system of protected areas will encompass a large network of sites that have *local* value and local constituents, along with a smaller set of sites that are protected for their *global* values. Both of these types of areas are important for the protection of biodiversity and other environmental values. But an important fact to keep in mind is that, historically, the benefits of these public goods, and the costs of maintaining them, have not accrued equally to local and global stakeholders.

Many, but by no means all, protected areas may have to be withdrawn from other uses, or subject to reduced intensity of use. In these cases, conservation programmes will often incur opportunity costs for those people who would otherwise have made some productive use of the resources. This may not always be the case, since some areas are of such amenity value that low-impact recreational use (such as ecotourism) may be the optimal economic activity. But usually the designation of protected area status incurs opportunity costs for society at large or at least for a subset of potential users of the economic products of the land.

Some advocacy groups have called for very large areas of land to be allocated for biodiversity conservation while showing considerable indifference to the opportunity costs that this implies. The fact that in many cases such costs would have to be borne by poor countries, or by very poor people in these countries, has been a major factor in the past polarization of the debate on conservation. Groups advocating the most extreme conservation measures often do not represent the people who would have to support the cost of these measures.

Governments have a pivotal role to play in rectifying this injustice. But the costs and benefits of conservation affect countries unevenly. Pressing economic and social development needs may tip the scale against safeguarding the interests of local people, and the long-term viability of national resources, in favour of the global interests of multinational companies or of small, privileged groups of powerful stakeholders.

WHAT CAN WE DO?

Conservation organizations need to pool their expertise and that of other stakeholders in order to achieve realistic solutions to these problems. For example, the principle of paying compensation for foregoing personal benefits for the sake of broader public interest is widely accepted in richer countries. It will have to become a more important element of conservation programmes in poorer countries. It is unrealistic – and unethical – to base conservation programmes on social and cultural values that are not shared by all stakeholders. Conservation programmes will rarely work if their costs are borne by poor forest-dependent communities, or by industries operating in a highly competitive economic environment, while their benefits accrue primarily to a small community of distant environmentalists.

One possible approach to reducing the economic costs of biodiversity conservation, particularly the opportunity costs, may be to minimize the areas that are alienated from all other economic use. Conflicts between people and protected areas should be further reduced if biodiversity objectives can be met in areas that are also used for other purposes. We need to move further in the direction of biodiversity conservation programmes based on fewer and more targeted total reserves in a matrix of multiple-use reserves (Zuidema et al, 1997). The systems of protected areas in the United Kingdom and France are good examples. There is an urgent need to apply the lessons of these integrated British and French models in poorer tropical countries.

A key scientific question is to determine how we can optimize biodiversity conservation in areas modified for extractive human uses. This requires knowledge of the tolerance of different components of biodiversity to different types of habitat modification and the development of 'adaptive management' techniques. It also needs defensible methods of decision-making on the desirable balance between biodiversity objectives and other economic objectives in areas allocated for multiple use.

This strategy implies basing conservation programmes on a minimum number and extent of totally protected areas, and using other approaches to maximize biodiversity conservation in the rest of the landscape. In summary, we must:

- Optimize the location of protected areas to capture maximum biodiversity value.
- Maximize the opportunities for conserving biodiversity in areas that are subject to other economic uses (such as multiple-use forests).
- Allocate habitat types at the landscape level to achieve an optimal compromise between biodiversity conservation and other economic interests.

To determine optimal systems for conserving biodiversity, we also need better scientific knowledge and tools. This requires:

- Efficient techniques for assessing the significance of different areas for biodiversity and for detecting changes in biodiversity under different management treatments and over time (Boyle and Sayer, 1995).
- Better understanding of methods that can be applied to maintain viable populations of species over long periods of time; this will be especially important in fragmented habitats where animals and plants have small population sizes.
- Knowledge of the optimal disposition of protected areas in relation to other landscape elements, including modified habitats and totally transformed artificial land uses, so as to optimize biodiversity and other economic benefits at a large scale; this requires knowledge of the impacts on biodiversity of connectivity between habitats and of the nature of the matrix environments in which protected areas are located. A key issue is to define the role of different types of modified (multiple-use or production) systems.

At the same time, we need to determine what kinds of national and international interventions (projects) are most likely to succeed in achieving biodiversity conservation goals. This requires a review of past attempts to influence biodiversity outcomes, particularly those that have attempted to reconcile conflicting interests in the use of resources. Some issues for consideration in this area include the following:

Cost-benefit analysis

How do we measure the impact of investments in biodiversity conservation? Which approaches to conservation have been the most cost effective, in which circumstances, and from whose perspective (see Chambers, 1997)?

Development versus regulation

Integrated conservation and development projects (ICDPs) have attracted very large international funding in recent years. Yet the results of this approach have often been disappointing compared with those that provide direct support for enforcing regulations, even though the latter approach has become unfashionable among development assistance agencies. It might be argued that while direct policing action will have a greater impact in the short term, ICDPs may show a greater impact over a longer term, say, 20 to 30 years, although this remains to be seen.

Time and scale

A similar set of arguments relates to landscape protection as embraced in the national park systems of the United Kingdom and France, which have been criticized as ineffective in securing biodiversity conservation. Again, this is based on assessing their impacts over relatively short time periods. Landscape-scale approaches must be assessed against the long-term viability of very small reserves, which appear to be the only other option in densely populated and intensively used landscapes and seascapes. Great scientific uncertainty remains over the relative merits of integrated or segregated approaches to biodiversity conservation.

Nature of management

The fact that much biodiversity conservation will be based on a fine balance between conflicting resource uses means that difficult issues of institutional arrangements for managing conservation programmes remain at the local, national and international levels. Careful analysis of institutional or governance arrangements for conservation is urgently needed.

Changing values

A society's commitment to, or tolerance of, biodiversity conservation programmes differs according to numerous attributes of that society, and especially according to its level of economic and social development. The nature and strength of 'civil society' has to be taken into account in any measures to conserve biodiversity, and it must be recognized that just as civil society varies over time and space, so conservation measures will have to respond to that variation. Different peoples have widely divergent visions of the value of biodiversity. There is not a single 'reality', and we have to be sure that we have adequately considered whose biodiversity reality counts (Chambers, 1997).

We should not assume that we already know how to achieve conservation in the globalized societies of the 21st century. It is not simply a question of throwing more money at the problem. We need more objective, value-neutral research, and this will have to address conservation issues in a holistic way with much more attention given to serious economic, social, political and institutional components of the problems.

REFERENCES

Boyle, T J B and Sayer, J A (1995) 'Measuring, monitoring and conserving biodiversity in managed tropical forests', *Commonwealth Forestry Review* 74:20–25

Chambers, R (1997) *Whose Reality Counts?: Putting the First Last*, Intermediate Technology, London

Kaimowitz, D, Flores, G, Johnson, J, Pacheco, P, Pavéz, I, Roper, J, Vallejos, C and Veléz, R (1997) 'Local government and biodiversity conservation in the Bolivian tropics', unpublished manuscript, CIFOR, Bogor, Indonesia

Korten, D C (1995) *When Corporations Rule the World*, Earthscan, London

Ohmae, K (1995) *The End of the Nation State*, Free Press, New York

Sayer, J A and Byron, R N (1996) 'Technological advance and the conservation of resources' *International Journal of Sustainable Development and World Ecology* 3:43–53

Sayer, J A, Zuidema, P A and Rijks, M H (1995) 'Managing for biodiversity in humid tropical forests', *Commonwealth Forestry Review* 74:282–287

Waggoner, P E (1996) 'How much land can 10 billion people spare for nature?' *Daedalus*, summer (409):73–93

Zuidema, P, Sayer, J A and Dijkman, W (1997) 'Forest fragmentation and biodiversity: The case for intermediate-sized protected areas', *Environmental Conservation* 23:290–297

Photo: WWF-Canon/Anthony B Rath

Shallow-water coral reef, Belize barrier reef

It is important to include all habitat types in protected areas. Many ecosystems still remain
under-represented, for example, apart from whaling sanctuaries, marine protected areas
make up less than 1 per cent of the ocean's surface.

PART II

ADOPTING NEW APPROACHES TO PROTECTED AREA SELECTION

Protected areas are supposed to represent examples of the world's most
valuable and important habitats. Importance may be measured variously in
terms of biodiversity, geology, cultural and historical associations, aesthetic
considerations or even spiritual values. But how are protected areas selected?
And do we always choose the best areas for protection? Research suggests that
this is frequently not the case. However, great efforts are now being made to
address this question. Over the last decade, a range of new selection techniques
have been developed and implemented. In the following section, some of the
people involved in making these advances discuss their work and its implications. Techniques addressed in the following chapters include bioregional and
ecoregional approaches, gap analysis, national systems planning and particular
activities related to indigenous territories and marine protected areas.

5 BIOREGIONAL PLANNING AND BIODIVERSITY CONSERVATION

Kenton R Miller

INTRODUCTION

For millennia governments and communities have been giving special protection to geographic areas that feature natural and cultural attributes considered by society to be of high material, cultural, historical, spiritual or ecosystem value. Over the years, these values have been redefined and new areas have been identified for evolving purposes. Presently, with the impetus of the Convention on Biological Diversity (CBD), the focus is on the protection, restoration and long-term in situ management of habitats, species and their genetic variations, and overall ecosystem functions and processes. The process of developing this convention has elevated the awareness of governments and communities as to the values of biodiversity to human health, nutrition and industrial potential. Also at this time, however, population growth, expansion of the agricultural frontier, resource extraction, pollution, urban sprawl, highway development and invasive species are acting to reduce the quantity and quality of the world's remaining wildlands, coastal and marine areas. Hence, the geographic space that is readily available for addressing the role of protected areas is limited and is declining rapidly. It consists of the existing protected areas of the world, as classified and characterised by IUCN and WCMC, and the remaining wildlands that potentially could be dedicated to these purposes.

One critical factor in planning a network of protected areas for biodiversity conservation is to work with geographic spaces of sufficient size to deal with whole ecosystems. Such areas, often referred to as bioregions, embrace local communities and the landscapes upon which they depend for their food, recreation, resources and other aspects of their livelihoods. They also provide the flexibility within which to establish and harmonize protected areas and the corridors needed to link such areas to allow for migration and adaptation to climate change and major disturbances. This chapter discusses the need for a bioregional approach and how these concepts can be developed.

Obstacles to future benefits and values of protected areas

From the analysis of WCMC (see Chapter 3), published scientific literature and the experience of WCPA members, it is clear that protected areas around the world face seven significant obstacles that will limit their capacity to meet growing demands for their full array of benefits and values.

Criteria employed for the selection of the original areas may not have identified the land and water resources needed to address biodiversity conservation goals per se. Many areas were identified and established to protect their scenic and recreational resources, charismatic megafauna and birds, historic and cultural sites, and other values of great importance to local, national and international communities. Society will continue to value these areas and they should remain as components of the nation's protected area network.

The *size* of most areas is too small to maintain the full complement of biodiversity should these areas become isolated patches in a landscape that retains only scattered remnants of wildland. What then of small protected areas? Do they continue to have value for biodiversity goals? Indeed, even as isolated patches they contribute by protecting critical habitats, and retaining those species that have more limited home ranges. They may also contain important water catchment basins, wetlands and other sites critical for their ecological functions and ecosystem services to the region. The issue, as we shall explain, moreover, is to develop the potential of the surrounding landscape to help maintain the native flora and fauna.

The *shape* of protected areas becomes particularly important once adjacent areas are no longer in biodiversity friendly uses. Many areas have shapes that, unlike the ideal circle shape, expose long edges per unit of wildland area to outside antagonistic influences (such as pesticides, exotic species and noise), or they feature long, narrow peninsulas that are insufficiently wide to contain effective inner core habitats.

Many marine protected areas have been established in locations that are directly *downstream* (in relation to prevailing currents) from land- or sea-based sources of pollution.

Most previously established protected areas lack *landscape linkages*, or connectivity, with neighbouring protected areas to permit the migration of flora and fauna, or to accommodate adaptation to changes in climate.

Organizations responsible for protected areas lack political and financial support consistent with the key role that these areas play in national development, sustainability, well-being and international commitments. A recent report by James and Green (1997) shows that for virtually every region of the world, protected area agency budgets reach half or less than half of the amount of funding requested to meet their basic management needs. Newly emerging alternatives for protected area management through decentralization mechanisms, comanagement arrangements, and by devolution of authority and responsibility to lower levels of government, or indigenous community-led or private initiatives, may provide important complementary back-up capacity to public services. Elsewhere, governments prefer to implement decentralization policies with caution to ensure the long-term viability of these options (Miller et al, 1997). Global Environmental Facility (GEF) projects are now making resources available to those protected areas that provide significant benefits to the world community, over and above those in the national interest. National environment funds and private sector involvement offer additional new opportunities to strengthen the capacity to manage at the national and local levels (IUCN, 1994b; McNeely and Weatherly, 1996; Bezanson and Mendez, 1995; Bruce, Ellis, Eisner and Beiring, 1994; Hansen, OECD, 1995; WRI, 1989).

Investments in *scientific, technical and managerial capacity, field management practices*, and the institutional mechanisms required to develop these capabilities and practices, are insufficient and inadequate to address biodiversity conservation goals.

This chapter addresses primarily the first six of these obstacles, but is also relevant to the seventh.

A NEW STRATEGY FOR PROTECTED AREAS IN THE 21ST CENTURY

At the bioregional scale, people and protected areas can coexist, both through the judicious use of categories that can consistently combine biodiversity conservation with human habitation and managed resource extraction, and by developing region-wide cooperative programmes among protected areas and neighbouring farmers, foresters, fishers, industry, villagers and visitors to the area. Cases on all continents already demonstrate that such options are viable and tend to foster social, economic and ecological sustainability. This new strategy can address the obstacles listed above and ensure that both terrestrial and marine protected areas can contribute to future human well-being and the survival of nature.

Several important elements are necessary for a bioregional approach (see Figure 5.1). The first and central element of 'bioregional planning' consists of core wild areas that contain the wild undomesticated plant and animal communities, their habitat or site requirements and ecosystems needed for their long-term survival. Tools for identifying and selecting the best areas to meet biodiversity goals have gained significantly in scientific rigor during the past two decades (Margules et al, 1994; Pressey et al, 1994; Jennings and Scott, 1992; Williams and Humphries, 1994). Core areas are kept relatively free from further human intervention except to restore and manage the area for its biodiversity goals (for instance, reintroduction of wolf and white rhino, control of invasive species, allowing or promoting periodic fire) and to manage compatible uses by people (recreation, tourism, research, education, spiritual renewal and cultural practices). Roads are kept to a minimum. Typically, core areas are formally established under national legislation, as national parks, or other IUCN Category I to IV areas. In some cases, core areas may be established by non-legislative means, especially on communal lands through community agreements (Zimbabwe Trust, 1990; Padilla, 1995). In many areas, strict core areas have been established in recognition of their primary or parallel role in producing high-quality water and regulated stream flow (Hamilton, 1997), or as 'replenishment areas' to augment depleted fish stocks in surrounding areas.

Secondly, buffer zones are established in the lands and waters immediately surrounding the core areas, where public, private and communal landowners and users are encouraged through legal and policy instruments and economic

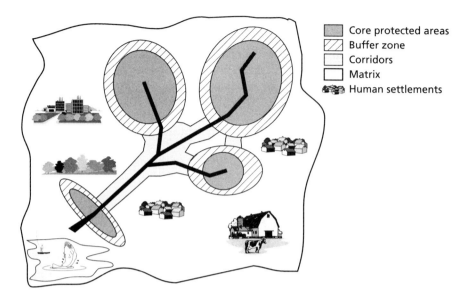

Figure 5.1 *The bioregional approach*

incentives to manage their resources in ways that minimize negative impacts upon the core areas, such as agricultural pesticides and fertilizers or clear-cut logging. As a quid pro quo, core area managers agree to minimize the negative impacts that the plants and animals of the wild core areas can have upon neighbouring farmers, foresters, and residents, including predation upon livestock, transfer of diseases and trampling or raiding of gardens and crops. International conservation and development projects (ICDPs) have been developed in various countries to help neighbouring peoples develop livelihoods that will not only capture benefits from core areas, but minimize the negative transfers in either direction.

Thirdly, these cores and their buffer zones are linked with other core and buffer zone areas by swaths of landscape or waterscape, or corridors, that provide suitable habitats for plant and animal migration and options for adaptating to climate change. While these areas usually fall into IUCN Categories V and VI, private or communal ownership, or are perhaps fully dedicated to economic activity, they may at the same time feature the communities, habitat structures and ecological processes needed to serve as biological corridors. Where this is not the case, legal mechanisms, economic incentives and technological assistance from government agencies can help encourage landowners to voluntarily shift their practices to more nature friendly uses.

Fourthly, these core areas, their buffer zones and the landscape-linking corridors are nested within bioregions where resident communities, landowners and resource users live and work. The goal of bioregional management is to establish voluntarily cooperative programmes across the entire region that provide appropriate treatment of those sites critical for biodiversity maintenance and restoration, while supporting local livelihoods and lifestyles. Normally, this involves restoring riparian vegetation, leaving wetlands undisturbed during migratory periods, retaining and promoting selected seral stages in forest harvesting regimes, minimizing road construction, removing invasive pests, and reintroducing native species. In many cases, the areas surrounding wild core areas consist of other IUCN protected area Categories V or VI, under public, private or comanagement arrangements, which allow for controlled and limited uses and resource extraction, as in the case of the La Amistad Biosphere Reserve in Costa Rica. In other instances, as with CAMPFIRE (Communal Areas Management Programme for Indigenous Resources) in Zimbabwe, the Cuna Comarca in Panama, or the Great Barrier Reef Marine Park in Australia, the surrounding areas are managed through agreements among local rural communities without the apparent need for formal government designation or legislation. The need is both to establish Category V and VI areas dedicated to protecting and maintaining biological diversity and the associated natural and cultural resources, but also to encourage better environmental care in the whole landscape. This is a 21st century challenge to protected area managers and to WCPA. This is stewardship on a regional scale.

GEOGRAPHIC AREA OF ACTION

The application of these ideas implies some important distinctions in the way that protected areas have been planned and managed in the past. They call for an expansion of the scale at which we conceptualize and plan our work, both in space and in time, and in the way we determine our partners and establish alliances. If we are to commit to supporting the protection of biodiversity, the 'geographic area of action' needs to be sufficiently large and secure to maintain ecological and evolutionary processes. This does not imply that protected area agencies are expected to extend further their already limited resources to engage in agriculture, forestry, fishing and community extension work. Rather, it means that in the years to come, protected area strategies will want to feature activities, capacity-building efforts and investments to promote new partnerships and alliances with neighbouring agencies, communities and individuals in ways that lead to broad bioregional programmes that will ensure biodiversity-related goals (McNeely, 1995). Therefore, our strategy is to *expand the scale of management* to embrace whole ecosystems and includes the following:

Habitat for viable populations

Studies by Newmark (1987) and others have shown that even the largest protected areas cannot support viable populations of all native species. For example, doubts have been raised whether the 898,349-hectare Yellowstone National Park can support viable populations of grizzly and elk.

Migration

Some bird species skip and jump across the landscape at large continental and global scales. The ECONET programme in Europe provides a 'stepping-stone' model that provides protection to those sites needed by bird migration. Similarly, marine mammals require protection of widely separated sites where different habitat requirements for feeding and breeding can be met. These cases illustrate the particular value of and need for small protected areas across the bioregion, and the need for linking them at the local level.

Rainfall patterns and ocean currents

These are vital components of ecosystems. For example, in the Amazon, forest cover provides moisture through evapotranspiration. Over 70 per cent of this moisture returns locally as rainfall, the remainder temporarily leaves the Amazon basin as precipitation over the Andes or runoff to the Atlantic. Without this forested land cover, the rain-laden clouds entering the basin on constant trade winds would produce rainfall that would primarily leave the area as runoff. Thus, unless land-use policies promote forest cover across the region, even relatively large protected areas may witness major climatic change in the near term.

Small- and large-scale natural disturbance

Fire, flood, cyclones, earthquakes, volcanism, drought and other natural disturbances bring about subtle or major changes to ecosystems on cyclical or stochastic time patterns. Effective protected areas and their surrounding buffer areas need to be sufficiently large to absorb these disturbances and adapt to their impact without irreversible loss to the overall ecosystems. For example, this means that where fire has been part of the overall evolution of ecosystems, it should be retained and permitted as a natural component of management. Alternatively, where protected areas are completely altered by natural or human disturbance (air or water pollution), they cannot be expected to maintain the full suite of natural biodiversity. In these cases, representative areas should be replicated across the same biogeographic region.

Human-induced climate change

Climate change will require that plant and animal species are able to shift their range in response to gradual or perhaps quite rapid change in temperature and rainfall. This may require altitudinal movement or longitudinal or latitudinal movement along the rainfall gradients. Whatever the case, areas need to cover as great a range of current ecosystems as possible.

Ecological linkages

These are needed to connect fragmented habitats found in small nature reserves or remnant forests in a largely agriculturally transformed landscape. The ECONET programme in Europe is promoting connectivity at various scales, including the use of wild hedgerows as corridors. In landscapes that have been long inhabited and intensively used, such a programme is of immense value. However, the goal should always be to enlarge the cores and widen the corridors so that biodiversity is maintained as best we know how, since narrow corridors have edge effects and are more vulnerable to invasion by aliens or to catastrophe.

New institutional arrangements

These ideas also call for some changes in our institutional arrangements. As we move out beyond the established boundaries of protected areas, we will need to establish ways in which to work with the neighbouring communities, residents, indigenous groups, corporations, or local levels of government that own, manage, use or otherwise care for the land and water. We will need to develop methods that can lead to cooperative agreements on resource use. Typically this involves participatory planning, negotiated goals and practices, adapted technologies for resource use, incentives, policy reform, and setting standards and criteria of performance.

Experience demonstrates that these programmes appear to work best when neighbours cooperate on a voluntary basis, stemming from their appreciation of the overall goals and their interest in the benefits they anticipate from incentives or other rewards (see Keystone Center, 1996; Yaffee, 1996; Zimbabwe Trust, 1990; Miller, 1996). In fact, in some countries, the most successful bioregional management cases are those that have been established by local groups and individuals who wish to resolve locally perceived problems. In several cases, non-governmental conservation groups and government agencies provide original facilitation and support to local initiatives (Keystone Center, 1996).

This implies proactive efforts on the part of protected area managers and conservation workers to engage neighbours, local governments, corporations, indigenous communities and civic groups in the goals and opportunities of bioregional programmes. It means creating alliances with other local and regionally based organizations (NGOs, civic groups, churches, farmers, ranchers, forestry and fishery associations, banks, etc).

Scientific and other types of information are more important than ever. Tools such as GIS are particularly helpful for mapping the relative location of key features, and enable local people to assess future land use options. Virtually all successful bioregional programmes feature voluntary or staff scientists who help with data collection and the preparation of information to assist others in making critical decisions. This may include collecting maps of land use patterns, surveys of roads and other infrastructure, assessing disturbance factors, and integrating other factors affecting management (Keystone Center, 1996; Miller, 1996; Pressey et al, 1994).

Finally, and above all, the potential for such bioregional programmes to work will depend upon having policies, economic instruments and institutional tools that will enable and encourage protected area agencies, communities and neighbours to establish cooperative alliances, develop appropriate programmes and keep the momentum over long periods of time. This means solid political, agency, community and financial support. It means that governments really do intend to meet the objectives of biodiversity conservation, according to the CBD, and that communities and neighbours find compelling reasons to join forces with conservation efforts that have often, in the past, been seen as land grabbing, anti-land rights or elite-serving programmes emanating from distant capitals. In many places the term buffer zone has an undesirable connotation to private landowners within it. What is needed are conservation areas of nature friendly management between and around core protected areas.

CONCLUSION

Lessons learned suggest that bioregional programmes that combine the pursuit of livelihoods for local residents, and national and global goals for biodiversity conservation, share in common a basic set of components. They feature institutional mechanisms for voluntary cooperation by stakeholders in the region. Incentives have been established to foster participation. Information is available to empower all stakeholders and to engender wise decisions. Science is employed and data analysed to provide constantly evolving guidelines to stakeholders and managers. Land and water tenure is clear for individuals, communal groups and corporations. Distribution of benefits is managed through broad tax-based mechanisms, direct payments to stakeholders or via non-monetary means. And the planning and implementation process evolves sequentially in order to adapt to new information and knowledge.

Protected areas within the context of bioregional programmes have the potential to foster a productive relationship between people and key biodiversity sites.

REFERENCES

Bezanson, K and Mendez, R (1995) 'Alternative Funding: Looking Beyond the Nation State', *Futures* 27(2)

Bruce, N and Ellis, G M (no date) *Environmental Taxes and Policies for Developing Countries*, Policy Research Working Papers, 1177, World Bank, Washington DC

Eisner, T and Beiring, E A (1994) 'Biotic Exploration Fund: Protecting Biodiversity through Chemical Processing', *Bioscience* 44(2)

Hamilton, L S (1997) 'Protected Areas, Watersheds and Development', *Wild Earth* 7(2)

Hansen, S (no date) *Debt for Nature Swaps: Overview and Discussion of Key Issues*, Environment Department Working Paper I, World Bank, Washington DC

IUCN (1994) 'Financing Protected Areas', *Parks* 4(2), IUCN, Gland

James, A N and Green, M J B (1997) *Financial Indicators and Targets for Protected Areas*, WCMC, Cambridge

Jennings, M and Scott, J M (1992) 'Building a Macroscope: How well do places managed for diversity match reality', *Renewable Resources Journal*

Keystone Center (1996) *The Keystone National Policy Dialogue on Ecosystem Management*, The Keystone Center, Colorado

Margules, C R, Cresell, I D and Nicholls, A O (1994) 'A Scientific Basis for Establishing Networks of Protected Areas', in Forey, P L, Humphries, C J and Vane-Wright, R I (eds) *Systematics and Conservation Evaluation*, Clarendon Press, Oxford

McNeely, J A (1995) *Expanding Partnerships in Conservation*, Island Press, Washington DC

McNeely, J A and Weatherly, W P (1996) 'Innovative Funding to Support Biodiversity Conservation', *International Journal of Social Economics*, 23 (4/5/6)

Miller, K R, McNeely, J, Salim, E and Miranda, M (1997) *Decentralization and the Capacity to Manage Biodiversity*, Issues and Ideas Paper, World Resources Institute, Washington DC

Miller, K R (1996) *Balancing the Scales: Guidelines for Increasing Biodiversity's Chances Through Bioregional Management*, World Resources Institute, Washington DC

Newmark, W D (1987) 'A Land Bridge Perspective on Mammalian Extinction's in Western North American Parks', *Nature* 325, 430–432

OECD (1995) *Making Markets Work for Biological Diversity: The Role of Economic Incentive Measures*, OECD, Paris

Padilla, G (1995) 'El programa legal de COAMA', *Revista COAMA* 1

Pressey, R L, Bedward, M and Keith, D A (1994) 'New Procedures for Reserve Selection in New South Wales: Maximizing the Chances of Achieving a Representative Network', in Forey, P L, Humphries, C J and Vane-Wright, R I (eds) *Systematics and Conservation Evaluation*, Clarendon Press, Oxford

Williams, P H and Humphries, C J (1994) 'Biodiversity, Taxonomic Relatedness and Endemism Conservation', in Forey, P L, Humphries, C J and Vane-Wright, R I (eds) *Systematics and Conservation Evaluation*, Clarendon Press, Oxford

WRI (1989) *Natural Endowments: Financing Resource Conservation for Development*, WRI, Washington DC

Yaffee, S A, Phillips, I, Frentz, P, Hardy, S, Maleki, S and Thorpe, B (1996) *Ecosystem Management in the United States: An Assessment of Current Experience*, Island Press, Washington DC

Zimbabwe Trust (1990) *People, Wildlife and Natural Resources – The CAMPFIRE Approach to Rural Development in Zimbabwe*, Zimbabwe Trust, Harare

6 SPATIAL ANALYSIS OF BIODIVERSITY INFORMATION: THE CANADIAN EXPERIENCE OF GAP ANALYSIS AND CONSERVATION VALUES ANALYSIS

Tony Iacobelli and Kevin Kavanagh

INTRODUCTION

The importance of completing a *representative* network of protected areas has won international acceptance in conservation planning fora. For example, the Fourth World Congress on National Parks and Protected Areas, held in Caracas in February 1992, concluded that:

> ...*we strongly urge all governments and appropriate national and international bodies: ... To take urgent action to consolidate and enlarge national systems of well-managed protected areas with buffer zones and corridors, so that by the year 2000 they safeguard the full representative range of land, freshwater, coastal and marine ecosystems of each country.*
>
> IUCN, 1993

The launch of World Wildlife Fund Canada's (WWF) Endangered Spaces Campaign added a different dimension to its previous conservation efforts: with the more rigorous analysis of spatial ecological information to assess conservation value and priorities. The campaign aims to represent each of Canada's terrestrial natural regions in a system of ecologically representative protected areas by the year 2000 and to similarly represent marine and Great Lakes systems by 2010.

WWF believes that a broad spectrum of biological diversity will be protected if the range of habitat types and environmental gradients in each region are adequately captured within a protected areas network, as defined by the approach described below. In WWF's vision of a completed protected areas system, sites designated for protection are chosen, designed and linked together in a system that has the capacity to maintain the evolutionary processes critical to conserving ecological systems. Adequate representation will require more than the mere presence of a protected area in a natural region; protected areas must also be judged to be in the right place, of the right size and the right configuration to help protect biological diversity over the long term.

As a result, WWF needed a way to measure progress towards the campaign goal: to describe how well the existing system of protected areas represents ecological diversity in each natural region and to identify how best to fill the gaps in ecological representation with new candidate sites. A method of *gap analysis* was therefore designed, tailored for the specific requirements of the campaign.

WWF's PROTECTED AREAS GAP ANALYSIS: A DESCRIPTIVE ANALYSIS

A gap analysis is an assessment of the protection status of biodiversity in a specified region, which looks for gaps in the representation of species or ecosystems in protected areas. The gap analysis methodology undertaken by WWF embraces the assumption that ecological diversity (and hence biodiversity) is largely an expression of abiotic factors such as climate, physiography, topography, and surface geology interacting over time.

GEOGRAPHIC UNIT

WWF and the Canadian Council on Ecological Areas therefore developed a coarse-filter conservation assessment of protected areas based on a landscape approach using 'enduring features' (essentially landforms or physical habitats) as geographic units that reflect biological diversity (Geomatics International, 1994). The gap analysis involves three main stages (see Table 6.1). Firstly, natural regional frameworks are reviewed to ensure that natural region boundaries reflect broad physiographic and climatic gradients. Next, within each natural region, WWF Canada identifies and maps enduring features using primarily a nationwide, terrain data base (Soil Landscapes of Canada – SLC) provided by Agriculture and Agri-Food Canada. Finally, the relationship of biodiversity to enduring features of the landscape is derived from more detailed tertiary sources (Kavanagh and Iacobelli, 1995).

An *enduring feature* is a landform or landscape element or unit within a natural region characterized by a relatively uniform origin of parent material, texture of parent material and topography relief. The steps required to identify enduring features within each natural region are as follows:

- categorization of soil polygons of the Soil Landscapes of Canada maps based on attribute fields describing parent material origin, parent material texture and surface form; the breakdown of the three factors is provided in Table 4 and Figure 16 of the 1995 gap analysis discussion paper (Kavanagh and Iacobelli, 1995); and

- use of digital elevation data and surficial deposit maps to interpret variation within enduring features.

Table 6.1 *Stages in gap analysis*

Stage	Scale	Information type
Broad environmental setting	1:5,000,000 scale, nationwide	Bostock's physiographic divisions; ecoclimatic regions of Canada; natural region boundaries
Ecological diversity	1:1,000,000 scale, natural region	Shape and substance of landscape leading to identification of enduring features
Biological communities	1:250,000 scale, larger enduring feature	Habitat types, environmental gradients, ecological processes, disturbance regimes

ASSESSMENT OF ECOLOGICAL REPRESENTATION

Each enduring feature is then evaluated based on the degree of ecological representation by existing protected areas. Sustaining key ecological processes and maintaining viable populations of all native species are general conservation criteria that guide the representation assessment. The difficulty is translating these broad conservation criteria which relate to ecosystem integrity into a numeric or spatial set of standards. This is done by judging the extent to which all physical habitats (high and low elevation areas, variety of slope classes and aspect, shorelines) are included in each enduring feature.

WWF also evaluates ecological representation of enduring features in relation to the typical spatial scales of key ecological processes, such as fire, insect outbreak, periodic flooding, or dune processes. To date, this has been translated as a general guide explained in Table 6.2.

The criteria listed above also depend on the size of the enduring feature. For smaller enduring features (<50,000 hectares), it is sufficient to capture in protected areas all environmental gradients and the diversity of physical habitats while also connecting to adjacent enduring features. For larger enduring features (>one million hectares), it is more important that the enduring feature is included in a protected area of sufficient size to address landscape-scale ecological processes. As an example, a 450,000-hectare protected area in the boreal forest that includes equal parts of three large enduring features (>one million hectares each with 150,000 ha in the protected area) may be sufficient to 'adequately' represent all three enduring features.

Knowledge of the amount and location of intact habitat, as well as the habitat condition within existing protected areas, is also important information for assessing ecological representation by protected areas. Where this information is available, the presence or absence of good-quality habitat associ-

Table 6.2 *General spatial guidelines for assessing the ecological representation of enduring features by existing protected areas*

Assessment	Description
Little or no representation	No protected areas or no protected blocks > 200 ha.
Partial representation	The enduring feature has at least one protected block of habitat > 200 ha. This is large enough to address stand or patch level dynamics, such as tree fall gaps.
Moderate representation	The enduring feature includes protected areas of sufficient size to begin to address landscape scale dynamics. For example, this criterion would be met if protected areas are of equivalent size to the average fire size. Lands in protected areas ranging from 1000 ha to 10,000 ha often meet this criterion, but depend on the characteristics of the natural region.
Adequate Representation	The enduring feature includes protected areas of sufficient size to address landscape scale dynamics and/or captures all environmental gradients and the diversity of physical habitats. For a fire-driven forest ecosystem, this may mean protected areas on the order of 500,000 ha.

ated with an enduring feature is factored into the assessment of ecological representation. Areas of intact habitat are more likely to serve as ecological benchmarks. Similarly, where habitat conversion and/or habitat fragmentation has occurred in existing protected areas, the general decision rules in Table 6.2 are applied to the amount of remaining interior habitat.

DATA REQUIREMENTS

The Soil Landscapes of Canada (version 2), used to identify enduring features, has proved to be an extremely useful data set. Other information in the SLC data base, such as drainage and soil development classes, helps to identify environmental gradients. Information from other data sources that could help to identify enduring features includes the location of eskers, moraines and relic beach ridges. A relatively detailed digital elevation model would be extremely useful to identify elevation gradients. WWF currently uses one:one million scale paper copy maps and a one-kilometre resolution Digital Elevation Model (DEM) for this purpose. Information pertaining to spatial scales of ecological processes is also of key importance in determining the contribution of protected areas to ecological representation. It would be useful, for example, to catalogue spatial information such as average and maximum fire size on an ecoregion basis. Other ecological processes should be included where relevant, such as the spatial scales of dune processes. Drainage basin maps indicate important headwater areas. A digital version of the Canada Land Inventory would help tp identify areas based on productivity levels relating to the underlying landform types, even though the area may have been converted from its natural vegetation types. Finally, data showing the amount and location of intact habitat would indicate key ecological benchmarks that should be represented in protected areas.

CONSERVATION VALUES ANALYSIS: A PRESCRIPTIVE APPROACH

In a further development of the gap analysis approach, WWF Canada has now developed an objective analysis for determining areas of high conservation value, based on the general application of composite and suitability mapping. The analysis consists of analysing primary ecological themes to derive a conservation score and then modifying the score with additional ecological themes. It highlights core areas of high conservation value based on the available information. As a result, this approach complements the descriptive analysis described above, which provides an assessment of the ecological contribution of existing protected areas. The conservation values analysis can be used to identify the 'best' sites for new protected areas to fill a gap in ecological representation.

This approach has been developed to support conservation efforts by the Partnership for Public Lands in response to Ontario's Lands for Life initiative, a land-use planning process covering the commercial forest base in Ontario. An outline is given below.

PRIMARY ECOLOGICAL THEMES

The primary ecological themes used in the analysis are:

* intact habitat measured as the distance from the nearest road;
* late successional forest;
* wetlands; and
* physical habitat heterogeneity.

The variation within each ecological theme was ranked according to conservation value, then the values were added quantitatively across all themes to portray their collective and overlapping distribution.

Roadless Areas

At the request of the Partnership for Public Lands, the Ontario Ministry of Natural Resources provided a raster file indicating the distance of each pixel (unit of measurement used in satellite imagery, such as remote sensing) to the nearest road or utility infrastructure (railway, powerline and pipelines) for the Lands for Life study area.

Distance intervals were given the following conservation values.

> *5000 metres, conservation value = 10*

2000 to 5000 metres, conservation value = 5

< 2000 metres, conservation value = 0

Late Successional Forest

At the request of the Partnership for Public Lands, the Ontario Ministry of Natural Resources provided a summarized version of the Forest Resource Inventory (FRI) data for the Lands for Life study area. Each polygon in the digital file represented the actual extent of a single FRI map sheet. The data normally found on each map sheet (thousands of polygons with attribute data) were summarized into approximately 30 data fields.

Forest composition was described by main forest types (softwood, hardwood, mixed wood) and forest age was divided into either 20-year or 30-year classes. The Partnership for Public Lands used the forest age data across all major forest types to rank the FRI data as shown below.

>30 per cent of the polygon (FRI map sheet) in age class > 121 years, conservation value = 10

>50 per cent of the polygon in age class 90–120 years, conservation value = 10

10 per cent–30 per cent of the polygon in age class > 121 years, conservation value = 7

30 per cent–50 per cent of the polygon in age class 90–120 years, conservation value = 7

10 per cent–30 per cent of the polygon in age class 90–120 years, conservation value = 5

all other scenarios, conservation value = 0

Wetlands

The Ontario Ministry of Natural Resources provided data on the occurrence of wetlands as part of a series of land cover data files. The raster files had a 200-metre resolution based on Landsat (thematic mapper used in remote sensing) reflectance values.

The Partnership for Public Lands summarized the data for wetlands for one kilometre by one kilometre blocks as follows.

50 per cent–100 per cent of a 1 km² block in wetlands, conservation value = 10

1 per cent–50 per cent of a 1 km² block in wetlands, conservation value = 5

0 per cent of a 1 km² block in wetlands, conservation value = 0

Physical Habitat Heterogeneity

The Partnership for Public Lands based the estimate of physical habitat heterogeneity on the distribution of enduring features as determined by WWF using the Soil Landscapes of Canada (SLC) data base (one:one million scale). The SLC digital file was converted to a raster file with a one-kilometre pixel. Each

INFORMATION LAYERS   INFORMATION SOURCES

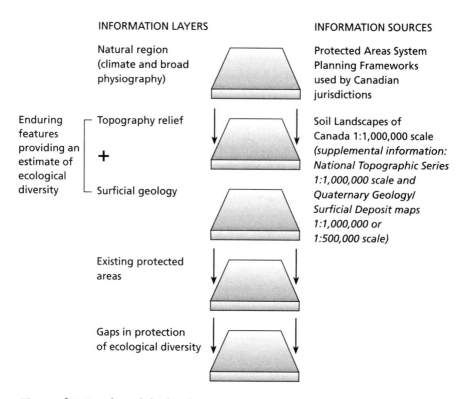

Natural region   Protected Areas System
(climate and broad   Planning Frameworks
physiography)   used by Canadian
                                      jurisdictions

Enduring   ┌ Topography relief   Soil Landscapes of
features   │   Canada 1:1,000,000 scale
providing an   │ **+**   *(supplemental information:*
estimate of   │   *National Topographic Series*
ecological   │   *1:1,000,000 scale and*
diversity   └ Surficial geology   *Quaternary Geology/*
                                      Surficial Deposit maps
                                      1:1,000,000 or
                                      1:500,000 scale)

Existing protected
areas

Gaps in protection
of ecological diversity

Figure 6.1 *Overlay of the landscape themes and data sources used in WWF*
gap analysis procedure

pixel was coded with its enduring feature number and analysed using the
FOCAL VARIETY function in Arc Grid based on a circular neighbourhood with
a radius of 18 pixels (approximately 100,000 hectares). Up to 20 different
enduring features for a 'neighbourhood' were determined using this method –
that is, pixels in the raster file had scores ranging from one to 20. The highest
scores comprising 15 per cent of the study area were given the highest conservation value (10). The next highest scores comprising 15 per cent of the study
area were given the second highest conservation value (5). All other scores
(making up the remaining 70 per cent of the study area) were given a conservation value of zero.

'MODIFIER' ECOLOGICAL THEMES

Several other secondary, but important, landscape values were added or
subtracted quantitatively from the four core ecological themes in order to
reflect other landscape values important in identifying protected areas at a
broad scale. The ecological themes used as 'modifiers' were given a maximum
value that was no more than 20 per cent of the value of the resulting sum of
the four primary ecological themes.

Enduring Feature Representation

The Partnership for Public Lands used the results of WWF's enduring feature gap analysis to modify the conservation priority analysis according to the current level of ecological representation by protected areas.

Species Occurrences

The Natural Heritage Information Centre provided species occurrence data to the Partnership for Public Lands. The presence of a species listed as vulnerable, threatened or endangered in a one kilometre by one kilometre pixel was recorded.

Cutover Data

The Ontario Ministry of Natural Resources provided information regarding previously logged areas based on Landsat data with a 200-metre resolution. The Partnership for Public Lands summarized the data for cutover areas for one kilometre by one kilometre blocks as follows.

> *50 per cent–100 per cent of a 1 km² block as cutover, conservation value = –2*
>
> *1 per cent–50 per cent of a 1 km² block as cutover, conservation value = –1*
>
> *0 per cent of a 1 km² block as cutover, conservation value = 0*

The conservation values of the cutover data are based on standardizing the resulting conservation score from the addition of the primary ecological themes from one to ten.

Old Growth Red and White Pine

From the Forest Resource Inventory summary data, an additional conservation value was assigned to areas where a range of conditions was met for a single FRI map sheet relating to the presence of certain proportions of red and white pine (which have declined to a large degree in the province).

DATA REQUIREMENTS

A measure of intact habitat is a key ecological theme for this type of conservation priority analysis. We have concentrated on obtaining surrogate data, such as road density, distance from roads or measures of fragmentation and edge effects. Suitable land cover data would also serve to provide a measure of habitat quality ranging from 'converted' lands to 'intact' lands.

The analysis is also more suited to quantitative data where a range of values can be determined within each theme. This works well for estimates of physical habitat heterogeneity and forest community diversity (if the latter data is available in the form of land cover classes), but is problematic for species occurrence data. In the approach used to date, species occurrence data provided by the Natural Heritage Information Centre was only used to indicate presence or absence of species listed as vulnerable, threatened or endangered. Mapping species concentration areas may be a more defensible approach to incorporating species occurrence data within the spatial analysis. However, the latter approach does not properly incorporate information pertaining to key indicator species, such as woodland caribou that range across large areas and naturally occur in low densities. For such species, it may be necessary to use a habitat suitability analysis to determine probability maps of their occurrence based on habitat data and other criteria related to fragmentation effects and home range.

CONCLUSIONS

WWF Canada continues to refine both the descriptive conservation assessment to determine the adequacy of existing protected areas systems and the prescriptive conservation values analysis to fill the gaps in ecological representation.

We have outlined some of the data sources that would further refine the two approaches:

- documenting spatial scales of ecological processes (such as fire) and ecosystem function on an ecoregion basis;
- a nationwide digital elevation model to determine elevation gradients and headwater areas;
- a land cover data set of sufficient detail to determine the quality of habitat as well as areas of high vegetation community diversity, including forest composition and age; and
- a flexible framework for recording species occurrence data.

REFERENCES

Geomatics International Inc (1994) *CCEA Studies on Ecoregion Gap Analysis: Final draft report*, Canadian Council on Ecological Areas
IUCN (1993) *Parks for Life: Report of the IVth World Congress on National Parks and Protected Areas*, IUCN, Gland
Kavanagh, K and Iacobelli, T (1995) *A protected Areas Gap Analysis Methodology: Planning for the conservation of biodiversity*, WWF Canada, Toronto

7 THE GLOBAL 200 INITIATIVE: A REPRESENTATION APPROACH TO CONSERVING THE EARTH'S DISTINCTIVE ECOREGIONS

David M Olson and Eric Dinerstein

INTRODUCTION

The current extinction crisis requires dramatic action to save the variety of life on Earth. Because funding for conservation is limited, governments, donors and conservation groups must be strategic and earmark the greatest amount of resources for protecting those areas richest in biodiversity. Most conservation biologists recognize that although we cannot save everything, we should at least ensure that all ecosystem and habitat types are *represented* within regional conservation strategies.

The representation approach has been applied at a number of geographical scales, from watersheds to states, ecoregions, countries and regions (see Chapter 6). Here we introduce a first attempt to achieve representation of habitat types at a global scale by identifying the world's most outstanding examples within each major habitat type (for example, tropical dry forests, large lakes, coral reefs).

The 'habitat representation' approach is soundly based in conservation biology. It incorporates the goal of maintaining species diversity (the traditional focus of biodiversity conservation) within conservation action at a higher level – the preservation of distinct ecosystems and ecological processes. While it is true that more than half of all species are likely to occur in tropical moist forests around the world, the other 50 per cent of species are found elsewhere. To conserve the latter half we must emphasize the importance of conserving and protecting a full representation of the world's diverse ecosystems. Tundra, tropical lakes, mangroves and temperate broadleaf forests are all unique expressions of biodiversity and contain species assemblages adapted to distinct environmental conditions and which reflect different evolutionary histories.

The World Wildlife Fund (WWF) Global 200 Initiative departs from past efforts to identify global conservation priorities, such as the hotspots (Myers, 1990; Conservation International, 1997) and the megadiversity country approaches (McNeeley et al, 1990; Mittermeier and Werner, 1990). Both of these approaches largely overlook marine and freshwater biodiversity, and distinctive ecological or evolutionary phenomena. Even within the terrestrial realm, these earlier studies fall short of the goal of representing distinct habitats and ecosystem types.

Although we recognize that conservation action must take place at the country level, patterns of biodiversity and ecological processes (such as migration) do not conform to political boundaries. Thus, we use *ecoregions* as the unit for conservation in creating the Global 200 Initiative. We define an ecoregion as 'a relatively large unit of land or water containing a characteristic set of natural communities that share a large majority of their species, dynamics, and environmental conditions' (Dinerstein et al, 1995).

Ecoregions function effectively as conservation units at regional scales because they encompass similar biological communities, and their boundaries roughly coincide with the area over which key ecological processes most strongly interact (Noss, 1996). The identification of ecoregions offers a valuable tool for protected areas planning. In particular, it provides the opportunity to consider the network of protected areas needed throughout an ecoregion for the long-term conservation of characteristic natural communities – including across national borders. It also enables conservation planners to identify the key underlying causes of biodiversity loss across an ecoregion so that these can be tackled – and ongoing losses of natural habitat restrained.

AN OBJECTIVE HIERARCHY FOR SELECTING THE GLOBAL 200 INITIATIVE

To maintain representation of biodiversity at a global scale, we first stratified ecoregions by realm (terrestrial, freshwater, and marine). We further divided realms by major habitat types (MHTs); these are geographic areas that share environmental conditions, habitat structure and patterns of biological complexity, and that contain species with similar guild structures and adaptations. MHT classifications are roughly equivalent to biomes. We identified 12 MHTs in the terrestrial realm, three in the freshwater realm and four in the marine realm. Each MHT was further subdivided by biogeographic realm (for example, Nearctic, Indian Ocean) to capture unique faunas and floras on different continents or ocean basins. Finally, we identified ecoregions within each biogeographic realm that represent the most distinctive examples of biodiversity for a given MHT – these form the Global 200 (actually 232 important ecoregions). A list of MHTs is given below and a full list of ecoregions is given in Olsen and Dinerstein (1997):

- tropical and subtropical moist broadleaf forests;
- tropical dry forests;
- tropical and subtropical conifer forests;
- temperate broadleaf and conifer forests;
- boreal forests and taiga;
- arctic tundra;
- temperate grasslands, savannahs and shrublands;

- tropical and subtropical grasslands, savannahs and shrublands;
- flooded grasslands and savannahs;
- tropical montane grasslands and savannahs;
- deserts and xeric shrublands;
- mediterranean shrublands and woodlands;
- small rivers and streams;
- large rivers;
- lake and closed-basin freshwater ecosystems;
- large deltas, mangroves and estuaries;
- coastal reef and associated marine ecosystems;
- coastal marine ecosystems; and
- polar and subpolar marine ecosystems.

This hierarchy is based on biogeographic and ecological principles. Firstly, to set priorities we only need to compare the biodiversity value of ecoregions that share the same MHT. Employing species richness and endemism as a discriminator among ecoregions is much more powerful if the MHTs are analysed separately, because the relative magnitude of these parameters varies widely among MHTs.

Secondly, incorporating biogeographic realms addresses another important aspect of global representation: ecoregions that share the same MHT, but occur on different continents support different species assemblages. For example, the deserts of central and north-western Australia support over 150 species of reptile, all of which are endemic to Australia. Using biogeographic realms also addresses higher-order taxonomic diversity. For example, the Chihuahuan and Sonoran deserts include the centres of diversity of cacti, a family absent from African and Asian deserts.

Thirdly, assessments of the relative intactness and degree of threat (conservation status) of ecoregions can be made more accurately if ecoregions are categorized within a framework of MHTs. This allows us to address the patterns of biodiversity, ecological dynamics and responses to disturbance that are specific to different MHTs.

DELINEATION OF ECOREGIONS

Terrestrial ecoregions

The boundaries of terrestrial ecoregions for the Global 200 Initiative are taken from intensive regional analyses of biodiversity patterns across five continents undertaken by the WWF-US Conservation Science Programme and others. All ecoregions approximate the original extent of their natural communities. Ecoregions are most finely delineated in tropical moist forests. Complexity is high within and among tropical moist forest ecoregions, as is turnover of species along environmental gradients or with distance (betadiversity). By contrast, tundra and boreal forests show only slight longitudinal or latitudinal variation and are therefore delineated as larger units.

Freshwater ecoregions

Separate analyses of freshwater and terrestrial ecoregions were conducted because the distribution of freshwater biodiversity in many cases diverges from terrestrial patterns. Except for the Nearctic and Neotropics, freshwater ecoregion boundaries are coarse approximations of biogeographic units.

Marine ecoregions

Marine ecoregions delineated by the Global 200 Initiative are nested within a large marine ecosystem framework, developed by the WWF Conservation Science Programme. Their delineation is intended to highlight general regions within which characteristic animals, plants, ecological interactions and biophysical processes occur. Relative to most terrestrial ecoregions, these are more spatially and temporally dynamic ecological and biogeographic units.

SELECTION CRITERIA

For five of the continents, detailed regional priority-setting analyses have been conducted by the WWF Conservation Science Programme in collaboration with a host of regional experts and supplemented with extensive literature reviews. Thus, the final Global 200 Initiative draws heavily from the results of intensive regional analyses of biodiversity conducted over the last several years. Within each MHT and biogeographic realm, ecoregions are classified by their *biological distinctiveness* at one of four levels:

* globally outstanding;
* regionally outstanding (eg Neotropics);
* bioregionally outstanding (eg Caribbean); or
* locally important.

Biological distinctiveness, as a discriminator, evaluates the relative rarity of different units of biodiversity. In conjunction with other parameters, it can be used to estimate the urgency of action based on the opportunity for conservation that exists. The criteria we used to prioritize ecoregions for the Global 200 Initiative are similar to those used for the regional assessments.

On a global scale, and within each biogeographic realm, we chose the set of ecoregions with the greatest biological distinctiveness based on the following parameters:

* species richness;
* endemism;
* higher taxonomic uniqueness (for instance, unique genera or families, relict species or communities, primitive lineages);
* unusual ecological or evolutionary phenomena;
* global rarity of MHT; and
* keystone habitats.

Biodiversity features were weighted and measured in the regional analyses using a method previously employed for terrestrial ecoregions of North America. The weight assigned to these parameters also varied by MHT. For example, tropical moist forest ecoregions – such as those that encompass the eastern slopes of the Andes and the western Amazonian piedmont – support the highest known species diversity of plants and animals for any terrestrial ecosystems on Earth. Thus, it is logical and appropriate to rely heavily on levels of *species richness and endemism* to discriminate among ecoregions within this MHT.

Some ecoregions are noted for biotas that contain *unique taxa at higher taxonomic levels than species*, such as unique genera and families, or for harbouring relict and primitive lineages. For example, most families and genera of birds and mammals in Australia are unique to the continent. Moreover, the moist forests of north-eastern Australia, northern New Zealand and New Caledonia are recognized as having a number of the most primitive lineages of conifers and flowering plants in the world. Madagascar is often considered a seventh continent from a biogeographic perspective because of its uniqueness at higher taxonomic levels.

Species richness and endemism are poor discriminators among the more depauperate terrestrial ecoregions found in boreal forests and tundra, the two northernmost terrestrial MHTs. For these MHTs and for some ecoregions of sub-Saharan Africa, we gave greater weight to *unusual ecological phenomena*, in these cases, examples of extensive intact habitats and large vertebrate assemblages, particularly those that still sustain top predators, large herbivores and larger frugivores that are highly sensitive to human disturbance and fragmentation. Large blocks of natural habitat where species populations and ecological processes still fluctuate within their natural range of variation are rapidly disappearing around the world (Bryant et al, 1997). Therefore, remaining intact ecosystems represent rare opportunities for conservation. In assessing the intactness of habitat and faunal assemblages for ecoregions, the presence of larger blocks of habitat is emphasized because principles of landscape ecology and conservation biology suggest that biodiversity is best maintained within such areas. Strategies that highlight the conservation of large vertebrates and the full complement of migratory species help to conserve intact faunal assemblages (see Balmford et al, 1995). Naturally occurring unusual ecological phenomena, such as long-distance caribou migrations or seasonal fish migrations in the flooded forests of the Amazon (várzea forests), were also given due recognition.

Unusual evolutionary phenomena – such as the extraordinary adaptive radiations seen in Hawaiian plants, birds and insects, the radiation of Galapagos finches, relict taxa of the Greater Antilles, and the radiation of cichuds in Rift Valley Lakes of Africa – also elevated some ecoregions to the Global 200 Initiative.

All ecoregions in *globally rare MHTs* are highly distinctive at this analytical scale. The species that manage to live in these habitats often have unusual adaptations to specialized conditions. Their community structures, assemblages and ecological processes are highly distinctive at a global scale. Examples of rare MHTs include the Mediterranean shrublands (there are five worldwide, and all of limited area) and the temperate rainforests that occur in seven relatively localized areas around the world. Paramos, or wet tropical

alpine shrublands, occur in restricted distributions in the Andes, on a few East
African mountain peaks and in Irian Jaya.

At regional scales, the persistence and ecological function of *keystone
habitats* may be critical for the species and processes of neighbouring biotic
systems. For example, strong ecological linkages between mangroves and their
surrounding terrestrial, marine and freshwater habitats, and the importance of
cloud forests for capturing and regulating water for downstream and adjacent
lowland habitats, make both mangroves and cloud forests keystone habitat
types. Coral reefs and gallery forests are other examples. Thus, we emphasized
the selection of mangroves, coral reefs and montane cloud forests in each
biogeographic realm where they occurred, and we included multiple ecoregions of these keystones where their biodiversity value was considered
extraordinary.

If a particular set of candidate ecoregions shared a similar MHT and
biogeographic realm, and showed similar levels of biological distinctiveness,
we selected the ecoregions that had relatively more intact habitats and faunas
based on assessments of their conservation status. We did not use ecological
function, conservation feasibility (political, social, economic, cultural factors)
or human utility as discriminators. The Global 200 Initiative focuses on biological values as the critical first step in setting global conservation priorities.

CONSERVATION STATUS OF THE GLOBAL 200 ECOREGIONS

Ecoregions vary greatly not only in their biological distinctiveness, but also in
their conservation status. Conservation status represents an estimate of the
current and future ability of an ecoregion to maintain viable species populations, to sustain ecological processes and to be responsive to short- and
long-term environmental changes. Conservation status assessments of the
Global 200 ecoregions were based on landscape or aquascape-level features,
such as total habitat loss, the degree of fragmentation, water quality and
estimates of future threat. Drawing heavily on regional conservation assessments, ecoregions were classified into one of three broad categories:
critical/endangered, vulnerable or relatively stable/relatively intact. For terrestrial ecoregions, the most prominent contributor to conservation status is
habitat loss, followed by the size of remaining habitat blocks, degree of
fragmentation, degree of degradation and degree of protection.

OUTSTANDING SITES FOR LARGE-SCALE MIGRATION AND SUBTERRANEAN BIOTAS

The conservation of large-scale ecological phenomena, such as bird and butter-
fly migrations, often requires hemispheric coordination of activities that
transcends ecoregion-level conservation efforts. Habitat conservation within
Global 200 ecoregions can contribute to this effort, but identification of critical stopover, breeding, feeding, wintering and resting sites for migratory birds,
bats, butterflies and cetaceans is necessary. We have made an initial effort, with

the assistance of BirdLife International and Wetlands International, to identify globally and hemispherically important sites for bird migration on the Global 200 map. Effective habitat conservation within Global 200 ecoregions can help conserve regional-scale terrestrial mammal migrations, such as those of caribou and wildebeest, and altitudinal movements of birds, insects, bats and some larger mammals. We have also included several of the known sites for outstanding subterranean biotas around the world. Widespread and dynamic pelagic ecosystems have not been adequately mapped up to this point, nor have hydrothermal vent communities and other abyssal ecosystems and cave and groundwater ecosystems. These gaps in information preclude their consideration in the analysis.

RESULTS AND DISCUSSION

We identified 232 ecoregions whose biodiversity and representation values are outstanding at a global scale, representing the terrestrial, freshwater and marine realms, and the 19 MHTs nested within these realms. Among the three realms, 136 (59 per cent) are terrestrial, 35 (15 per cent) are freshwater ecoregions, and 61 (26 per cent) are marine. The preponderance of terrestrial ecoregions reflects both the tendency of terrestrial biodiversity to display more fine-scale biogeographic patterns than marine biotas, and the greater gaps in biogeographic information from freshwater and marine biodiversity. Ongoing analysis and the availability of new data may lead to the identification of a small number of additional ecoregions – particularly freshwater ecoregions – sufficiently outstanding at the global level to be included in the Global 200 Initiative.

CONSERVATION STATUS OF ECOREGIONS

Global 200 ecoregions depict estimates of the original extent of natural habitats. Ecoregion boundaries do not reflect the extensive habitat loss, fragmentation and degradation that have occurred in many of the terrestrial ecoregions. In ecoregions that have been dramatically altered, characteristic species and communities survive only in the few remaining small blocks of habitat. Among the terrestrial MRTs, ecoregions falling within the tropical dry forests, temperate grasslands, Mediterranean shrublands and temperate broadleaf forests are the most threatened. Virtually all biotas on small islands are vulnerable or critical/endangered due to their limited habitat area and extreme sensitivity to anthropogenic disturbance and alien species invasion. Island ecoregions are projected to experience a wave of extinctions over the next two decades given the fragility of island ecosystems, the sensitivity and endemicity of island species, and the severe threats native island biotas face worldwide.

Among all terrestrial Global 200 ecoregions, 47 per cent are considered critical or endangered, 29 per cent vulnerable, and 24 per cent relatively stable or intact. The Global 200 map does not attempt to assess the status of each freshwater and marine ecoregion because regional analyses are incomplete. However, preliminary analysis shows that freshwater ecosystems, particularly flooded forests, cataracts and freshwater communities in xeric areas, are endangered worldwide. Moreover, most temperate freshwater biotas are threatened by invasion of exotics, pollution, dams and habitat degradation. In marine MHTs, upwelling areas are heavily overfished, enclosed seas are degraded and coral reefs and mangroves are severely affected by habitat destruction, degradation and overfishing around the world.

DEGREE OF OVERLAP OF TERRESTRIAL, FRESHWATER AND MARINE GLOBAL 200 ECOREGIONS

The linkages among terrestrial, freshwater and marine conservation are often overlooked. Among the Global 200, 33 (25 per cent) of the 136 terrestrial ecoregions overlap extensively with freshwater ecoregions (more than 50 per cent of the original extent of the terrestrial ecoregion is covered by a freshwater unit). Twenty-nine (22 per cent) of the terrestrial ecoregions share at least 50 per cent of their coastline with a marine ecoregion. And 13 (10 per cent) of the terrestrial ecoregions do both, overlapping extensively with a freshwater ecoregion and sharing at least 50 per cent of their coastline with a marine ecoregion. The exceptional terrestrial ecoregions of this third group are the Madagascar dry forests, Congolian coastal forests, Greater Antilles moist forests, Pacific temperate rainforests, Queensland tropical moist forests, south-eastern Australia *Eucalyptus–Acacia* forests, New Caledonia moist forests, New Caledonia dry forests, New Guinea lowland forests, Sulawesi moist forests, Philippines moist forests, North-East Borneol/Palawan moist forests, and Russian Far East temperate forests. Carefully designed conservation activities in these 13 units could ultimately affect 39 ecoregions.

APPLYING THE GLOBAL 200 INITIATIVE AS A TOOL FOR GLOBAL BIODIVERSITY CONSERVATION

The Global 200 Initiative is an effective tool for targeting distinctive biogeographic units of biodiversity and providing a solid approach for promoting ecosystem-level representation at global scales. It broadens the goals of conservation from a primary focus on preserving species diversity to an encompassing view of habitat diversity (in terms of structure, composition and ecological processes), evolutionary phenomena and adaptations of species to different environmental conditions around the world. In some cases, it also distinguishes representative ecoregions that are relatively more intact than other examples, highlighting the best opportunities for long-term conservation.

However, it is a global-scale analysis. It is a first step intended to provide a global context for refining and developing regional strategies, not to replace them. It does not try to identify particular sites within priority ecoregions for conservation action. Many of the ecoregions, or clusters of ecoregions, are so large that several finer-scale analyses will be necessary to guide conservation investment. More detailed and fine-scale analyses are essential to identify important sites and to assess the timing, sequence and level of effort needed for different conservation activities within each ecoregion. Widespread and dynamic pelagic ecosystems have not been adequately mapped up to this point, nor have hydrothermal vent communities and other abyssal ecosystems and cave and groundwater ecosystems. The Global 200 Initiative also does not explicitly target large-scale ecological phenomena such as migrations of marine mammals, sea turtles, birds or fish that depend on conservation activities coordinated at hemispheric scales. Ecoregion-level conservation strategies must also address regional-scale ecological phenomena such as intratropical and altitudinal migrations of bats, birds and insects.

MATCHING THE CHALLENGE OF BIODIVERSITY LOSS

Global 200 identifies targets for a global biodiversity conservation strategy which, through appropriate timing, sequence and coordination of conservation investments, can eventually be achieved by the global conservation community and the world's nations. Moreover, the greater understanding of how globally outstanding biodiversity is distributed can help investors of development organizations to better recognize and mitigate the effects of projects, or to carefully consider the wisdom of development in particularly important and sensitive ecoregions. The Global 200 Initiative can enhance regional and national-level conservation strategies by lending weight to shared priorities and by providing a global perspective for local conservation. We also suggest that the geographic overlap and adjacency of many priority terrestrial, freshwater and marine ecoregions means that carefully designed conservation activities in some areas can effectively conserve several Global 200 ecoregions. Because many of the Global 200 ecoregions have already been heavily altered, opportunities to conserve biodiversity in these units, especially those that are critical and endangered, are much reduced. In other words, certain conservation activities are only feasible in a much smaller subset of the ecoregions than all those depicted on the map.

In the context of protected areas, the Global 200 analysis can help to identify gaps in the representation of particular habitat types in protected area networks. The approach can also help to prioritize the channelling of conservation resources to protected areas that are particularly significant from a global perspective – for example, to those which harbour globally endangered habitats and species.

Most importantly, the grave and widespread destruction of the Earth's biodiversity that is taking place today must be matched by a response an order of magnitude greater than the current effort of the global conservation community. Thus, the Global 200 Initiative provides a necessarily ambitious template for conservation action. If we are not ambitious in trying to conserve a representative example of the Earth's biodiversity now, future generations will be less concerned with hotspots than with the 'last spots' left on Earth.

REFERENCES

Balmford, A, Leader-Wiliams, N and Green, M J B (1995) 'Parks or arks: where to conserve threatened mammals?', *Biodiversity Conservation* 62, 115–125

Bryant, D, Nielsen, D and Tangley, L (1997) *The Last Frontier Forests: Ecosystems and economies on the edge*, World Resources Institute, Washington DC

Conservation International (1997) 'Global biodiversity hotspots: field reports', Web site: http://www.conservation.org/web/fieldact/hotspots/hot97.htm

Dinerstein, E, Olsen, D M, Graham, D J, Webster, A L, Primm, S A, Bookbinder, M P and Leduc, G (1995) *A Conservation Assessment of the Terrestrial Ecoregions of Latin America and the Caribbean*, The World Bank, Washington DC

McNeely, J A, Miller, K R, Reid, W V, Mittermeier, R A and Werner, T B (1990) *Conserving the World's Biological Diversity*, IUCN, WRI, CI, WWF-US and World Bank, Gland and Washington DC

Mittermeier, R A and Werner, T B (1990) 'Wealth of plants and animals unites "megadiversity" countries', *Tropicos* 4, 4–5

Myers, N (1990) 'The biodiversity challenge: expanded hot-spots analysis', *The Environmentalist* 10, 243–256

Noss, R F (1996) 'Ecosystems as conservation targets', *TREE* 11, 351

Olsen, D M and Dinerstein, E (1997) *The Global 200: A representation approach to conserving the Earth's distinctive ecoregions*, WWF–US, Washington DC

8 INDIGENOUS PROTECTED AREAS: A NEW APPROACH TO THE USE OF IUCN CATEGORIES V AND VI IN AUSTRALIA

Peter Bridgewater, Ian Cresswell, Steve Szabo and Richard Thackway

INTRODUCTION

A new approach to protected areas is evolving in Australia which it is hoped will improve coverage in the developing national system of protected areas. The concept of indigenous protected areas (IPAs) in Australia, distinct from government-run parks and reserves, is gathering momentum. At present, the only aboriginal and Torres Strait Islander-owned national parks are those established or continued as a precondition to the granting of indigenous land. Although indigenous landholders have a major say in managing those national parks via boards of management and other joint management arrangements, they had no original choice as to whether the national park was declared.

Existing jointly managed national parks have been established to accommodate indigenous interests in managing a predetermined conservation framework. To date, indigenous landholders have not voluntarily entered into cooperative arrangements in respect of land they already own. Voluntary cooperative agreements which fall short of establishing a statutory protected area are currently being negotiated. Going beyond this step to a new process where indigenous landholders voluntarily establish protected areas on their land will depend on their maintaining control of the process, including the act of declaration.

Many unique features of biodiversity at all levels occur only on lands owned or leased by indigenous Australians. Most indigenous landholdings occurs in arid central Australia, in areas where no additional lands are available for dedicated government-run parks and reserves. The Australian government has begun investigating the feasibility of using the *IUCN Guidelines* (see pages xiv–xv) as a mechanism for allowing indigenous people to 'self-declare' protected areas on indigenous lands (Thackway et al, 1996). The federal, state and territory nature conservation agencies wish to enter into voluntary partnerships and agreements with indigenous communities and organizations as an alternative to traditional reserve establishment methods of land acquisition. While all IUCN protected area categories could be included in these partnerships, Categories V and VI seem the most promising.

A significant factor in following this course of action comes from the understanding that indigenous people are keen to protect and enhance the cultural and natural values of their lands but are often hampered by the lack of appropriate support and recurrent resources. The adoption of this concept will ensure a reliable flow of resources to indigenous communities to implement land use and land conservation management.

GAPS IN THE NATIONAL SYSTEM OF PROTECTED AREAS

The federal and the state and territory nature conservation agencies are cooperating to develop a national overview of protected areas in Australia. All agencies have agreed to use the IUCN system for categorizing existing parks and reserves.

Indigenous owned and managed land encompasses about 15 per cent of the land area of Australia (AUSLIG, 1993). Australia's system of protected areas encompasses about 7.6 per cent of the land area (Cresswell and Thomas, 1997) and comprises a variety of areas of many different designations proclaimed and managed by the federal and state and territory governments. While this system of protected areas occupies a relatively large area, it does not represent the full range of ecosystem biodiversity found in Australia (Thackway and Cresswell, 1995a). Historically, areas have been selected as national parks and reserves for their spectacular scenery, naturalness, value for recreation, or as sites for the protection of threatened species (Pressey and Tully, 1994). Consequently, most of the effort and resources in establishing protected areas has favoured conservation of only a limited extent of Australia's ecosystem diversity. These deficiencies in Australia's system of protected areas have been recognized since the early 1970s (House of Representatives Select Committee, 1972).

A bioregional planning framework encompassing all of Australia's major ecosystems, known as the Interim Biogeographic Regionalization for Australia (IBRA), has been developed and endorsed by all Australian governments as the framework for developing a national system of protected areas (Thackway and Cresswell, 1995b). This framework provides the basis for identifying gaps in the existing systems of protected areas and is used as the basis for setting priorities to fill these gaps.

The federal and the state and territory nature conservation agencies have developed a set of conservation planning attributes for each IBRA region: reservation status, bias in the degree of comprehensiveness of ecosystems represented in protected areas, and constraints and limitations to planning the national system of protected areas (threatening processes). High priority IBRA regions for improving the protected area systems are those which have:

* no protected areas, or which have a small proportion of the region in protected areas;
* current protected areas missing major ecosystems within the region; and

- exceptional circumstances regarding long-term viability of the region's biodiversity due to threatening processes.

Many of the priority IBRA regions for biodiversity conservation contain significant tracts of aboriginal-owned or managed lands.

DEFINING THE INDIGENOUS PROTECTED AREAS CONCEPT

The concept of indigenous protected areas (IPA) involves indigenous landowners announcing their intention to manage their lands primarily for the protection of natural and cultural values in accordance with the *IUCN Guidelines*. Management would be by local and resident indigenous people with government support providing resources, training and advice. Government assistance could include devolution of enforcement powers as applicable under various legislation, and would generally be formalized through legal agreements and partnerships (Szabo, in press).

THE USE OF THE IUCN GUIDELINES IN INTERPRETING THE NEEDS OF INDIGENOUS LANDHOLDERS

Category VI was initially considered most appropriate because it gives specific recognition to largely natural areas while also ensuring the supply of a sustainable flow of goods and services to local indigenous groups. Though the *IUCN Guidelines* for Category VI do not specifically refer to indigenous peoples' interests, the reference to sustainable use of natural ecosystems as a management objective, and the recognition of local custom as a management mechanism, make this category potentially attractive to indigenous landholders declaring and managing their land for nature conservation while also allowing sustainable use of natural resources (Thackway et al, 1996).

Category V is also directly relevant to much of Australia, where the interaction of indigenous people and nature over time has produced a great diversity of Australian landscapes with distinct character and significant aesthetic, ecological and/or cultural values, and often with high biological diversity. Safeguarding the integrity of this traditional interaction is vital to the protection, maintenance and evolution of much Australian biodiversity. Other IUCN categories could also meet the requirements of an indigenous protected area.

EMPOWERING INDIGENOUS COMMUNITIES

The IPA concept provides indigenous people with the opportunity to state that they are managing their land for cultural and natural resource values in accordance with recognized international standards (Thackway et al, 1997). By accepting the requirements laid down in the *IUCN Guidelines*, indigenous owners may attract the perceived benefits of government funding and recognition. Federal and state and territory governments benefit from being able to recognize these lands as part of the national system of protected areas to conserve biodiversity.

As IPAs begin to be implemented in Australia using IUCN Categories V and VI, appropriate government support will be needed to encourage effective conservation without impeding, but in fact enhancing, indigenous peoples' rights and capacity to control and manage their land. In some Australian states, aboriginal land councils and nature conservation agencies see the establishment of indigenous protected areas as contributing positively to the resolution of aboriginal land claims under various statutory claim mechanisms and/or the recognition of native title. For example, where nature conservation agencies may currently object to the granting of an aboriginal land claim on the grounds that the land in question is of high conservation value, they may support the land grant if there is a commitment by the indigenous landowners to manage the area in accordance with the IUCN categories. Similarly, the option of establishing an indigenous protected area may provide an additional avenue for negotiation in the formal mediation of native title claims (Thackway et al, 1997).

BIOREGIONAL PLANNING

Appropriate establishment and management of IPAs will enable greater coordination of conservation management on a bioregional basis. The National Strategy for the Conservation of Australia's Biological Diversity calls on all levels of government to establish better lines of communication and coordination in bioregional planning, particularly with regard to providing mechanisms for genuine, continuing community participation (Commonwealth of Australia, 1996). For instance, many existing national parks are located adjacent to aboriginal land. If such aboriginal land were to be managed as an IPA, in cooperation with the state or territory conservation agency, the opportunity for a more regional approach to management would occur. The adoption of a bioregional planning framework in many regions of Australia will fail without the inclusion of indigenous landholders. Indeed, indigenous Australians have been using a bioregional approach for millennia; it is the rest of Australia which is only now beginning to understand the benefits of a whole landscape approach inclusive of all stakeholders.

FORMING NEW PARTNERSHIPS

Both indigenous organizations and conservation agencies have raised the prospect of improved coordination as a possible outcome of establishing IPAs (Thackway et al, 1997). For indigenous people, the advantages may come from being accepted by conservation agencies as legitimate protected area managers in their own right, and hence on a more equal footing with government agencies than may have previously been the case. For conservation agencies, the advantages may come from having the opportunity to develop long-term partnerships in managing protected areas, a greater mutual understanding of common and different goals, and the prospect of a more regional approach to conservation.

While indigenous people and conservation agencies may have long been aware of the need for improved cooperation, the opportunities and resources to build such relations have not been generally available. IPAs may therefore provide an opportunity for nurturing new relationships at an organizational and personal level.

MAINTAINING CONTROL, RIGHTS AND RESPONSIBILITIES

An issue of major concern to indigenous organizations is the extent to which the establishment of protected areas on aboriginal or Torres Strait Islander lands may compromise existing rights to use, control and manage their lands and resources. Indigenous people have long struggled to secure the return of their land and the recognition of their indigenous rights, often in the face of concerted opposition from the government agencies which now seek conservation partnerships with them. This history of distrust, therefore, is a fundamental issue to be addressed in establishing and managing any indigenous protected area. Lessons learned from overseas experiences will be important in overcoming our history.

> *Rebuilding the relationship between conservation authorities and local people, after a history of policing and exclusion, has proved difficult and some government authorities have been unwilling to support participation, especially if it is seen to be a threat to central authority... Numerous examples exist where coercive methods rather than interactive dialogue have been employed, whilst project managers continually underestimate the time, human resources and commitment necessary to rebuild trusting relationships with communities.*
>
> IIED, 1994

FORMALIZING EXISTING CONSERVATION MANAGEMENT INITIATIVES

Over the last decade indigenous landholders have increasingly developed their capacity to manage the natural and cultural resources of their land and sea, both by strengthening traditional management practices and by embracing contemporary management practices with and without the assistance of government agencies. Examples of these initiatives can be found in all states and the Northern Territory.

Some of these, such as the Kowanyama Trust Area on Western Cape York Peninsula and the north-east tip of Arnhemland (managed by the Dhimurru Aboriginal Land Management Corporation), have developed to the stage where aboriginal land is being managed as a de facto protected area consistent with the *IUCN Guidelines*. Other initiatives, such as the development of a marine strategy for Torres Strait by the Islander Coordinating Council, and conservation planning exercises conducted by land councils and their equivalents in all states and territories, are creating the building blocks for establishing protected areas if indigenous landholders choose to proceed towards that goal (Thackway et al, 1997).

MARINE PROTECTED AREAS

While the focus to date has been on terrestrial protected areas, the *IUCN Guidelines* can be equally applicable to marine protected areas. Several indigenous organizations have shown considerable interest in using the IUCN categories to establish indigenous marine protected areas, or to secure greater recognition for indigenous peoples' interests in existing marine protected areas.

Recognition of indigenous peoples' interests in Australia's marine environment has historically been more difficult than on land. Generally, statutory land claim processes do not apply to the sea, and as yet there have been no native title determinations with respect to aboriginal or Torres Strait Islander customary marine estates (though several such determinations are currently pending). Indigenous groups who expressed an interest in the management of the coastal and marine environments observed that the involvement of indigenous people in this domain has not progressed to the same extent as in terrestrial national parks, especially Uluru and Kakadu. Nevertheless, in the Kakadu region there is much discussion on how the management of the marine component, and adjacent reefs, can be progressively achieved.

CONSULTATIONS WITH INDIGENOUS ORGANIZATIONS AND COMMUNITIES ON THE IPA CONCEPT

Consultations to date with aboriginal and Torres Strait Islander organizations have been undertaken as an exploratory, scoping process. They have not intended to reach all indigenous Australians with a potential interest in environmental management. Rather, an effort has been made to explore the concept with major indigenous organizations in each Australian state and territory with experience and interest in environmental management issues (Thackway et al, 1997).

Two main consultative mechanisms have been adopted to involve indigenous Australians in the exploration of the IPA concept:

• meetings with selected land councils and other indigenous organizations with an interest in land acquisition and management; and
• a national working group meeting held with representatives of indigenous organizations and conservation agencies.

An unanticipated outcome of the consultations so far has been the strongly held view by indigenous people that the value of the IPA concept is not restricted to those indigenous people who had ownership or occupation of their traditional lands (Thackway et al, 1997). A commonly held view is that establishing IPAs only in central and northern Australia where most aboriginal land is located would increase the division between the 'haves and have nots' among the indigenous groups. Accepting this clear position, the federal government agreed that the IPA concept would be broadened to include existing and future publicly funded protected areas (Thackway et al, 1997). With regard to publicly funded protected areas, the government's role would be to facilitate, encourage and resource the establishment of management partnerships between indigenous groups and relevant state and territory agencies.

IMPLEMENTING THE IPA CONCEPT

In order to test the feasibility of the IPA concept at the local community level, the federal government and an indigenous taskforce on protected areas selected a range of pilot projects across Australia. Projects were selected to ensure coverage of each jurisdiction and a range of land tenure categories. In addition, projects were chosen to represent different stages in the capacity of the local communities to develop the IPA concept (Szabo, in press).

There are already indigenous communities (Dhimurru and Kowanyama) who are demonstrating their capacity and willingness to manage their lands for nature conservation with minimal support or direction from government (Thackway et al, 1997). However, many indigenous communities who have expressed interest in managing their lands for nature conservation need support from government with directed programmes to develop their capacity at a local level without compromising local control. 'Aboriginal people will be willing to support internationally recognized conservation regimes only if management decision-making and implementation occur at the local level' (Pearson, 1995).

Ongoing liaison with local indigenous communities involved in undertaking the IPA pilot projects shows a strong sense of commitment to managing natural and cultural resources in a sustainable way, and a willingness to evaluate the usefulness of the IPA concept for their needs. While it is early days, one emerging outcome is that IPAs have a positive empowering role to play in assisting indigenous people to state their position more effectively and to negotiate equitable solutions for their local communities.

Overseas experiences also provide valuable guidance to ensuring that realistic approaches are taken in the design and testing of pilot projects (Possiel et al, 1995). In the past the involvement of indigenous people in protected area management has been perfunctory, and has promised much but yielded little. The real problems and benefits of incorporating indigenous peoples' views and knowledge within day-to-day management of existing protected areas are substantial (IIED 1994).

DISCUSSION

As landowners and managers in both a traditional and a contemporary sense, indigenous people have long called for recognition of their rights, responsibilities and capacity to be fully involved in natural and cultural resource management activities. Numerous recent reports have identified indigenous involvement in managing natural and cultural resources as an important social justice issue (Commonwealth of Australia, 1991a; Commonwealth of Australia, 1995a and 1995b). The Ecologically Sustainable Development Working Group on Fisheries noted that government agencies needed to:

> *...find ways to engage indigenous communities in all aspects*
> *and levels of management, and that an appropriate framework*
> *must be found to work within the customary tenure systems*
> *which extends over the land–sea interface, and coastal waters*
> *by the indigenous groups in much of Australia.*
>
> Commonwealth of Australia, 1991b.

Further support for empowering indigenous communities came in 1992. The United Nations Conference on Environment and Development (UNCED) recommended that nations find ways to empower their indigenous people and communities through a wide range of measures, which included the:

> *...enhancement of capacity-building for indigenous communi-*
> *ties, based on adaptation and exchange of traditional*
> *experience, knowledge and resource management practices, to*
> *ensure their sustainable development.*
>
> United Nations, 1992.

One of the benefits identified by indigenous groups and communities is the potential for IPAs to provide another avenue for national and international recognition of aboriginal and Torres Strait Islander rights, responsibilities and capabilities. In this sense, the establishment of IPAs could play a positive role in the current process of reconciliation between indigenous and non-indigenous Australians.

This may be particularly so if the act of formally declaring and establishing protected areas is undertaken by indigenous landholders or their representative organizations, rather than by government conservation agencies. This could make the establishment of such protected areas an explicit act of self-determination. In that event, conservation agencies would be invited to recognize the protected area status as part of any funding, training or cooperative management agreement. The act of self-declaration of protected areas has great potential for further enabling self-determination within indigenous communities. As this system takes hold it is possible that indigenous Australians will show the wider Australian, and global, community how 'caring for country' without a strict legislative framework is the best form of biodiversity conservation and management.

It is interesting to note that while our initial investigations focused on IUCN Categories V and VI, work performed by Environment Australia during the implementation of the IPA pilot projects has shown that there is no impediment to indigenous peoples self-declaring their land as a protected area under any of the IUCN Categories I to VI. Once a management plan has been agreed upon by the custodian landholders, such protected areas could be recognized by an appropriate government agency or non-government nature conservation agency (Thackway and Brunckhorst, in press).

CONCLUSIONS

The IPA pilot projects will help to determine the resources necessary for implementing the IPA concept more widely across Australia as partnerships between nature conservation agencies and local communities. It is hoped that the IPA concept will be widely supported by governments and the wider community given its potential benefits for social justice, regional planning and economic independence of indigenous people.

The success of indigenous protected areas will depend upon effective and equal partnerships between indigenous land owners and nature conservation agencies. The marks of such partnerships will be recognition:

- that traditional owners have a right to access land management information required to assist them in the stewardship of their land;
- that traditional cultural management of the land (caring for country) by indigenous people is a legitimate basis for the maintenance of natural biodiversity;
- that traditional owners who have responsibility for customary law for a site or area should remain the stewards of that country;
- that traditional owner knowledge of land management is on an equal basis to 'scientific' understanding of the land as espoused by nature conservation agencies; and
- by nature conservation agencies that effective management of lands can be achieved where indigenous people are empowered with appropriate resources and information.

The issue of greater access to traditional lands in proclaimed national parks is being actively pursued by indigenous people through some 30 proposals for joint management of protected areas under consideration across Australia (De Lacey, 1994). The survival of indigenous rights in many proclaimed national parks is a relevant and significant development which state and territory nature conservation agencies are struggling with. Claims over these areas have raised a number of issues where indigenous people have expectations which have not been resolved. These include: subsistence, ecotourism, ethnoecology, and employment and training. If these changes were adequately addressed in favour of aboriginal people then: 'they will have a profound impact on the culture and nature of protected area management in Australia. They could also contribute to social justice for aboriginal people' (De Lacey, 1994).

REFERENCES

AUSLIG (Australian Surveying and Land Information Group) (1993) *Digital Land Tenure Data Set*, AUSMAP, Department of Administrative Services, Canberra
Commonwealth of Australia (1991a) *Royal Commission into Aboriginal Deaths in Custody*, Australian Government Publishing Service, Canberra
Commonwealth of Australia (1991b) *Ecological Sustainable Development Working Group on Fisheries*, Australian Government Publishing Service, Canberra

Commonwealth of Australia (1995a) *Recognition, Rights and Reforms – Report to Government on Native Title Social Justice Measures*, Australian Government Publishing Service, Canberra

Commonwealth of Australia (1995b) *Council for Aboriginal Reconciliation, 'Going Forward – Social Justice for the first Australians*, Australian Government Publishing Service, Canberra

Commonwealth of Australia (1996) *National strategy for the conservation of Australia's biological diversity*, Department of Environment, Sport and Territories, Canberra

Cresswell, I D and Thomas, G (1997) *Terrestrial and Marine Protected Areas in Australia – 1997*, Biodiversity Group, Environment Australia, Department of Environment, Sport and Territories, Canberra

De Lacey, T (1994) 'The Uluru/Kakadu model – Anangu Tjukurrpa: 50,000 years of Aboriginal law and land management changing the concept of national parks in Australia', *Society and Natural Resources* 7, 479–498

House of Representatives Select Committee (1972) *Report on Wildlife Conservation*, Australian Government Publishing Service, Canberra

IIED (1994) *Whose Eden? An overview of community approaches to wildlife management*, International Institute for Environment and Development, London

Pearson, N (1995) 'The future: Aboriginal management of Cape York Peninsula', in *Habitat* 23(4), 19

Possiel, W J, Saunier, R E and Meganck, R A (1995) 'In-Situ Conservation of Biodiversity', in *Conservation of Biodiversity and the New Regional Planning*, Saunier, R E and Meganck, R A (eds) Organization of American States and the IUCN – The World Conservation Union

Pressey, R L and Tully, S L (1994) 'The cost of ad hoc reservation: a case study in western New South Wales', *Australian Journal of Ecology* 19, 375–384

Szabo, S G (in press) 'Indigenous Protected Areas: Managing natural and cultural values – a two way street', in The 1996 Commission for National Parks and Protected Areas Regional Conference: Australia and Pacific/New Zealand Regions, 8–10 June 1996, Sydney

Thackway, R and Brunckhorst, D J (in press) 'Alternative Futures for Indigenous Cultural and Natural Areas in Australia's Rangelands', *Australian Journal of Environmental Management*

Thackway, R and Cresswell, I D (1995a) 'Towards a systematic approach for identifying gaps in the Australian system of protected areas', in *Ecosystem monitoring and Protected areas*, Proceedings of the 2nd International Conference on the Science and the Management of Protected Areas, Halifax, Nova Scotia, May 1994, 473–483

Thackway, R and Cresswell, I D (eds) (1995b) *An interim biogeographic regionalisation for Australia: a framework for establishing the national system of reserves*, version 4.0, Australian Nature Conservation Agency, Canberra

Thackway, R, Szabo, S and Smyth, D (1996) 'Indigenous protected areas: a new concept in conservation of biodiversity, 18–34', in *Biodiversity, broadening the debate 4, the beat goes on...* Richard Longmore (ed), Australian Nature Conservation Agency, Canberra

Thackway, R, Szabo, S and Smyth, D (1996) 'Indigenous protected areas: new opportunities for the conservation of biodiversity', in *Conservation Outside of Nature Reserves*, Conference paper given at the Centre for Conservation Biology, University of Queensland, Brisbane, 5–8 February

United Nations (1992) *Earth Summit Agenda 21*, The United Nations Programme of Action held in Rio de Janeiro, United Nations Publication, New York

9 FUTURE DEVELOPMENTS IN MARINE PROTECTED AREAS[*]

Sue Wells and Will Hildesley

INTRODUCTION

Marine protected areas (MPAs) are an essential tool for conserving and restoring marine ecosystem health, and in many places are considered to be effective fishery management tools. Consequently, increasing attention is being paid to establishing new MPAs and ensuring that existing ones are effectively managed. This chapter outlines some of the key issues which are being, and will need to be, addressed by those involved in MPA establishment and management.

ECOLOGICAL DIFFERENCES BETWEEN MARINE AND TERRESTRIAL ENVIRONMENTS

Conservation science and practical experience show that marine and terrestrial protected areas are most effective when they encompass complete ecological units. However, the nature of water is such that marine ecological boundaries are often less well defined than terrestrial boundaries, and tend to be less static. For example, the boundary between freshwater flowing out of a river and salt water in the receiving ocean changes shape and location depending upon the amount and speed of the freshwater flow, which can change on a daily, seasonal and annual basis. The design of MPAs must take this variability into account, which may require designating larger areas and using flexible management approaches that can respond to changing ecological conditions.

Linkages between marine ecosystems are often more complex and occur on a larger scale than in terrestrial ecosystems. For example, nutrients and larvae can be carried over large distances on ocean currents and transferred between many different ecosystems (Roberts, 1997a); and larvae may even move directionally between different areas (Wolanski et al, 1997). The design of individual MPAs and MPA systems must take these long-distance processes

[*] Thanks to Charlotte de Fontaubert, Marine Programme Officer, IUCN, and Janet Gibson.

into account. For example, if giant clams in one area grow from larvae produced many kilometres away, it will be necessary to protect both the adult habitat and the source of larvae. Furthermore, even though terrestrial protected areas can be damaged by pollution produced hundreds or thousands of kilometres away, MPAs are particularly vulnerable to this and other kinds of downstream effects.

Highly migratory species occur both on land and in water, but are particularly prevalent in the oceans. Cetaceans, large pelagic fish and turtles, for example, migrate enormous distances, both as adults and during different growth stages in their life cycles. These migrations are often linked to feeding and breeding behaviour. Many species are also closely associated with large ocean current systems (such as the Atlantic bluefin tuna in the Gulf Stream) and migrate annually, following a current to stay in water of a suitable temperature or to find sources of food. Protecting such species requires the establishment of MPAs at key sites (for instance, feeding and breeding areas) along the migratory routes. In addition, migratory species will also require broader regulations outside these protected areas to ensure their long-term survival.

These features of the marine environment underline the need for MPAs to be established as part of both regional and global systems, designed to ensure full representation of all ecosystems, and to take into account the linkages between them (Kelleher et al, 1995). Well-designed networks of effectively managed MPAs are essential. However, alone they will not result in adequate conservation of marine biodiversity, anymore than national parks alone can conserve terrestrial biodiversity, and a framework of integrated coastal and marine management must be established.

MANAGING MARINE ECOSYSTEMS

Attempts to protect marine environments and manage use of marine resources are influenced by two fundamental aspects of humankind's relationship with the oceans. Firstly, in comparison with terrestrial systems, very little is known about ocean processes and populations. Filling the gaps in this knowledge is costly and complex compared to carrying out similar research on land. Lack of scientific knowledge on which to base sound management may lead to the wrong decisions being taken; and it can also be used as an excuse to delay or obstruct the establishment of an MPA.

Secondly, unlike on land, the oceans have historically been perceived and managed as an open access commons. Private ownership of the seabed and marine resources is rare although, in some regions such as the South Pacific, systems of communal customary tenure have developed in coastal waters. The 'high seas' (all areas of the oceans outside exclusive economic zones – EEZs) are, however, defined as open access commons under the United Nations Convention on the Law of the Sea (UNCLOS). Establishment and management of MPAs on the high seas therefore requires international cooperation.

Managed as a commons, ocean and coastal areas are normally subject to multiple, conflicting use. Frequently, the same resource or population is targeted by a variety of user groups, such as recreational fishers, long-liners, scuba divers and traditional fishers. Thus establishment and management of

an MPA, particularly in coastal areas, often involves a greater number of stakeholders and consideration of a wider range of issues than is common for
terrestrial protected areas.

Many protected areas include terrestrial as well as subtidal areas, which
usually come under the jurisdiction of different government agencies; this may
also occur even where the entire area is intertidal or subtidal. If these agencies
have conflicting aims or management approaches, this may create an obstacle
to successful management. For example, a protected area managed by a
national parks department may contain mangroves subject to the regulations
of a forestry department, and fish fry that are the responsibility of a fishery
department.

DEFINITIONS AND CATEGORIES OF MPAS

The main objective of most legally designated MPAs is biodiversity conservation, including protection or restoration of depleted populations, endangered
species and critical habitats. However, MPAs also have other roles. Large,
zoned, multiple-use areas, such as Australia's Great Barrier Reef Marine Park,
play a role in reducing conflict between different uses of the marine environment; many, such as the Galapagos Marine Reserve and Banc D'Arguin National
Park, play an important role in regulating resource use. As human uses of the
marine environment expand and intensify, the aims, definitions and management approaches of MPAs are becoming increasingly flexible. Contemporary
MPA designations represent a continuum of approaches, with 'no-disturbance'
zones and strict protection at one end and 'multiple-use' management areas at
the other.

These changes have been accompanied by new approaches to MPA establishment and management, including:

- alternatives to statutory designation, such as customary tenure and voluntary protected areas;
- management by local communities, with or without active participation of
  governments;
- the increasing use of zoning schemes within MPAs to balance conservation
  and human use; and
- participation of industry, including tourism and fisheries.

Although these trends have been welcomed in many cases, they have also
raised questions as to whether conservation objectives are being met in full. In
order to ensure that the global network of MPAs adequately protects marine
biodiversity, national systems must be designed so that they protect the full
range of marine ecosystems and species. At the same time, they must take into
account the relevant different cultural, economic and political situations.

The term MPA means different things in different places, a point that is
reflected in national legislation and, to a lesser extent, in global treaties and
agreements. In some countries, such as Canada, a dichotomy has arisen
between MPAs established for fisheries management, and those designated to
serve broader conservation objectives. In Europe, the European Union (EU)
Habitats Directive recognizes as MPAs only those sites designated to protect

biodiversity, representative habitats or threatened species, and does not consider areas closed to fishing, under fisheries legislation, as protected areas. Recent calls by scientists for the establishment of MPAs have further confused the picture since the basis for these statements has been research on fisheries management and the specific benefits of no-fishing zones (NFZs).

An MPA is defined by IUCN as: any area of intertidal or subtidal terrain, together with its overlying water and associated flora, fauna, historical and cultural features, which has been reserved by law or other effective means to protect part or all of the enclosed environment (Kelleher and Recchia, 1998). This definition is intentionally very broad, encouraging the use of the term MPA generically to cover areas established for a variety of purposes, including fisheries management, provided there is a conservation objective. The IUCN definition includes areas protected by 'effective means' other than statutory legislation, and thus includes areas set up under customary tenure or voluntary agreements, provided these are deemed 'effective', a qualification that has yet to be defined. In some countries, these may be the only sites accepted by local communities and effectively managed. However, in many cases, these areas are not recognized by governments as contributing to national protected area systems.

Under the IUCN protected area management categories, Categories V and VI, protected areas could be most effective in both marine and terrestrial environments since they tend to encompass larger areas and a greater range of interdependent ecosystems. MPAs in these categories often have 'core areas' with strict protection, in a larger area of integrated management. Category V areas closely fit the biosphere reserve model of a highly protected core area, surrounded by a less stringently protected buffer zone, surrounded in turn by a transition area which may contain human communities. Many multiple-use MPAs are zoned and, if IUCN categories were to be applied to each zone, a much clearer picture of the management objective of the area would be obtained (Kelleher and Recchia, 1998). Therefore, the Great Barrier Reef Marine Park is Category VI but includes a number of zones that meet the criteria for other categories (Tanzer, 1998). Categories I and II protected areas may, in fact, provide less protection since they may be harder to establish because they prohibit so many human activities, and they are often small, isolated areas in a larger landscape of unsustainable resource use, vulnerable to outside influences.

Effective national systems of protected areas, both marine and terrestrial, are most likely to need a combination of categories, provided that those in the 'less strict' categories are established and managed according to the criteria (Dudley and Stolton, 1998). However, the potential for abuse of the categories has raised the question of whether minimum standards should be established. For example, WWF Canada's Endangered Spaces Campaign has suggested that minimum standards for MPAs should include, as well as statutory designation, the prohibition of activities such as non-renewable resource development, bottom trawling and dredging. However, such criteria might easily discourage the establishment of new MPAs.

As Dudley and Stolton (1998) suggest, the key issue may be judging the proportion of a national protected area system that needs to fall under each category. A balanced network of categories, covering a representative proportion of all ecosystems and with objectives that meet a range of ecological and social goals, will be optimal. Once such networks are established, however, it is also essential that their management effectiveness is assessed on a regular basis (see Chapter 27).

SPECIFIC TYPES OF MPAs

There are a number of issues that need particular consideration when setting up MPAs that may not arise in the terrestrial situation. These include the role of MPAs in fisheries management and the particular problems encountered with offshore MPAs and those beyond national jurisdiction.

No-fishing zones (NFZs)

Once, technological and economic constraints provided de facto NFZs in the form of inaccessible fish populations, but now modern boats and gear leave few stocks out of reach. However, for centuries, subsistence fishers in the tropics have recognized the value of enforcing seasonal or permanent area closures to minimize the risk of overexploiting fisheries resources. Today, such areas are gaining increasing attention as the overfishing crisis mounts.

Several terms are used for areas in which fishing is excluded, including no-fishing zones (NFZs), 'fishery reserves', 'harvest refugia' and 'no-take zones'. Such areas also vary in the extent to which non-extractive activities such as scuba diving are allowed, and whether extractive activities such as dredging and oil production are allowed. In this chapter, NFZ is used for those areas closed to all fishing activities on a permanent basis, regardless of whether other activities are permitted. NFZs have been designated as stand-alone measures under protected area or fisheries legislation, as in Bermuda where 20 per cent of the continental shelf has been closed to fishing, or as zones within larger multiple-use protected areas – for example, in several marine reserves in Belize and in the Great Barrier Reef Marine Park in Australia.

There is growing evidence that closing areas to fishing can benefit fisheries while meeting a broad range of other marine management objectives (Roberts, 1997b). Fisheries benefits, demonstrated in many situations including New Zealand (Walls, 1998), the Philippines (Russ and Alcala, 1996), the Caribbean (Roberts, 1995) and Kenya (McClanahan and Kaunda-Arara, 1996), include:

- increased abundance and size of individuals within NFZs;
- emigration of target species from reserves to adjacent fishing grounds – 'the spillover effect';
- increased production of eggs and larvae and export of these to adjacent fisheries, and increased fertilization success due to density effects; and
- protection of habitat for spawning and settlement of eggs and larvae.

Full NFZs also have management benefits. They serve as an 'insurance policy' against failure of existing regulations. Enforcement may be easier and less expensive, since any observed fishing within an NFZ is a proof of breach. Furthermore, once fishers find that NFZs result in increased catches outside the area, they often enforce the area themselves.

Since they are one type of MPA, NFZs also contribute to the protection of biodiversity, including rare species and populations especially vulnerable to fishing. They maintain ecosystem structure and function by preventing direct fishing impacts such as bottom trawling and trap damage, and indirect impacts such as removal of predators. Like other MPAs, they may help to improve public understanding of the marine environment and the need for its management, and to provide opportunities for economic diversification through tourism, recreation and educational opportunities.

Where the benefits of NFZs have been demonstrated, they are being established with relative ease, particularly when they are part of an MPA system which provides alternative sources of income through tourism, for example in Belize (where some 19 per cent of the total area of MPAs is closed to fishing – Wells et al, unpublished) and The Philippines (where numerous small fish sanctuaries have been established by village communities). In contrast, establishing NFZs remains a controversial issue in countries where MPAs have not traditionally involved closure to fishing. In the US, only 0.14 per cent of the total area of over 100 MPAs is closed to fishing (McArdle, 1997). The draft management plan for the Florida Keys National Marine Sanctuary proposed a network of closed areas covering 6 to 8 per cent of the sanctuary, but this was reduced to one NFZ covering 0.5 per cent through public pressure. Even in Australia, only 4.6 per cent of the Great Barrier Reef Marine Park is designated as NFZs (Prideaux et al, 1998).

There are a variety of reasons for this resistance. Most research into the benefits of NFZs has been carried out in coral reef environments, where fish are relatively sedentary and entire populations can theoretically be protected. However, modelling suggests that a wide variety of fisheries will benefit (Lauck et al, 1998). Benefits to highly mobile and migratory species would logically be fewer as NFZs, although providing the same level of protection to habitats will directly protect individuals only while they are inside an area.

For species which form seasonal aggregations at a certain location – for example, groupers when spawning – NFZs can play a key role on a seasonal basis (Johannes, 1998). In other cases, the benefits of seasonal closures are less clear. For example, the North Sea 'Plaice Box' is closed for the second and third quarters of each year in order to protect juvenile plaice. The relative abundance of undersized plaice has increased since 1989, but fishing effort has grown markedly within the Plaice Box during the fourth quarter of each year (Gubbay, 1996). Seasonal closures of this kind are unlikely to provide many of the conservation benefits predicted for permanent closures.

Another problem is that increased fishing effort outside an NFZ or, in the case of seasonally closed areas, in the fishing season may ultimately negate the value of the closed area itself. NFZs are likely to result in initial reductions in yields; increased catches may not appear for three to five years (Nowlis and Roberts, 1997) and this may lead either to pressure to reopen the fishery before the benefits appear, or demands for compensation. It is therefore essential that NFZs are established as part of a broader fishery management and MPA plan, and that alternative sources of income are considered for those previously dependent upon the closed area. For example, in Samoa, giant clam aquaculture and subsequent restocking of reefs were promoted concurrently with the establishment of village-based NFZs.

Further work is also needed on optimal designs, sizes and locations of NFZs. Large areas are likely to be most effective, but small NFZs may provide adequate protection for largely sedentary species (as demonstrated in South Africa – Buxton, 1996) or for critical habitats (such as nursery areas or spawning grounds) of more mobile species. However, for many species such 'critical habitat' is hard to identify. Where species use one habitat as juveniles and another as adults both areas may need protection. As with MPAs in general, a network is probably essential, designed to reflect larval dispersal patterns, and providing an insurance mechanism if one site is degraded, for example by pollution (Roberts, 1997a; Ballantine, 1995).

MPAs in offshore waters and beyond national jurisdiction

So far the majority of MPAs have been established close, if not adjacent, to shore. However, areas of high productivity and diversity exist offshore, as do critical habitats such as spawning areas, nursery grounds and migration routes (WWF–UK, 1997). Offshore areas are also subject to similar threats as inshore areas, such as overfishing, dumping and oil pollution, and, owing to the interconnected nature of marine environments, may indirectly suffer from negative impacts such as pollution originating from land or coastal waters.

Therefore, there is a clear need for offshore MPAs. An increasing number are being established, such as Elizabeth and Middleton Reefs in Australia, the Flower Gardens National Marine Sanctuary in the US, and Hertha's Flak in Denmark. However, in many regions there is a reluctance to accept the need for such areas, partly due to potential difficulties in enforcement and implementation, and partly because their out-of-sight, out-of-mind nature may mean that it is difficult to gather public support for them.

MPAs are generally established under national jurisdiction, within a nation's territorial waters or EEZ (where they may be either inshore – close to the coast – or offshore). Growing recognition that marine ecosystems do not respect political boundaries, and increasing access to the deep sea via improved technology, mean that such designations alone may no longer be sufficient. Deep sea and open ocean ecosystems include vast plankton blooms and swarms of krill, act as nursery areas for great and small whales and include little understood geological features of scientific interest such as geothermal vents and deep trenches (McCloske, 1996). Attention is therefore being given to the potential and feasibility of establishing MPAs on the high seas or in international waters.

This, however, presents particular legal and institutional challenges. In international waters, nations can regulate only the activities of their own citizens and flagged vessels; two or more nations can agree by treaty to protect an area of international water, but they will only be able to control the activities of ships subject to their own national legislation. For example, the Indian Ocean Sanctuary and the Southern Ocean Sanctuary, established by the International Whaling Commission (IWC), together provide a permanent no-take zone for whales of approximately 100 million square kilometres, largely in international waters (Phillips, 1996). Enforcement, however, is limited to the commitment of IWC member nations to the sanctuary concept. Japan, for example, continues to exploit the IWC provision for scientific research and hunts up to 440 minke whales a year from the Southern Ocean Sanctuary, an activity over which the other participating nations have no direct control.

UNCLOS contains provisions for the International Seabed Authority to place parts of the sea floor off-limits for mineral extraction if and when this poses an environmental threat, and would be another global treaty under which MPAs on the high seas could be designated. UNCLOS provides for habitat protection, unlike the IWC sanctuaries but given current international maritime law, enforcement would still be as difficult.

Several regional agreements are also addressing the issue of MPAs on the high seas and may provide models and principles for international cooperation. The Antarctic Treaty Environmental Protection Protocol includes a provision for designating special areas for protection and scientific study to protect species or habitats, including areas in the high seas under its jurisdiction. The Barcelona Convention also allows for MPAs on the high seas in the Mediterranean. However, in neither area have such MPAs yet been established.

Transboundary MPAs and regional networks

Transboundary MPAs are protected areas that straddle the frontiers of two or more countries. Although these are important on land, since no ecosystems or ecological processes respect political boundaries, they may be particularly important in the marine environment given the interconnectedness of marine ecosystems, processes and populations, and the prevalence of migratory species.

These areas require good cooperation between participating states to be effective, and legislative, institutional and political differences are often major obstacles. Legal precedents for states to cooperate in managing and conserving marine resources that straddle their boundaries can be found in the joint exploitation zones that have been agreed between states as temporary or permanent solutions to intractable boundary disputes. These include a joint fishing zone between Colombia and the Dominican Republic, the Joint Red Sea Common Zone between Saudi Arabia and Sudan for exploitation of minerals (Blake, 1987), and the agreement between the UK and Argentina over fishing around the Falkland Islands.

Jointly formulated networks of MPAs, where states collaborate to select sites and then manage them jointly or independently, are another form of transboundary cooperation. Such initiatives may result in protection over entire ecosystems or regions but demand high levels of cooperation between the states involved, as illustrated by the Wadden Sea Conservation Area designated as a joint initiative by Denmark, Germany and The Netherlands (Enemark et al, 1998).

CONCLUSIONS

The marine environment is still poorly represented in the global protected area. Within the MPA network itself, many marine ecosystems and species are underrepresented, with most MPAs established in coastal waters and/or for large, charismatic marine vertebrates such as turtles and marine mammals.

The 'connectivity' of the oceans means that it is particularly important to establish networks or systems of MPAs, carefully designed to take into account the movements of migratory species and the dispersal patterns of larvae and nutrients. Such networks must be established with the recognition that marine ecosystems and processes take no account of national boundaries, territorial waters or EEZs. Mechanisms must therefore be found which allow implementation and effective management of MPAs outside national jurisdiction. In the marine environment, regional and global treaties and agreements may have a particularly important role to play in protected area management.

Equally important, given that MPAs are so vulnerable to pollution and other impacts taking place outside their boundaries, more attention is needed to ensure that MPA systems are firmly grounded in broader integrated coastal and marine management programmes that address land-based activities and fishing. As on land, there is no single model for a protected area in the sea, and a careful balance of different types of MPAs are required, reflecting the needs of both species and ecosystems and of the human communities that depend upon them. In particular, protected area managers and fishery managers need to develop closer collaborative relationships and to recognize that carefully designed MPAs can benefit them both, protecting marine biodiversity and contributing towards sustainable fisheries.

REFERENCES

Ballantine, W J (1995) 'Networks of "no-take" marine reserves are practical and necessary', in Shackell, N L and Willison, J H M (eds) *Marine Protected Areas and Sustainable Fisheries*, 2nd International Conference on Science and the Management of Protected Areas, Halifax, 13–20

Blake, G (1987) *Maritime Boundaries and Ocean Resources*, International Geographical Union Study Group on the World Political Map, Croom Helm, London

Buxton, C (1996) 'The role of marine protected areas in the management of reef fish: a South African example', in *Developing Australia's Representative System of Marine Protected Areas*, Ocean Rescue Workshop Series, 114–124

Dudley, N and Stolton, S (1998) *Protected Areas for a New Millennium: the implications of IUCN's protected area categories for forest conservation*, WWF/IUCN Discussion Paper, WWF-International and IUCN – The World Conservation Union, Gland

Enemark, J, Wesemuller, H and Gerdiken, A (1998) 'The Wadden Sea: an international perspective on managing marine resources', *Parks* 8(2): 36–40

Gubbay, S (1996) *Marine Refuges: the next step for nature conservation and fisheries management in the North-East Atlantic?* Report to WWF-UK, Godalming

Johannes, R E (1998) 'The case for data-less marine resource management: examples from tropical nearshore finfisheries', *Trends in Ecology and Evolution* 13(6): 243–246

Kelleher, G, Bleakley, C and Wells, S (eds) (1995) *A Global Representative System of Marine Protected Areas*, vols 1–4, The World Bank, IUCN and the Great Barrier Reef Marine Park Authority, IUCN, Gland

Kelleher, G and Recchia, C (1998) 'Editorial – lessons from marine protected areas around the world', *Parks* 8(2): 1–4.

Lauck, T, Clark, C W, Mangel, M and Munro, G R (1998) 'Implementing the precautionary principle in fisheries management through marine reserves', *Ecological Applications* 8(1) supplement: S72–S78

McArdle, D A (ed) (1997) *California Marine Protected Areas*, University of California, La Jolla

McClanahan, T R and Kaunda-Arara, B (1996) 'Fishery recovery in a coral-reef marine park and its effect on the adjacent fishery', *Conservation Biology* 10, 1187–1199

McCloskey, M (1996) 'MPA Problems and Solutions for the High Seas', Paper presented to the IUCN World Conservation Congress (WCC), 13–23 October 1996, Montreal

Nowlis, J S and Roberts, C M (1997) 'You can have your fish and eat it too: theoretical approaches to marine reserve design', Proceedings of the 8th International Coral Reef Symposium, *Panama*, 2, 1907–1910

Phillips, C (1996) 'Conservation in practice: agreements, regulations, sanctuaries and action plans', in Simmonds, M P and Hutchinson, J D (eds) *The Conservation of Whales and Dolphins*, John Wiley and Sons Ltd, 447–465

Prideaux, M, Emmett, J and Horstman, M (1998) 'Sustainable use or multiple abuse?', *Habitat Australia*, April 1998

Roberts, C M (1995) 'Rapid build-up of fish biomass in a Caribbean marine reserve', *Conservation Biology* 91(4): 815–826

Roberts, C M (1997a) 'Connectivity and management of Caribbean coral reefs', *Science* 278, 1454–1457

Roberts, C M (1997b) 'Ecological advice for the global fisheries crisis', *Trends in Ecology and Evolution*, 12(1): 35–38

Russ, G R and Alcala, A C (1996) 'Do marine reserves export adult fish biomass? Evidence from Apo Island, central Philippines', *Marine Ecology Progress Series* 132, 1–9

Tanzer, J (1998) 'Fisheries in the Great Barrier Reef Marine Park – seeking the balance'. *Parks* 8(2): 41–46

Walls, K (1998) 'Leigh Marine Reserve, New Zealand', *Parks* 8(2): 5–10

Wells, S M, McField, M D, Gibson, J, Carter, J and Sedberry, G R (unpublished) *Marine protected areas in Belize and their potential in fisheries management*, Paper presented at symposium on marine protected areas, Centre for Marine Conservation, Bahamas

Wolanski, E, Doherty, P and Carleton, J (1997) 'Directional swimming of fish larvae determines connectivity of fish populations on the Great Barrier Reef', *Naturwissenschaften* 84, 262–268

WWF-UK (1997) *The Value of Protecting Offshore Areas as Marine Reserves*, WWF-UK Briefing, Godalming

10 National System Planning for Protected Areas[*]

Adrian G Davey

Introduction

The major threats to conservation in most countries lie outside the protected area system. Unless the linkages between protected area management and external factors are identified and addressed, fundamental conservation issues are difficult to resolve. Protected area system plans cannot therefore focus solely on protected areas, but must address broader issues of concern to society.

A *system plan* is the design of a total reserve system covering the full range of ecosystems and communities found in a particular country. The plan should identify the range of purposes of protected areas and help to balance different objectives. The plan should also identify the relationships among the system components – between individual areas, between protected areas and other land uses and between different sectors and levels of the society concerned. It should help demonstrate important linkages with other aspects of economic development and show how various stakeholders can interact and cooperate to support effective and sustainable management of protected areas. Lastly, a system plan should be a means to establish the priorities for a workable national system of protected areas.

A system approach improves the probability of substantial progress in conservation. It also promotes a truly integrated approach to linking conservation with other human endeavours.

The need for system planning

Protected areas will not survive unless they enjoy broad public support and this will not exist unless people's fundamental needs are met. Land use and

* This chapter is based on Adrian G Davey (1998) *National System Planning for Protected Areas*, WCPA: Best Practice Protected Area Guidelines Series No 1, IUCN, Gland, reproduced here with the kind permission of IUCN.

resource management conflicts, inequities or impacts do not go away simply because an area is given protected status. When they are established by nation states or related entities, protected area boundaries often reflect considerations of sovereignty, governance and tenure as much as the environment types they seek to protect. For all these reasons, the planning and management of protected areas must be coordinated with the use and management of other areas rather than treated in isolation. The long-term success of protected areas must be seen in the light of the search for more sustainable patterns of development in general. System planning offers a practical way of putting protected areas management into this wider context.

Protected area system plans are called for under Article 8 of the Convention on Biological Diversity (Glowka et al, 1994) in which protected areas are identified as having an important role in the conservation of biodiversity. Thus, governments have now agreed a clear mandate under the convention for coordinated protected area planning at the national level. The system plan is a means of carrying this out since protected areas also serve many functions other than biodiversity conservation. It is essential that protected area system planning is integrated with national biodiversity strategies, national conservation strategies, ecologically sustainable development strategies and other national-level planning.

Although there is no one model which is universally appropriate, a number of countries have developed system plans in recent years. System planning does have an extensive body of knowledge and field experience on which to build (Mackinnon et al, 1986; Thorsell, 1990; McNeely and Thorsell, 1991; Lucas, 1992; Harmon, 1994; IUCN, 1994), as well as an extensive technical literature in conservation biology and conservation evaluation.

The core idea of protected area system planning is simple enough: that effective planning and management of protected areas requires a coordinated approach both with respect to the various units within the system, and with other land uses and management activities.

SYSTEM PLANNING

When system planning is applied to protected areas, it aims to maximize the desirable characteristics of a national protected area system. This should be done in a way which recognizes prevailing conditions in each country arising from its environmental inheritance, history, and social, political, economic and cultural context.

In relation to protected areas, system planning is about defining the relationships between (a) different units and categories of protected areas, and (b) protected areas and other relevant categories of land. This entails taking a more strategic view of protected areas by defining the roles of key players in relation to protected areas and the relationships between these players; this may include building support and a constituency for protected areas (as a means to that end, not as an end in itself). It is important to identify gaps in protected area coverage (including opportunities and needs for connectivity) and deficiencies in management, and to identify current and potential impacts – both those affecting protected areas from surrounding lands and those emanating from the protected areas which affect surrounding lands.

CHARACTERISTICS OF A SYSTEM

Protected areas are a key part of in situ conservation under the Convention on Biological Diversity (CBD). By switching the focus from individual protected areas to looking at the relationships between them, and putting the whole protected area network into its broader context, system planning provides the means for ensuring that the total significance and effectiveness of a national protected areas system is much more than the sum of the parts.

There are at least five key characteristics of a system of protected areas. These are listed below.

Representativeness, comprehensiveness and balance

This includes the highest quality examples of the full range of environment types within a country, as well as the extent to which protected areas provide balanced sampling of the environment types they purport to represent. This characteristic applies particularly to the biodiversity of the country (at relevant levels, such as genetic, species and habitat) but should also apply to other features such as landform types and to cultural landscapes. Since it is most unlikely that any one protected area could be representative of the full range of biogeographic diversity within a single country, representativeness will nearly always require the development of a network of individual protected areas.

Often protected areas do not sample biodiversity in any systematic way, having been created in an ad hoc, opportunistic fashion. In many countries, there appears to be a need for fresh surveys to identify the environment types and biodiversity at the national level, with a view to redesigning protected areas in order to maximize representation of biodiversity and of natural and related cultural landscapes.

To assess representativeness, it is necessary to compile one or more relevant classification types. The main requirement is that the typologies are appropriate to the scale of planning and that they are based on the best available science. There is an extensive technical literature on this subject. Mackinnon et al (1986) remains an excellent overview but should be read in association with more recent contributions (Theberge, 1989; Bedward et al, 1992; Belbin, 1992; Pressey et al, 1993; Scott et al, 1993; Margules et al, 1994; Pressey and Logan, 1994; Peres and Terborgh, 1995).

It may be necessary to combine assessments of reserve coverage which are based on environmental representational objectives (the biogeographic approach) with assessments based on species and habitat conservation objectives (the key species approach). However, a reserve system should not be designed to be representative alone. It should also take account of the need to give protection to refugia areas, rare species' habitat, breeding habitat of migratory species and landform features.

Adequacy

This comprises integrity, sufficiency of spatial extent and arrangement of contributing units, together with effective management, to support viability of the environmental process and/or species, populations and communities which make up the biodiversity of the country.

A wide range of issues must be considered when selecting between alternative designs of national protected area systems. The final location, size and boundaries of contributing areas will be influenced by factors such as habitat area requirements of rare or other species and their minimum viable population sizes. Connectivity between units (corridors) to permit wildlife migration, or occasionally isolation to minimize transfer of disease, predators and the like, need to be considered, along with perimeter area relationships. Similarly, natural system linkages and boundaries, such as watersheds (surface and groundwater), volcanism, ocean currents, aeolian or other active geomorphic systems, should influence design. The following will also need consideration: accessibility to undertake management operations or inaccessibility to deter potentially impacting activity; existing degradation or external threats; traditional use, occupancy and sustainability; and cost of achieving protected area status (most commonly land acquisition compensation or transfer costs, or costs of establishing comanagement mechanisms).

Coherence and complementarity

This is defined as the positive contribution of each site towards the whole. Each site needs to add value to the national system of protected areas, in quality as well as quantity. There is little point in increasing the extent or number of protected areas unless this brings benefits at least in proportion to the costs.

Consistency

This implies application of management objectives, policies and classifications under comparable conditions in standard ways, so that the purpose of each unit is clear to all and to maximize the chance that management and use support the objectives.

Consistency focuses on the links between objectives and action. One of the main purposes of the IUCN protected areas management classification (see pages xiv–xv) (IUCN, 1994) is to promote a scheme of protected area types based on management objectives, emphasizing that management should flow consistently from those objectives.

Cost effectiveness, efficiency and equity

This is defined as the appropriate balance between the costs and benefits, and appropriate equity in their distribution; it also includes efficiency: the minimum number and size of protected areas needed to achieve system objectives.

The establishment and management of protected areas is a kind of social contract. They are set up and run for the purpose of realizing certain benefits for society. People will therefore need to be assured that they are effective, represent value for money and are managed in a way that is equitable in terms of their impact on communities.

INTEGRATING SYSTEM PLANS INTO THE INTERNATIONAL CONTEXT

The overriding objective of a national system plan is to increase the effectiveness of in situ biodiversity conservation. IUCN has suggested that the long-term success of in situ conservation requires that the global network of protected areas comprise a representative sample of each of the world's different ecosystems. In order to maximize the efficiency with which this is done, a global view is needed. For example, if a country no longer has a significant proportion of its natural forests remaining, it will be necessary to compensate for this shortfall by protecting a relatively larger proportion of such forests in neighbouring countries. Therefore, it is important that effective national system planning promotes cooperation between states.

Viewing the national system plan in an international context may also help to identify opportunities to increase conservation efficiency through cooperation. Transboundary protected areas may offer opportunities to increase the effectiveness of protected areas, and at a lower cost overall. As a result, it is necessary that each country's system plan acknowledges the conservation needs of the region and especially those areas of land and sea that adjoin neighbouring states. Possibilities for cooperative approaches should be identified and joint conservation initiatives should be fostered.

OUTLINE OF A MODEL SYSTEM PLAN

A system plan should be appropriate to its context. There is no one best process, structure or scope. It should be the product of the environment, state of development and institutional capacity of the country at the time of its preparation. Plans must change with time. It follows that the form of a plan that is appropriate also depends on where a country has progressed in evolving its protected area system at the time a particular plan is compiled.

Nonetheless, there are some critical elements that should be included in any national system plan for protected areas:

- a clear statement of objectives, rationale, categories, definitions and future directions for protected areas in the country;
- assessing conservation status, condition and management viability of the various units;
- a review of how well the system samples the biodiversity and other natural and associated cultural heritage of the country;
- procedures for selecting and designing additional protected areas so that the system as a whole has better characteristics;
- identifying the ways in which activities undertaken at national, regional and local levels interact to fulfil national and regional objectives for a system of protected areas;
- a clear basis for integration and coordination of protected areas with other aspects of national planning (for example, with national biodiversity strategies and so forth, but also with land use, economic and social planning);

- assessing existing institutional framework for protected areas (relationships, linkages and responsibilities) and identification of priorities for capacity-building;
- priorities for further evolution of the protected area system;
- procedures for deciding the management category which is most appropriate to each existing and proposed unit, to make best use of the full range of available protected area categories, and to promote ways in which the different system categories support each other;
- identifying investment needs and priorities for protected areas;
- identifying training and human resource development needs for protected area management; and
- guidelines for preparing and implementing management policies and site-level management plans.

OUTLINE OF A PROCESS FOR DEVELOPING A SYSTEM PLAN

If it is to be effective, the plan that is eventually developed for any country must reflect on-ground needs and priorities and must be 'owned' by those who will have to implement it. Therefore, adopting a plan should be mainly the task of the people responsible for protected area matters, although many other stakeholders will need to contribute to its initiation, development and implementation. It will be most effective if it evolves out of a constructive partnership between people, according to the structure of government in the country concerned, at district, provincial and national levels, together with interested NGOs and other stakeholders. It is desirable to include the participation of the local people who live in and around the protected areas (or have other traditional or economic links with them) in developing the plan. It will necessarily take time for the process to reach a stage where a set of integrated programmes will be identifiable as 'the system plan'.

In devising a process that is appropriate to local needs and realities, it should be noted that there is no one 'right' process that can be used in every case. To be effective inputs are required from staff at all levels in a protected area agency, including field staff. Since the aim of the process should be to build up local capacity, there is a need to use external consultants carefully, as much of the learning and institutional memory will be lost when the consultant leaves.

IMPLEMENTATION

Plans are only as good as the action in which they result. Too many plans are long on content and short on delivery. If national system plans for protected areas are to avoid this fate, a realistic appraisal should be made during their preparation of what can be achieved with the resources likely to be available so that the recommendations are recognized as being viable. The plan itself should identify the resource implications of its proposals and the action needed to secure these. It should be prepared through a process which involves building the support needed from government, local communities and other stakeholders and should clearly identify who is to do what; it must encourage institutions so that implementation is sustainable and improve their prospects for self-sufficiency. The plan should also be clearly presented, attractive and easy to read; it may, for example, need to be accompanied by supporting materials (for instance, summaries for different audiences) and a strategy for its promotion.

There should be direct links between the system plan as a national tool and the local action required to give effect to it (such as a clear connection between the system plan and site-based management plans). Finally, there should be arrangements for monitoring and evaluation so that priorities can be adjusted in the light of experience.

REFERENCES

Bedward, M, Pressey, R L and Keith, D A (1992) 'A new approach for selecting fully representative reserve networks: addressing efficiency, reserve design and land suitability with an iterative analysis', *Biological Conservation* 62, 115–125

Belbin, L (1992) 'Environmental representativeness: regional partitioning and reserve selection', *Biological Conservation* 66, 223–230

Glowka, L, Burhenne-Guilmin, F, Synge, H, McNeely, J A and Gündling, L (1994) *A Guide to the Convention on Biological Diversity*, IUCN, Gland, IUCN Environmental Law Centre, Environmental Policy & Law Paper No 30

Harmon, D (ed) (1994) *Co-ordinating research and management to enhance protected areas*, IUCN, Gland

IUCN (1994) *Guidelines for protected area management categories*, IUCN Commission on National Parks and Protected Areas with the assistance of the World Conservation Monitoring Centre, IUCN, Gland

Lucas, P H C (1992) *Protected landscapes: a guide for policy-makers and planning*, Chapman & Hall, London

Mackinnon, J, Mackinnon, K, Child, G and Thorsell, J (1986) *Managing protected areas in the tropics*, IUCN, Gland

Margules, C R, Cresswell, I D and Nicholls, A O (1994) 'A scientific basis for establishing networks of protected areas', in Forey, P L, Humphries, C J and Vane-Wright, R I (eds) *Systematics and conservation evaluation*, Clarendon Press, Oxford

McNeely, J and Thorsell, J (1991) 'Guidelines for preparing protected area system plans', *Parks* 2(2): 4–8

Peres, C A and Terborgh, J W (1995) 'Amazonian nature reserves: an analysis of the defensibility status of existing conservation units and design criteria for the future', *Conservation Biology* 9(1): 34–46

Pressey, R L, Humphries, C J, Margules, C R, Vane-Wright, R I and Williams, P H (1993) 'Beyond opportunism: key principles for systematic reserve selection', *Trends in Ecology & Evolution* 8(4): 124–128

Pressey, R L and Logan, V S (1994) 'Level of geographical subdivision and its effects on assessments of reserve coverage: a review of regional studies', *Conservation Biology* 8(4): 1037–1046

Scott, J M, Davis, F, Csuti, B, Noss, R, Butterfield, B, Groves, C, Anderson, H, Caicco, S, D'Erchia, F, Edwards, T C, Ulliman, J and Wright, R G (1993) 'Gap analysis: a geographic approach to protection of biological diversity', *Wildlife Monographs* No 123 (supplement to Journal of Wildlife Management 57(1))

Theberge, J B (1989) 'Guidelines to drawing ecologically sound boundaries for national parks and nature reserves', *Environmental Management* 13(6): 695–702

Thorsell, J (ed) (1990) *Parks on the borderline: experience in trans-frontier conservation* IUCN, Gland

North Yorkshire Moors, UK

Most protected areas contain human communities. The goodwill of these people is
therefore crucial to the long-term security of these areas. In Europe, for example, most
national parks are at least partly integrated with working landscapes.

PART III

BUILDING STRONGER ALLIANCES WITH PEOPLE

The old concept of a protected area as an uninhabited wilderness set-aside for
wildlife is now being comprehensively revised. Many if not most protected
areas have people living inside them; others have human communities
scattered around their edges. Building a good relationship between human
communities and protected areas is therefore of critical importance to the
success of any conservation programme. This involves new approaches, new
skills and in some cases also a major change in attitudes. The following section
summarizes some recent experiences with approaches to protected areas that
are carried out in association with – and sometimes driven by – local communities, rather than being imposed from above. This includes the process of
building alliances with indigenous people, an extractive wetland reserve in
Brazil and marine reserves in Africa and Central America. The section
concludes with a critical overview of the success of such people-orientated
approaches to conservation to date.

11 BUILDING ALLIANCES WITH INDIGENOUS PEOPLES TO ESTABLISH AND MANAGE PROTECTED AREAS

Gonzalo Oviedo and Jessica Brown

INTRODUCTION

Indigenous and traditional peoples inhabit nearly 20 per cent of the planet, mainly in places where they have lived for thousands of years (Martin, 1993), including many of the remaining significant areas of high natural value left on earth. Indigenous peoples depend directly or indirectly upon the wealth of these ecosystems for their livelihoods, and are the keepers of traditional knowledge and management systems essential to sustainable use. They have a tremendous stake in, and much to contribute to, the stewardship of protected areas.

Historically, many protected areas have been created without consultation with indigenous and other local people living in or near these areas. Often these populations have been displaced or have lost their traditional access to land, waterways and resources. At the same time, the fragile ecosystems and cultural landscapes contained within these protected areas have suffered from the removal of the people who were their traditional stewards (Kempf, 1993).

As a recent draft policy of WWF and IUCN/WCPA recalls (see below), many indigenous peoples' organizations have demanded that protected areas established on their lands and territories:

- effectively protect their lands, territories, waters, coastal seas and other resources, as well as their communities and cultures, from external threats;
- help protect especially valued areas, such as sacred groves and mountains, from external threats;
- recognize indigenous rights to their lands, territories, waters, coastal seas and other resources, as well as their rights to control and manage these within protected areas;
- strengthen traditional institutions and transfer power to them within their lands and territories;
- recognize the rights of indigenous peoples to self-development, that is to say, to determine their own development priorities;

- be declared only at their initiative and/or with their free and prior informed consent; and
- incorporate traditional land-use and conservation patterns.

These claims do not contradict the objectives and integrity of protected areas. However, they demand a new understanding of the rights, roles and responsibilities of indigenous peoples living within protected areas, as well as new partnership arrangements that are respectful of rights and cultures, and at the same time establish the necessary conservation commitments.

This chapter explores how emerging trends in protected areas management offer the potential to address indigenous and traditional peoples' rights, roles and responsibilities. It notes the growing interest of conservation organizations in this area, and reviews recent progress of IUCN and WWF in developing policies related to indigenous peoples and conservation. It reviews how the IUCN protected area management categories offer potential to incorporate indigenous peoples' interests and concerns. It presents key principles that can serve as a foundation on which to forge productive partnerships with indigenous peoples in protected areas management.

THE MEANING OF EMERGING TRENDS IN PROTECTED AREAS FOR INDIGENOUS AND TRADITIONAL PEOPLES

Significant changes in the way protected areas are currently conceived, established and managed in many regions of the world signal the emergence of a 'new paradigm' – one which will be better adapted to the current context of global change related to expanding democratization, the restructuring of nation states, and the growing integration of biodiversity conservation within planning for sustainable development. These trends have important implications for indigenous and traditional peoples living in protected areas.

The struggle of indigenous peoples and oppressed national minorities worldwide for recognition of their rights to self-determination and for respect of cultural diversity is having an important impact on the evolving protected area paradigm. There is growing recognition that the prevailing protected areas model cannot be imposed at the expense of local peoples' rights and cultural traditions, but must be adapted in ways that respect these rights and cultures.

Responding to demands by people all over the world for greater control of decisions affecting their lives, there is a global trend toward devolution of power to the local level and decentralization of authority. Accordingly, there is a trend in many regions away from *exclusive* management models of protected areas and toward *inclusive* models that allow for a high degree of local participation.

Everywhere, but especially in the developing world, governmental agencies responsible for protected areas find themselves in a crisis of political and financial support, and are progressively losing their capacity to manage and conserve the lands under their care. Responding to these challenges, new actors from the non-governmental and private sectors are playing a greater role, and there is expanding participation by local populations in matters related to protected areas. Meanwhile, there is growing conviction among all

---

BOX 11.1 BOLIVIA – COMANAGEMENT OF PROTECTED AREAS

General Regulations of Protected Areas

Title II of the General Regulations of Protected Areas, approved in July of 1997, contemplates the regime of 'shared administration' with private and public persons, including indigenous or aboriginal peoples or communities. This administration would mediate agreements for, among others, collective access to protected areas.

Agreement on procedures and management among the Moxeños, Yuracares and Tsimanes peoples and the Ministry for Sustainable Development

In July 1997, the Bolivian government recognized the double category of protected area and indigenous territory within the framework of the agreement and joint management agreement signed by the Ministry for Sustainable Development and Environment and the organization Subcentral Indigenous Territory and National Park Isiboro Secure (TIPNIS), representing the Moxeños, Yuracares and Tsimanes peoples. Among the objectives of this instrument is that of section 4.2(c), which aims to 'Permanently prevent and assure the integrity, intangibility and the inviolability of the TIPNIS, respecting settlements, incursions and uses or exploitation incompatible with the category of *Indigenous Territory and Protected Area*' (emphasis added).

Agreement on co-administration and management between the local indigenous authority and the state: Kaa-Iya del Gran Chaco National Park, Bolivia

The framework agreement for coadministration of Kaa-Iya del Gran Chaco National Park and integrated management natural area, signed in 1995 between the Ministry of Sustainable Development and the Captaincy of Upper and Lower Izozog, made possible the participation of local indigenous authorities in the administration and management of the park. Among the principal objectives were to prevent and assure the territorial integrity of the area against settlements, incursions and uses and exploitation incompatible with the categories of management, zoning and use regulations.

---

actors that protected areas cannot exist in isolation, and that the rights of indigenous peoples and other people who inhabit protected areas must be respected and their involvement ensured. Effective adaptation to this evolving context requires the development of new concepts, categories and tools.

Continuing this trend, all the indications are that in the next century the old model of protected areas, based fundamentally on the idea of critical areas, or hot spots, will, over time, be replaced by a bioregional model (see Chapter 5). In this new model, conservation strategies will be developed on the scale of ecosystems, and the emphasis will move from complete protection of isolated areas to a more comprehensive and dynamic concept of conservation and management of working landscapes. This will imply, among other things, greater reliance on the biosphere reserve concept, and on those categories of protected areas which value the interactions between people and nature and/or which view management activities as a critical aspect of protection, as is the case for IUCN Categories V and VI.

At the same time, there is a growing understanding of the link between nature and culture – that healthy landscapes are shaped by human culture as well as the forces of nature, that rich biological diversity often coincides with cultural diversity, and that conservation cannot be undertaken without the involvement of those people closest to the resources. The concept of biodiversity conservation is evolving to recognize that the world's biological diversity has coevolved with humans and that conservation must contribute to sustainable development by sustaining livelihoods, providing ecological services and ensuring the sharing of benefits.

Among the fundamental changes underway is a progressive shift toward acceptance that people who have traditionally lived in areas now protected can continue living there, while practising management methods which are compatible with the primary objectives of these areas. This shift, in turn, assumes the parallel creation of mechanisms for negotiation, conflict resolution, self-regulation (for example, through the use of incentives) and collaborative management.

It is possible that, in the future, land outside of formal protection will be incorporated within national systems of protected areas as buffer zones and corridors to enhance the effectiveness of the system of protection. As well, it is conceivable that private lands will be incorporated within national systems of protected areas, with landowners maintaining their property rights and the responsibility for direct management. It is also possible that, in the future, many indigenous lands and territories will be recognized as protected areas, under a system of categories and norms appropriate to their reality, and where the indigenous peoples and communities will obtain the right to autonomous management and control of these areas. One can anticipate, equally, a strength-

---

BOX 11.2 THE FINAL DECLARATION OF THE FIRST LATIN AMERICAN CONGRESS ON NATIONAL PARKS AND PROTECTED AREAS

The First Latin American Congress on National Parks and Protected Areas (Santa Marta, Colombia, May 1997) stated in its final declaration that:

- When protected areas, whatever form they might take, are superimposed on indigenous lands or territories, the fundamental rights of local communities should be respected, such as the right those communities have to their own land, to different forms of autonomy, and to use and manage the resources that exist on those lands.
- Dialogue with indigenous peoples on the basis of a recognition of the important role they have to play in preserving the environment is extending the possibilities of cooperation between communities and government in ensuring that their land or territories will continue to be managed in a way that will contribute to preserving biodiversity, while at the same time guaranteeing their legitimate rights and interests.
- Wherever possible, internationally accepted management categories should be adopted, taking into account the need to make human presence compatible with protecting biological diversity, with special reference being made to the rights and interests of indigenous peoples.

ening of the trend of establishing transboundary protected areas, conceived not solely as eco and bioregional tools for conservation, but also as opportunities for peace and reconciliation, as well as for a better understanding, appreciation and recognition of the local people who live in border areas.

In the next century, state protected areas will be managed increasingly by means of collaborative agreements between protected area authorities and local populations, non-governmental organizations, municipalities and other local actors. The role of governmental agencies in regulation, supervision and monitoring will decrease progressively. At the same time, systems of management and protection will become more decentralized, progressively transferring power to local entities. In some countries, this will create the conditions to expand considerably the systems of protected areas, guided by an approach that is more sensitive to social equity and sustainable development.

In these conditions, the fundamental requirement to ensure the survival of systems of protected areas will be the effective establishment of a social contract, through which the entire society can commit itself to participating in the shared mission of protecting its natural and cultural heritage.

TOWARDS A POLICY ON INDIGENOUS PEOPLES AND PROTECTED AREAS: THE WWF AND IUCN/WCPA PRINCIPLES AND GUIDELINES

Conservation organizations have become increasingly sensitive and responsive to the claims of indigenous and other traditional peoples about protected areas overlapping with their terrestrial, freshwater and coastal or marine domains. In an important example of this trend, WWF and IUCN recently developed a draft joint statement of principles and guidelines on indigenous and traditional peoples and protected areas. It states that:

> *In line with current understanding of the concept of sustainable development, as well as with the Convention on Biological Diversity, ILO Convention 169, Agenda 21 and the Rio Declaration on Environment and Development, WWF and IUCN recognize that:*
> - *Protected areas will survive only if they are seen to be of value, in the widest sense, to the nation as a whole and to local people in particular (Resolution 1.35 – IUCN 1996).*
> - *The territorial and resource rights of indigenous peoples inhabiting protected areas must be respected (Resolution 1.53 – IUCN 1996).*
> - *Knowledge, innovations and practices of indigenous peoples have much to contribute to the management of protected areas (IUCN, 1992).*
> - *Governments and protected area managers should incorporate customary and indigenous tenure and resource use and control systems as a means of enhancing biodiversity conservation (IUCN, 1992).*

The document also states that WWF and IUCN recognize that indigenous peoples have the right 'to participate effectively in the management of the protected areas established on their lands or territories', (Resolution 1.53, IUCN, 1996) and that agreements should be reached with them 'prior to the establishment of new protected areas in their lands or territories' (Resolution 1.53, IUCN, 1996).

Resolution 1.53 of the IUCN World Conservation Congress (WCC) requests IUCN to 'endorse, support, participate in and advocate the development and implementation of a clear policy in relation to protected areas established in indigenous lands and territories', based on the recognition of land/territorial and resource rights, the necessity for prior agreements for the establishment of new protected areas on their lands or territories, and rights to effective participation in protected area management.

In addition, the congress requested the IUCN World Commission on Protected Areas (WCPA) to: 'establish closer links with indigenous peoples' organizations, with a view to incorporating the rights and interests of indigenous peoples in the application of the IUCN Protected Area Management Categories' (Resolution 1.35 – IUCN 1996).

THE POTENTIAL OF THE IUCN SYSTEM OF PROTECTED AREA MANAGEMENT CATEGORIES TO ACCOMMODATE PROTECTED INDIGENOUS TERRITORIES

A review of the 1994 IUCN Guidelines for Protected Areas Management Categories (see Appendix 1) reveals that the system offers considerable scope to incorporate indigenous peoples' interest and concerns. Most of these revised protected area management categories explicitly recognize that indigenous and local communities may occupy and/or use such areas and *none of them is, by definition, opposed to indigenous peoples' claims with regard to protected areas established on their lands*. Therefore, the system as a whole has the potential to accommodate a range of models of protected areas, according to the degree of human intervention, in a way that both indigenous and other traditional peoples' rights and conservation objectives can be respected.

For example, none of the IUCN protected area management categories establish public ownership of the lands falling within the protected area as a requirement for protection. An important implication here, as recognized in the above-mentioned WCC resolution, is that land rights of communities living within protected areas must be respected regardless of the category in question, since the degree of human intervention and management objectives are not necessarily linked to public ownership of lands and resources, but rather to regulation of uses. In this respect, the current system of categories presents greater flexibility than existed before 1994, now that it appropriately separates the ownership of land and resources from the requirements and objectives of management. The IUCN guidelines state that 'whatever the ownership, experience shows that the success of management depends greatly on the good will and support of local communities'.

Apart from the issue of land ownership and the general concept of involvement in management, the definitions and guidelines of the IUCN categories

BOX 11.3 PRINCIPLES ON INDIGENOUS AND TRADITIONAL PEOPLES AND PROTECTED AREAS

The key principles presented in the WWF and IUCN/WCPA document are as follows:

Principle 1

Indigenous and other traditional peoples have made significant contributions to maintaining many of the Earth's most fragile ecosystems, through their traditional sustainable resource use practices and their profound, culture-based respect for nature. Therefore, there should be no inherent conflict between the objectives of protected areas and the existence, within and around their borders, of indigenous and other traditional peoples practising sustainable use of natural resources; and they should be recognized as rightful, equal partners in the development and implementation of conservation strategies that affect their lands, territories, waters, coastal seas and other resources, in particular the establishment and management of protected areas.

Principle 2

Full respect of the rights of indigenous and other traditional peoples to their lands, territories, waters, coastal seas and other resources should be the foundation of agreements drawn up between conservation institutions, including protected area management agencies, and indigenous and other traditional peoples for the establishment and management of protected areas affecting those lands, territories, waters, coastal seas and other resources. Simultaneously, such agreements should be based on the recognition by indigenous and other traditional peoples of their responsibility to conserve biodiversity and natural resources harboured in those protected areas.

Principle 3

The principles of decentralization, democratization, participation, transparency and accountability should be taken into account in all matters pertaining to the mutual interests of protected areas and indigenous and other traditional peoples.

Principle 4

Indigenous and other traditional peoples should be able to share fully and equitably in the benefits associated with protected areas, with due recognition to the rights of other legitimate stakeholders.

Principle 5

The rights of indigenous and other traditional peoples in connection with protected areas are often an international responsibility, since many of the lands, territories, waters, coastal seas, and other resources which they own, occupy or otherwise use, as well as many of the ecosystems in need of protection, cross national boundaries.

do not cover matters related to the rights, responsibilities and roles of local people. However, in principle, each of the categories offers the opportunity to incorporate the concept of *protected indigenous territory*. This is possible now that the IUCN categories, as expressed in the revised guidelines, do not exclude private lands (of communities, individual or corporations). At the same time, indigenous lands and territories, including bodies of water and coastal and marine zones, have a wide range of uses and degrees of human intervention – from heavily modified, to virtually untouched sacred areas – which may correspond to one or more of the IUCN protected area management categories.

With its emphasis on the value of the interactions between people and nature over time, *Category V (protected landscape and seascape)* is particularly appropriate to the characteristics of indigenous lands and territories. The IUCN definition notes that 'safeguarding the integrity of this traditional interaction is vital to the protection, maintenance, and evolution of such an area'. The protected landscape/seascape category can comprise a mosaic of land ownership patterns, including private and communally owned property, which leaves room for the recognition of indigenous rights to land, territory, bodies of water, coastal zones and other resources. Similarly, it can accommodate diverse management regimes, including customary laws governing resource management. The Category V designation builds on existing institutional responsibilities, and therefore offers possibilities to develop collaborative management agreements and other flexible arrangements for management of natural and cultural resources. Finally, it has important specific objectives related to the conservation of cultural heritage, and seeks to bring benefits to local communities and contribute to their well-being through the provision of environmental goods and services.

The Category V approach has proven to work well in certain indigenous territories where strict protected areas have failed, because it reinforces local responsibility for the area and accommodates traditional uses and customary tools for resource management. This category can be applied to the protection of indigenous territories that might have a particular scenic value (where, therefore, tourism, recreation and education could be important objectives of public use), as well as those with special natural features (such as mountains, coasts and islands) and cultural features (for example, artefacts of ancient civilizations).

Category VI (managed resource protected area) aims basically to ensure the sustainable use of natural ecosystems to meet community needs, while ensuring long-term protection and maintenance of biological diversity. This category embraces the concept of an 'area of multiple use'. It also permits private and communal ownership of land and considers specifically the option of management by local institutions, as well as collaborative management between public entities and local communities.

Under Category VI, a protected indigenous territory must comply with criteria specified in the guidelines which include: the area should be managed for the long-term protection and maintenance of its biodiversity; at least two-thirds of the area should remain in its natural state; it must be large enough to absorb sustainable resource uses without detriment to its overall long-term natural values; it should contain predominantly unmodified natural systems, whereas the management of the remaining area must not be in conflict with that primary purpose.

Sacredness is a particular issue that must be recognized and addressed in the context of protected areas (see Chapter 15). Usually, sacredness of natural sites is a cultural, religious or mythological expression of the recognition of critical vital functions. Similarly, taboos tend to be established in relation to especially valued species and other elements of nature. Sacredness imposes regulations on use, generates exclusion rules, creates a sense of respect and care, and even determines active management when degradation occurs.

The features of *Category Ia (strict nature reserve)* overlap quite closely with many of the sacred areas established at the initiation of indigenous and traditional peoples and communities, for the protection of their resources and the biological, cultural and spiritual values of nature. In these sacred areas the restrictions of access and use frequently parallel those which are established by protected area agencies for sites corresponding to Category Ia. In terms of management, therefore, there does not appear to be any fundamental discrepancy. The only important difference is that many sacred areas tend to be relatively small – increasingly the case, due to the physical limitations of indigenous territories – whereas the guidelines require that Category Ia areas be 'large enough to ensure the integrity of its ecosystems and to accomplish the management objectives for which it is protected'.

The definition for *Category Ib (wilderness area)* explicitly includes a reference to natural areas in which indigenous peoples are living, and states that one of the management objectives for these areas is: 'to enable indigenous communities living at low density and in balance with the available resources to maintain their lifestyle'. This category therefore is applicable to protected areas, including largely unmodified ecosystems, where indigenous communities are interested in keeping their interventions at a low level and do not foresee any significant anthropogenic conversion of ecosystems.

Category III (natural monument) is very often applicable to areas where indigenous peoples, for cultural and spiritual reasons, have established certain access restrictions and management regulations. Many sacred places which include special natural features of outstanding importance, but which do not meet the criteria of a strict nature reserve, might be included in this category. Taking this into consideration, the guidelines list, among other features, 'natural sites which have heritage significance to indigenous peoples'. It includes as a management objective: 'to deliver to any resident population such benefits as are consistent with the other objectives of management'.

Although its practical application on or near indigenous lands and territories has, in many cases, met with problems, the definition of *Category II (national park)* explicitly addresses issues related to indigenous peoples. It includes as a specific management objective to: 'take into account the needs of indigenous people, including subsistence resource use, insofar as these will not adversely affect the other objectives of management'. In terms of institutional responsibilities, the guidelines specify the option of ownership and management being vested in indigenous peoples' organizations. In a number of cases worldwide, national parks have largely included indigenous peoples' lands and traditional resource management, and have very often accommodated their practices in management planning and implementation.

Category IV (habitat/species management area) requires 'active intervention for management purposes so as to ensure the maintenance of habitats and/or to meet the requirements of specific species'. Applied to indigenous lands and territories, this category might correspond to an area under traditional management practices or protected by customary law as breeding or nursery areas (such as wetlands, coral reefs and forests). This category also includes as a management objective to 'deliver such benefits to people living within the designated area as are consistent with the other objectives of management'.

An approach that could particularly suit many indigenous territories with protected area status is *multiple classification*, due to the complexity of human uses, management objectives and degrees of intervention that characterize those territories. A large territory could, for example, include areas of categories Ia and Ib corresponding to sacred areas where strict protection is sought, and Category V and VI areas for places dedicated to sustainable use and conservation of cultural landscapes.

Biosphere reserves have been also frequently suggested as appropriate models for indigenous lands including protected areas; the Yanomami Reserve is a well-known example of this. Another example is the proposal by the Tawahka Indigenous Federation in Honduras to create a biosphere reserve within their territory, with responsibility for management and administration to be held by the Tawahka people.

CONCLUSIONS

A worldwide trend toward more inclusive protected area management models, and growing recognition by conservation organizations of indigenous and traditional peoples' interests, create the conditions for new partnerships in protected areas management. Further, the recently revised IUCN guidelines for protected area management categories present concrete opportunities to develop these partnerships and to create indigenous protected territories according to a diverse range of models.

However, lasting alliances can only be forged in an atmosphere where indigenous peoples are full partners in developing conservation strategies that affect their lands and resources – with the rights, roles and responsibilities this entails. These relationships must be based on respect for indigenous peoples' cultures and institutions, including traditional knowledge and resource management systems. Protected areas must recognize and support the land and resource rights, as well as other fundamental human rights of indigenous peoples. Management models must allow for meaningful participation by indigenous peoples, as well as other legitimate stakeholders, all of whom must be able to share fully and equitably in the benefits associated with protected areas.

With these principles as a foundation, strong and lasting alliances can be built with indigenous peoples as stewards of their traditional lands and resources.

REFERENCES

IUCN (1992) *Parks for Life*, Report of the IV World Congress on National Parks and Protected Areas (84), IUCN, Gland
IUCN (1996) *World Conservation Congress*, October 1996, IUCN, Gland
Kempf, E (1993) 'In Search of a Home', in *The Law of the Mother, Protecting Indigenous Peoples in Protected Areas*, World Wide Fund For Nature, Gland
Martin, C (1993) 'Introduction', in *The Law of the Mother, Protecting Indigenous Peoples in Protected Areas*, World Wide Fund For Nature, Gland

12 MAMIRAUÁ SUSTAINABLE DEVELOPMENT RESERVE, BRAZIL[*]

Sandra Charity and Don Masterson

INTRODUCTION

The process for implementing protected areas (IUCN categories I, II and III) in Brazil follows a typical 'parks-no-people' approach. Local communities are seldom involved in park designation or in the design and implementation of management plans, and intense land tenure conflicts arise as a result. However, some projects in the Amazon, such as the Mamirauá Sustainable Development Reserve, demonstrate the feasibility of an alternative approach to protected area implementation, based on the involvement of local communities throughout the process, from design of the management plan to the application of its management prescriptions. This approach is in line with the concept of integrated conservation and development programmes (ICDPs), which have the dual objective of conserving biological diversity and promoting improved standards of living. Such a model, if it is successful, could have far wider applications throughout the Amazon region and beyond.

THE MAMIRAUÁ RESERVE

Várzea whitewater floodplain forests cover less than 2 per cent of the Amazon, but contain many unique species of fish and wildlife. In 1990, a 1,124,000-hectare protected area was set up near Tefe, in the Brazilian state of Amazonas, to help preserve *várzea* biodiversity. The area was recognized as an internationally important wetland under the Ramsar Convention in 1992. The Mamirauá flooded forests are inundated for up to six months a year. Biological diversity is high and the area contains many rare or endangered species, such as the threatened white uakari monkey (*Cacajo calvus calvus*) and the recently discovered blackish squirrel monkey (*Saimiri vanzolinii*), as well as manatees

* Thanks to the many people involved in the project who have provided material for this chapter, including Rosa Maria De Sa, José Márcio Ayres, Bob Buschbacher, Joao Paulo Viana and Miriam Marmontel.

(*Trichechus inunguis*). Flooded forest habitats are among the most vulnerable in Amazonia because of their sediment-rich soils, productive fisheries and accessibility to timber. Biodiversity, therefore, continues to be at risk in the region with overexploitation damaging forests, fish stocks, shorebird and turtle communities, ornamental fish and other commercially valuable wildlife such as manatees and black caiman (*Melanosuchus niger*).

The Mamirauá Reserve is also home to around 5000 people who survive by fishing, hunting and some small-scale logging and agriculture. Much of the populations lives in conditions of serious poverty, with poor or non-existent educational facilities and health care. Infant mortality is 85 per 1000 individuals due mainly due to poor sanitation.

THE MAMIRAUÁ RESERVE PROJECT

The Mamirauá project is a collaboration of many partners, both national and international. The key problems the project is trying to address are:

- *social problems:* inadequate educational and health services, inequitable economic relations with urban centres and limited productive options;
- *unsustainable resource use:* over-exploitation of economically important fisheries and timber resources, uncontrolled sacking of shorebird and turtles nesting areas and caiman hunting, and over exploitation to supply the ornamental fish trade;

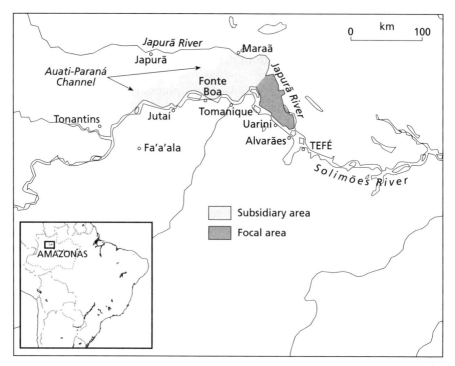

Figure 12.1 *Location of the Mamirauá focal and subsidiary areas*

- *threats to biodiversity:* illegal hunting and commerce of endangered species (manatees and caimans), regressive genetic pressure and loss of key species caused by selective logging.

The project began with the recognition that conservation will only be possible if it is both supported by, and in the long-term interests of, the local population. As Dr José Márcio Ayres, the Mamirauá project coordinator, stresses:

> *The idea is to awaken the interest of the local population to conserve the region, without having to abandon it, since they also depend upon the natural resources. Preserving biodiversity islands isn't feasible, but integrating biodiversity conservation and human populations is, if we can reduce environmental impacts.*

The integration of conservation and social development objectives was formally recognized when the original protected area, an ecological reserve established by the government of the state of Amazonas in 1990, was reclassified (following recommendation by the project) as a *sustainable development reserve* in 1996, thus legalizing the continued presence of people within the reserve and reinforcing the management model developed by the project. The creation of the new category sets a critically important precedent for in situ conservation in Brazil. Although Brazilian legislation on protected areas recognizes some categories of protected areas where direct resource use is allowed (such as extractive reserves, FLONAs – national forests and APAs – environmental protection areas), none of them have conservation of biodiversity as a primary goal. The sustainable development reserve reconciles the need to conserve biodiversity with the needs and aspirations of local people. The category is particulary important in areas such as Amazonia, where all the protected areas have people living within them.

MANAGING CHANGE

The project has been divided into two phases (phase I from 1992–1996 and phase II from 1997–2001). The goal of phase I was to assure conservation of the biodiversity of *várzea* flooded forests through two immediate objectives: the production of a management plan for the focal area of the reserve; and the improvement of local livelihoods through sustainable use of natural resources and improved social services. The goal of phase II includes the same basic elements; the objective is to conserve and manage the reserve in partnership with residents, users, local people and institutes – in other words, to implement the management plan in partnership with local people. The outputs of phase II are:

- *regulatory systems implemented and refined:* agreement of rules and adherence by reserve users;
- *community organization for planning and management of resources consolidated and improved:* quality of representation in decision-making processes, effectiveness of community organization;

- *quality of life (local livelihoods) improved through extension:* raised levels of income, greater stability of cash flow, use of innovative technologies, improved planning and management techniques for resource use;
- *educational processes implemented that support management, community participation and improvement of quality of life:* wider understanding and practice of sustainable resource use;
- *systems established for monitoring project impact:* records on use of key economic species over time, biodiversity trends, trends in natural resource populations;
- *information base for informing management decisions improved through applied and basic research:* quality and relevance of new research information, research results applied to management;
- *external linkages consolidated:* strength of political and public support, public knowledge about the reserve;
- *institutional structure of project management of phase II established:* effectiveness of structure, organization and staffing; and
- *long-term financial sustainability ensured:* endowment fund and revenue from ecotourism.

Even before the project started, local people were worried about declining natural resources. Over the last decade self-imposed fishing regulations were drawn up with encouragement from the local church; these include the identification of no-fishing zones and 'controlled-use' lakes to help take pressure off of commercial fish stocks.

The current project builds on this awareness, and on existing community participation, by involving local people in planning the reserve's future. It is initially targeted at a focal area of 260,000 hectares, covering almost a quarter of the total reserve, and which is used by approximately 5000 people living in 62 communities in and around the reserve. The area's biological importance derives from the fact that it is located at the confluence of a major white-water river (Solimões) and a vast black-water river (Japurá); these are connected by a canal (Parano do Aranapu) which represents the boundary between the focal area and the rest of the reserve.

During a preparatory phase in 1991–92, reserve residents and local authorities were asked what they considered to be the major issues and the problems to be resolved, and were invited to discuss the project's objectives. Following this, project staff concentrated on deeveloping a management plan, drawing on the results of both field research and the participation of a full range of local actors. The plan has a number of objectives:

- *participatory mechanisms* – mainly through organizing general and sector assemblies where local people can discuss options and make management decisions.
- *sustainable use and biodiversity zoning plan* – where the focal area is divided into three zones: fully protected areas, buffer zones for subsistence use and areas of permanent settlement.
- *resource management regulations* – such as a ban on large-scale commercial fishing and the zoning of fishing to allow stocks to recover. Fisheries is the main economic activity in the region. Pirarucu (*Arapaima gigas*) is one of the prized economic fish species and is sold fresh, dried or salted.

The pirarucu is the world's largest scaled freshwater fish, reaching three metres in length and weighing 150 kilogrammes. Researchers on the project are working with local fishermen to promote the awareness that fishing smaller pirarucus and the use of gill nets will reduce future stocks.

- *research and monitoring programme* – mainly applied research on key resources such as fisheries, timber and agroforestry, and endangered species. Fish landing data has been continuously collected for over three years, forming the largest data base on fish landing in the Amazon. Information on a daily basis indicates where fishermen are fishing, the species, volume fished and seasonal variation. This information is then used to establish management rules on fishing which are negotiated with local fishermen. For example, the project is planning to develop a sustainable trade in a local species, discus (*Symphydodon aequifasciatus*), which is currently endangered through overcollection for the ornamental fish trade.
- *health, education and community organization programme* – including establishing 20 health posts and supplying the region's first environmental educational materials and teacher training.
- *economic extension programme* –established in phase II. This will include activities in agroforestry, agriculture, fisheries, wildlife management and the involvement of local people in the provision of services in ecotourism, research and logistical support.

Initial discussions led directly to the formation of general and sector assemblies, which discuss and decide upon resource management and zoning decisions within the reserve. All communities in the focal zone, and those located nearby across the Solimões and Japurá rivers, are represented in the assemblies – a total of around 80 people – and are thus directly involved in, and responsible for, decision-making. General assemblies take place once a year and sector assemblies (involving six to ten communities) every two months.

Operationally, local communities are also responsible for overseeing compliance with resource use and zoning regulations in the reserve. When violations are detected, members of the community approach infractors, confiscate their catch and explain reasons for the rules. Communities receive organizational and logistical support to implement fisheries conservation practices and to take part in the reserve conservation model. For the first time in Brazil, IBAMA (the federal environment agency) has accredited 30 members of the local communities to act as voluntary rangers – an innovative form of community-based protection of a protected area. Project staff work in cooperation with local communities on extension activities related to public health, environmental education and agroforestry. Some material support is also provided, in the form of health and education and the free distribution of fruit tree seedlings and improved varieties of seed.

Planning is backed up by careful research about resource options and community needs. Information has been gathered on nutritional and health requirements, land use and habitat types, wildlife management techniques tested in the subsistence zones, baseline information for monitoring ecological impacts, and management strategies for fish species of economic importance.

Training is an important component of the project and covers resource protection, prenatal care for pregnant mothers, training for community health extensionists and midwives, and construction of latrine and drinking water facilities. Training also includes resource management. For example, the project is promoting the use of fishing gear that is selective to larger specimens of the pirarucu to help maintain population levels.

An environmental education programme is coordinated with municipal education authorities. The project has provided teacher training and negotiated the reconstruction of several schools within the reserve. In addition, local capacity is being developed through interchanges with other community conservation projects in the Amazon.

Recently, an ecotourism component of the project has been implemented. The purpose is to develop a community-based ecotourism programme which, it is hoped, will help finance reserve management and maintenance, as well as provide an alternative source of income to local residents. This exciting initiative is still at a preliminary stage, and an economic feasibility study has recently been carried out to assess the ecotourism potential of the area.

ASSESSMENT

Although the project was initially viewed as a threat by many people, it is now accepted by much of the community. General support for regulations and zoning is growing within the reserve, although compliance is reduced when rules conflict with immediate needs. In general, community-based resource use only works when pragmatic resource management rules are devised, which are based where possible on balancing the restriction of harvesting practices with short-term gains within communities – in other words, when costs and benefits are balanced and incentives maintained.

Practical problems still exist. Probably the foremost issue is that most of the local population live very close to the edge, savings are limited, and people literally live hand to mouth much of the time. During the height of the flood waters, or at the extreme low-water level when access to resources is much more limited, violating minimum size limits for pirarucu, cutting small diameter logs or endangered tree species such as samauma (*Ceiba pentandra*), or fishing in protected lakes may be the only option for providing income and food.

Secondly, in order to work, the system requires that community wardens enforce rules not only against outsiders, but also within their communities. Here, the reluctance to risk damaging personal relations and gaining enemies is high. Thirdly, individuals opposed to the conservation rules and the project tend to avoid participating in meetings and assemblies. Their non-participation is used as a justification for not complying with assembly decisions, and at the same time increases the difficulty of understanding their perspective and identifying solutions.

On the ground, however, there are a number of examples of developments which have taken place which benefit the local community. These include the following:

- *Improved sanitation:* the six to eight month flood typical of the *várzea*, makes conventional sanitation systems impossible to use. The project develops a sceptic tank which is adapted to *várzea* conditions, following the results of the baseline health survey which indicated high infant mortality, with 40 per cent of mothers losing one or more child under the age of five.

- *Development of education primers:* the workbooks and teachers' manuals developed by the project are the only adequate school materials on environmental education available in local schools, which receive little support from municipal education authorities. The teaching-training programmes promoted during phase I are the only training many teachers in the area have received.
- *Contributions to community infrastructure:* for instance, the installation of solar cells in local schools, the construction and equipping of health posts and the provision of community radios for resource protection and general communication.

The project has also gained political support and is now generally accepted, although lack of resources has limited the degree to which local government officials have taken part in field activities.

CONCLUSIONS

Mamirauá is currently the only protected area in Brazil which can genuinely claim to have a management plan which has both a solid scientific basis and was developed in a participatory fashion. The project is a bold, innovative initiative which could well become a model for protected area implementation in Brazil. It is, however, still an experiment, and thus should be seen as a learning experience. As has been indicated above, community-based management of resources is a long-term process. It took the first two years of the project to gain the trust of local people and government officials and to neutralize the effects of mistrust. The project was initially seen as a threat. The local people thought that the children, manatees and fish were to be exported (studies on nutrition required measuring the diameter of the forearm of children under five); and the government officials thought that the funds, which came from the UK, were being used to 'take over' the area.

Even so, the project has already had some positive impacts:

- the creation of the category of sustainable development reserve (SDR), which sets a new precedent for in situ conservation in Brazil;
- a credible protection programme covering most of the focal zone;
- an agroforestry extension programme, including the introduction of the 'camu camu' fruit (*Myrciaria dubia*) which has more vitamin C than any other known fruit; and
- the improvement of health and educational services.

The project has also received a high profile and generally supportive attention by local, national and international press. This in turn has led to donors and federal and state authorities accepting the feasibility of managing an internationally important protected area using a participatory, comanagement approach rather than traditional coercive methods.

On the other hand, some problems remain to be solved:

- The challenges involved in implementing the plan in a participatory fashion are truly daunting. The plan is only for the focal area (260,000 hectares, a quarter of the reserve), and, even in this area, general buy-in from local residents for implementation still needs to be achieved for a significant proportion of the 60 or more communities in the area.
- There is an ongoing need within the reserve to conserve fish stocks. However, balancing the needs of all the user groups can potentially cause problems. For example, negotiations with the urban-based fisheries union (*Colonia de Pescadores*) have fallen through. Resource users who live in the reserve have decided to exclude urban Colonia fishermen from fishing inside the reserve. This might pose potential conflicts in future, in particular following the creation of the Amana reserve (see below), which theoretically further reduces the availability of 'free-for-all' fishing grounds.
- Community representation is more easily assumed than achieved – for example, power structures in communities led to the 'election' of representatives who are not necessarily 'representative' of the communities' interests.
- It has proved difficult to involve women in formal meetings and therefore in the decision-making process. However, in phase II the project plans to organize women in 'mothers' clubs', which will develop handicrafts in fibres and clay, as well as vegetable gardens and other income-generating activities.
- One of the seven indigenous communities within the reserve has resisted management restrictions on their use of natural resources and remains unhappy about the project, although it is hoped that this will change when short- and longer-term incentives are perceived.
- Although attempts are being made to extend the comanagement to other resources (timber, turtles, caiman and game), these have so far met with less success.

Despite these problems, the Mamirauá project is already providing a good example of protected area management in the Amazon. A second sustainable development reserve has recently been created adjacent to Mamirauá: the Amana SDR. This is also a state reserve covering 2,350,000 hectares (an area the size of Belgium and twice the size of Mamirauá), which joins the Mamirauá reserve and the Jau national park (Brazil's largest national park which is under the jurisdiction of IBAMA, the federal environment agency). The three protected areas together form a vast continuous block of legally protected rainforest, covering a total area of 5,766,000 hectares (larger than Switzerland or Costa Rica), the largest block of officially protected forest on the planet. The initiative to create the Amana reserve was triggered by Mamirauá coordinator José Márcio Ayres and stems from the ambitious Brazilian government's Parques e Reservas programme (to be funded by the G-7), which aims to establish seven large corridors of protected forests in the Amazon and the Atlantic Forest, by joining several protected areas together.

REFERENCES

Alexander, B (1994) 'People of the Amazon Fight to Save the Flooded Forest', *Science* 265(29) July, 606–607

Lima, D (1997) 'Equity, Sustainable Development and Biodiversity Preservation: some questions on the ecological partnership in the Brazilian Amazon', in Henderson A, Padoch, C and Ayers, J (eds) *Ecology, Conservation and Development of Amazonian Várzea*, NY Botanical Gardens Press, New York

SCM (1996) *Mamirauá: Plano de Manejo*, SCM, CHPq-MCT, IPAAM, Brazil

Stolton, S and Dudley, N (1997) *Spotlight on Solutions: A Peoples' Agenda: A Handbook of Case Studies on Local Implementation of Agenda 21*, WWF International, Gland

13 INVOLVING PEOPLE IN MARINE PROTECTED AREAS: EXPERIENCES IN CENTRAL AMERICA AND AFRICA

Sue Wells and Meg Gawler

INTRODUCTION

The oceans have immense significance for humankind's social and economic well-being. It has been estimated that the oceans provide goods and services worth US$20.9 trillion, or 63 per cent of that provided by all the world's ecosystems (Costanza et al, 1997). Commercial and small-scale fisheries probably give direct employment to some 200 million people (McGinn, 1998) and perhaps as many as 500 million people draw their livelihoods indirectly from the sea (Weber, 1994): processors, packers, shippers and distributors of seafood; shipbuilders and outfitters; those working in marine-based tourism; and the recreational fishing industry amongst others. Inevitably, protection of marine biodiversity and sustainable management of marine resources will only be successful if human needs are taken into account. Over the last decade, this has been increasingly recognized particularly in relation to the management of tropical fisheries and other inshore resources (see Christie and White, 1997; White et al, 1994)

Experience shows that marine protected areas (MPAs), like terrestrial protected areas, only work if they have the support and the involvement of local communities (Borrini-Feyerabend, 1996; and Chapter 11 in this book). This has been demonstrated in regions such as the Pacific, where customary tenure has often provided a foundation for marine resource management, and where seasonal or permanent closed areas have traditionally been imposed and maintained by local communities (Ruddle et al, 1992; and see Chapter 25). The participatory approach has also been extensively used and documented in South-East Asia, where some of the earliest efforts at community-based management of MPAs were initiated (see White and Savina, 1987; Pomeroy, 1995). In this chapter, we review projects in other parts of the world, specifically Central America and Africa, where the needs of people and biodiversity have been combined, and draw some general conclusions.

Belize

The economic role of Belize's coral reefs, the largest areas of reef in the Western Hemisphere, has increased steadily since early this century. Initially, their importance lay in the fishing industry, with a wide range of species being hunted including turtles, sharks and finfish. Other marine products such as sponges and seaweeds are also harvested. Today, lobster and conch contribute most of the total value of exported wild-caught seafood, estimated at over US$10 million in 1995. Much of this is still harvested with traditional wooden sailing boats, or dories, and dug-out canoes. Belize has not, as yet, suffered the serious overfishing experienced in other countries, but catches of several species are declining. Illegal fishing of undersized conch and lobster is frequent, and there are fears that overexploitation is now occurring.

The main use of the Belize Barrier Reef is currently tourism. This is the country's largest source of foreign exchange and generated an estimated US$75 million in 1994, when nearly 90,000 tourists visited. The reefs, along with over 1000 islands, known as *cayes*, are major attractions: most of the hotels are in the coastal zone and about 80 per cent of tourists go snorkelling and diving. Tourism is, however, creating a new set of pressures (Gibson et al, 1998).

Since the early 1980s, Belize has been developing a remarkably ambitious marine protected area programme given the size of the country, with several sites designated (Half Moon Caye Natural Monument, Hol Chan Marine Reserve, South Water Caye Marine Reserve, Sapodilla Cayes Marine Reserve, Bacalar Chico National Park and Marine Reserve, Glovers Reef Marine Reserve, Blue Hole Natural Monument and Laughing Bird Caye National Park). Other protected areas are being planned for Caye Caulker, the Port Honduras area in the south of the country, and for parts of Turneffe Atoll. Many of these areas are now part of the Belize Barrier Reef World Heritage Area.

All these sites have, or will have, zoning schemes providing for recreational activities, small-scale fishing by traditional users, and total protection of key habitats and species in no-fishing zones. The no-fishing zones cover a small area at present but potentially could play an important role in managing the reef fisheries by protecting breeding stocks that may eventually repopulate other depleted areas. This is best illustrated in Hol Chan Marine Reserve, with its enormous groupers and shoals of snapper. This reserve was established in 1987, largely as a result of the community of San Pedro, the neighbouring town, recognizing that some form of management would be necessary to reconcile the conflict developing between fishermen and tourist operators, both dependent upon the reef for their livelihoods.

Direct responsibility for marine protected areas in Belize lies with either the Belize Fisheries Department (for Marine Reserves) of the Department of Forestry (natural monuments, national parks and other designations), with the Belize Coastal Zone Management Authority playing a coordinating role. The designation of protected areas requires extensive consultation and the holding of public forums, a process that will be made obligatory once new legislation is passed. Advisory committees are set up for each protected area, made up of representatives of all the main stakeholder groups and of the agencies and NGOs responsible for management. Public participation also occurs in more direct ways. Fishermen take part in monitoring and assessing the main commercial fisheries' stocks. Dive operators play a role in the installation and maintenance of mooring buoys, which prevent damage to corals from anchors. All tour guides belong to local associations and these will help to provide a good basis for improving management of reef tourism.

A rapidly growing number of Belizeans are now receiving training in marine resource management and are learning about the importance of reefs to their country (Wells, 1996). School children visit the Marine Research Centre, students from the university help out on research programmes, and numerous young Belizeans have learned to dive with volunteer programmes such as Coral Cay Conservation and Raleigh International. These activities, combined with the innovative environmental education and public awareness programmes run by non-governmental organizations (NGOs), such as the Belize Audubon Society and the Toledo Institute for Development and Environment (TIDE), are helping to generate a solid constituency for reef protection and management within the country.

MAURITANIA

The Banc d'Arguin, the largest marine park in Africa, is a site of unparalleled importance for marine biodiversity and ecological processes. It also constitutes Mauritania's most important reproduction and nursery area for fish and crustaceans – the country's major economic resource. However, as catches decline along the coast of West Africa, fishers are increasingly attracted to this area, where many resources are more abundant as a result of their protection.

An early strategy, dating from the creation of the park in 1976, was to maintain – within the limits of the park – the small communities of resident fishers, the Imraguen, and to give them exclusive fishing rights to the area, using traditional non-motorized methods. By protecting their own resources, the Imraguen have become the 'defenders' of the park, providing a level of surveillance from their own sailboats that the park administration would be unable to carry out alone.

However, the rapid evolution and globalization of the world's fisheries is posing ever increasing threats. For example, the Imraguen, who are among the poorest people in Mauritania, are now solicited by middlemen for the shark-fin market in Asia, where prices exceed US$100 per kilogramme. In recent years an important shark and ray fishery has developed within the park, and some species, such as the saw-fish, have already disappeared.

In order to address problems such as these, the Banc d'Arguin National Park, with the technical and financial support of its partners, has developed a ten-year master plan, negotiated with all major stakeholders and approved by the Mauritanian government. The master plan is based on five major objectives:

- establishing efficient management systems;
- protecting the park and its resources;
- scientifically demonstrating the biological and economic importance of the park;
- improving the Imraguen's living conditions together with the park's economic and aesthetic values; and
- strengthening partnerships.

In order to implement the plan, new park regulations have been defined in collaboration with representatives of the Imraguen communities, and these are currently under consideration by the Mauritanian authorities. One important accomplishment of this participatory planning was reaching agreement to limit the total number of Imraguen boats to 100, in the interest of ensuring a sustainable level of fishing effort.

However, not all problems have been solved. Among the most difficult are the pirate fishers: small-scale fishers from Mauritania and Senegal, and industrial vessels, often from Europe. In response to these threats, the park and its partners have raised funds for three rapid patrol boats.

In spite of the concerted efforts of the Imraguen, the park, and its partner organizations, the future gives great cause for concern. Never have the internal and external pressures on the park been so great. As marine resources outside are increasingly depleted, it becomes more and more difficult to protect the vast areas and rich resources of the Banc d'Arguin. What is needed is not only adequate funding, but also more enlightened fisheries policies in Europe and Asia, and an end to irresponsible and destructive practices by distant water fishing fleets – in short, greater international solidarity – to help Mauritania safeguard this complex and beautiful World Heritage site.

MOZAMBIQUE

The Bazaruto Archipelago consists of five islands: Bazaruto, Santa Carolina, Benguerua, Magaruque and Bangue. The latter three are located in the southern part of the archipelago, and together with their adjacent waters were declared a national park in 1971, although no legislation accompanied the decree. The economy of the 60 communities on the inhabited islands is based upon artisanal fishing, boat-building, and transport services. As early as the 1950s, the archipelago began to attract tourists owing to its natural beauty, exotic location, lure of fishing and adventure, and international tourist facilities. Mozambique's national tourism policy advocates the promotion of high-class, low-impact tourism, and aims to ensure the involvement of local communities in order to guarantee sustainable development of both the sector and the communities themselves (Republic of Mozambique, 1995).

The islanders, in addition to fishing to provide their own food, sell crayfish, squid and sand oysters to lodges and hotels, and supply other marine products to the mainland. However, these artisanal fishing communities need to improve their economic viability and state of empowerment in order to avoid being ousted by insensitive foreign tourism developments. The main problem to be addressed is the establishment of balanced and sustainable use of the archipelago's natural resources, while strengthening the long-term economy of the inhabitants.

Sound structures for comanagement by government authorities and stakeholders are seen as vital for ensuring success, and this has proved to be difficult. It is, however, essential for the development of joint management structures that the park management is able to communicate with associations such as fisher groups and agricultural women's groups. An important aim of the Bazaruto project is to get all user groups to give their opinions, to assist in forming management policies, and to benefit from these. The recruitment of a social scientist, who speaks the local language and has an easy and natural contact with the islanders, helped to ease the process of forming small groups. The most positive sign of success was when small associations or groups met together themselves when they had a problem. For example, when collectors from Zenguelemo, having virtually wiped out their own stocks of sand oyster (*mapalo*), an important local resource, started to collect in the Sitone region, the collectors of Sitone joined ranks to work out how to keep out collectors from other areas.

As in Belize, much of the conflict was resolved by developing a zoning plan in consultation with all stakeholders. Five types of areas were identified:

(1) *Wilderness zones:* these apply specifically to the mobile sand dunes that are afforded the highest protection. No structures or roads can be built on them, vehicular traffic (other than essential limited management traffic), agriculture and fuelwood collection is prohibited.

(2) *Total protection areas:* these cover marine areas, mangroves, forests and certain lakes and swamps. Fishing or collection by any method and anchoring are prohibited. Only activities that have a low impact are permitted, such as boating, scuba diving, snorkelling and underwater photography in marine total protection areas.

(3) *Limited community resource use areas:* these include inshore seagrass beds, sand oyster zones and the older stabilized dunes where millet is cultivated. These areas may only be used by the local inhabitants; extraction of staple foods resources, such as sand oysters, crabs, sipunculid worms, crayfish and fish, is permitted using traditional methods, or those specified by the park management. Boat passage and careful anchorage are permitted.

(4) *Multiple-use zones:* these are marine areas, open to both islanders and people from the mainland. Extraction of sand oysters, crabs, crayfish, squid, and non-reef fishes, using only sustainable fishing techniques as advocated by the park management, is permitted. Boating and anchoring are permitted, as long as care is taken not to moor on corals.

(5) *Extensive-use zones:* these are used for various commercial and service-oriented purposes such as commercial tourism developments, the national park headquarters and outposts, markets, and government services (such as schools, clinics, police, administration). When protected zones, such as mangroves, forests or sand dunes, overlap with tourism concession areas, primary consideration is given to protecting these from extraction and building activities.

The two primary objectives now are the establishment of greater Bazaruto National Park, including all five islands and the surrounding sea, and the adoption of legislation that promotes both conservation and sustainable use of the existing natural resources. The legislative framework for expanding the park is under review by the government. A management plan for the park's development has been produced and partnerships with government have been strengthened at all levels. At a local level there have been advances in sustainable resource management and a general improvement in the conditions of islanders through schools, credit systems for obtaining fishing nets (which encourages the use of legal mesh size of at least two centimetres), boat-building tools, and channelling of revenues from hotels and park fees to islands (in Benguera Islands these funds are being used to finance the building of a school).

LESSONS LEARNED

The three case studies illustrate the importance of ensuring that participation is equitable. All stakeholders must be involved from the outset and not be thought of as the recipients of a management plan, but rather as partners who will share in the responsibility of planning and implementation. This can be achieved through the early establishment of advisory or management committees, with careful representation of all the stakeholder groups. In Belize, this has proved to be relatively easy in that many interest groups (such as fishers and tour operators) are already organized into associations or cooperatives. In Bazaruto, efforts must go into forming or ensuring effective functioning of such user groups before the participatory process could become truly representative. The objectives and anticipated benefits of an MPA should be communicated to all stakeholders in a language that they can understand, particularly when the site is being established at the initiative of the government or an outside agency. Models for ensuring participation of user groups can now be found in many other countries, including, for example, the multi-stakeholder process set up for management of the Galapagos Marine Reserve, and the committees and working groups established to run voluntary marine reserves in the UK (WWF, 1998).

Full participation invariably takes time. Stakeholders must not be coerced into participation since it is only if participation is voluntary (rather than mandatory) that full support will be given. A minimum of five years or more may be necessary to gain the trust of local stakeholders, a time span that generally exceeds most projects. In Belize, the concept of community involvement only really took hold once the benefits of Hol Chan Marine Reserve became apparent and news of this spread to the rest of the country. In some instances, particularly in developing countries, basic needs must be met before conservation will be considered by a community. For example, in the Bazaruto Archipelago, a community programme for sustainable use was carried out alongside the more traditional protected area work. Such approaches involve long-term commitment and investment of resources, but are likely to build the kind of relationships with local stakeholders that can facilitate the establishment and enforcement of an MPA.

Despite the move to community-based management in many countries, a sound legal basis is often essential to ensure the long-term survival of an MPA and to support the efforts of local people. In all three case studies, the enacting of appropriate legislation, and the development of legally binding management plans, has been, or will be, a vitally important component. This is also evident in many other MPA projects. For example, in Menai Bay, Zanzibar, local communities took the initiative to form their own managment committee and subsequently to establish a conservation area. External assistance was sought to help with formal designation of the area, which was needed to provide the legislation necessary to halt destructive fishing. Traditional authorities and institutions can also play an important role, but even in countries with strong customary tenure traditions, as in Samoa, government support is often important (see Chapter 25).

Where public support has been successfully generated for an MPA, enforcement costs can be low (Kelleher and Kenchington, 1991). Communities that have a sense of 'ownership' of an MPA, having been involved in its establishment, and who receive direct benefits from it, are more likely to adhere to the regulations voluntarily. In the Banc d'Arguin, Imraguen fishers have a vested interest in enforcing MPA regulations since they have exclusive fishing rights within the boundaries of the park. In other MPAs, for example in Mafia Island Marine Park in Tanzania, local communities have been provided with radios and have reported illegal activities to the police. This is only feasible if both partners see an advantage in the partnership. Local communities receive additional resources from controlling encroaching pressures from beyond the protected areas, while conservation authorities get valuable help with biodiversity conservation.

As in Belize, it is increasingly clear that local people can play an important role in both gathering baseline information about an area and in monitoring the effectiveness of an MPA. These roles extend both to biological monitoring of marine environment, particularly where coral reefs are involved – simple monitoring methodologies are being developed that can be used by non-experts – and to monitoring of socioeconomic parameters, such as fishery information (by fishers) or tourism use of reefs (by dive operators) (Johannes, 1998; Wells, 1995). For such programmes to be effective over the long term however, attention must be paid to training and capacity-building, and to ensuring that the community sees the benefits of such inputs (Borrini-Feyerabend, 1996).

CONCLUSIONS

Many marine coastal areas face combined pressures from diminishing fish stocks, intensification of fishing practices, pollution and tourist development. Addressing these issues through protected areas will involve a complex mixture of approaches, as is the case in the terrestrial environment. These include: community participation, partnership between different interest groups, educational programmes and the careful zoning of kinds of protection, to balanced sustainable use with conservation. Greater communication and sharing of experience is needed between those involved in protected area management in the terrestrial and marine environments.

REFERENCES

Borrini-Feyerabend, G (1996) *Collaborative Management of Protected Areas, tailoring the approach to the context*, Issues in Social Policy, IUCN, Gland

Christie, P and White, A (1997) 'Trends in development of coastal area management in tropical countries, from central to community orientation', *Coastal Management* 25, 155–181

Costanza, R et al (1997) 'The value of the world's ecosystem services and natural capital', *Nature* 387, 253–260

Gibson, J, McField, M and Wells, S (1998) 'Coral reef management in Belize, an approach through integrated coastal zone management', *Ocean and Coastal Management* 39, 229–244

Republic of Mozambique (1995) *The Strategy for the Development of Tourism in Mozambique (1995–1999)*, Direcção Nacional de Turismo, Maputo

Johannes, R E (1998) 'The case for data-less marine resource management, examples from tropical nearshore finfisheries', *Trends in Ecology and Evolution* 13(6): 243–246

McGinn, A P (1998) *Rocking the Boat, conserving fisheries and protecting jobs*, Worldwatch Paper No 142, Worldwatch Institute, Washington DC

Pomeroy, R S (1995) 'Community-based and co-management institutions for sustainable coastal fisheries management in South-east Asia', *Ocean and Coastal Management* 27(3), 143–162

Ruddle, K, Hviding, E and Johannes, R E (1992) 'Marine resources management in the context of customary tenure', *Marine Resource Economics* 7, 249–273

Weber, P (1994) *Net Loss, Fish, Jobs and the Marine Environment*, Worldwatch Paper No 120, Worldwatch Institute, Washington DC

Wells, S M (1995) *Reef assessment and monitoring using volunteers and non-professionals*, Report compiled for the International Year of the Reef, University of Miami

Wells, S M (1996) 'Capacity building for science and management in Belize, essential goals for sustainable reef management', *Proceedings of the 8th International Coral Reef Symposium, Panama*, 2, 1991–1994

White, A T, Hale, L Z, Renard, Y and Cortesi, L (eds) (1994) *Collaborative and community-based management of coral reefs, lessons from experience*, Kumarian Press, West Hartford, Connecticut

White, A T and Savina, G (1987) 'Community-based marine reserves, a Philippine first', in *Proceedings of Coastal Zone 87*, American Society of Civil Engineers, Seattle, 2022–2036

WWF (1998) *Marine Protected Areas, WWF's Role in their Future Development*, WWF International Discussion Document, WWF International, Gland

14 PEOPLE-ORIENTED CONSERVATION: PROGRESS TO DATE

Sally Jeanrenaud

INTRODUCTION

A recurrent theme of this book is the increasingly important role of people-oriented conservation initiatives in protected area management. Various 'social' elements are now often factored into the design and implementation of integrated conservation and development projects (ICDPs), the collaborative management of protected areas, joint forest management, community-based conservation and community wildlife management (Borrini-Feyerabend, 1997ab; Western, Wright and Strum, 1994). This chapter examines some common assumptions made about 'people-oriented' conservation, examines progress made and makes recommendations relating to how people-oriented conservation can be further improved in the future.

DEFINITIONS

The new conservation literature includes many terms which imply a simultaneous interest in the welfare of people and nature – for example, community-based conservation, integrated conservation and development, collaborative, joint and comanagement, sustainable resource utilization, participatory natural resource management and self-mobilized conservation initiatives. Each expresses particular assumptions and meanings. The term people-oriented conservation attempts to capture what is assumed to be common to them all: the idea that environmental care and local livelihoods go hand in hand.

The term needs to be qualified. It was first coined by conservation organizations during the 1970s and can reflect the thinking and priorities of conservationists, tending to signify donor concerns rather than the plural perspectives of local people. This implies definitions of both people and conservation imposed 'from above'. However, it can also be used in another sense to include self-mobilized and grassroots attempts to secure rights to the environment. This suggests people-oriented conservation as it might be defined 'from below'.

This distinction is critical. Different actors have different perceptions of, interests in, and relationships with, nature, and therefore frame environmental problems in various ways. People-oriented conservation must involve analysis of the values, interests and activities of a wide number of actors (Blaikie and Jeanrenaud, 1996).

A number of common 'policy prescriptions', or emergent 'principles' for people-oriented conservation reflect the extent to which conservation organizations have reframed their perceptions of environmental problems and local people over the past 15 years. A central theme of this new approach is that conservation efforts: 'need to identify and promote *social processes* that enable local communities to conserve and enhance biodiversity as part of their livelihood systems' (Pimbert and Pretty, 1995, p24, emphasis added)

COMMUNITY

The new conservation literature makes extensive reference to communities. It is often implicitly (and sometime explicitly) assumed that communities 'exist'; that local people have collective or shared interests and consensual decision-making processes; that people can agree on community membership; and that communities are conservation minded. Where social differences are recognized, it is often assumed that diverse perspectives, priorities and goals can be negotiated and promoted through stakeholder analysis. However, as many analysts point out, attempts to implement these ideas raise many complex questions for development and conservation agencies. What is a community? Who is local? Should incomers be included? What is the difference between local, indigenous and traditional communities? Do communities have the same priorities as conservationists (Agrawal, 1997)? There are also more radical questions concerning whether communities actually exist at all, or whether they are just fictitious abstractions to serve policy-makers' needs (Anderson, 1983).

Ideas about what constitutes a community in natural resource management are frequently disputed. People have multiple and overlapping identities and interests, and the unity and identity of a community is best considered as an ideal. Groups of people are not homogenous. For example, in Nepal community was associated with a *panchayat* or local political–administrative unit until the revolution in 1990 when the system broke down. It has subsequently been associated with forest-user group, a concept promoted by aid agencies. However, this concept can also cause problems because there are often differences between traditional forest users and incomers who rely on forests for subsistence purposes (Hobley, 1996).

Understanding who has access to, and control of, resources has significant implications for who bears the costs of protected areas and who reaps the benefits of resource management. Projects sometimes make blanket prescriptions, which have a differential impact on local groups and can exacerbate environmental degradation and human welfare. In seeking solutions to environmental problems, addressing *socially different needs* should play a key part.

Stakeholder analysis has emerged largely as a response to problems with the notion of community. While acknowledging plural interests, it sometimes fails to address unequal power relations and power processes. Stakeholder participation can become a focus and stage on which power relations are played out. It is thus important to understand the dynamic processes of inter-action between groups, and the means people use to reach their goals. It is also important to consider positive discrimination for poorer subgroups (such as the landless and women) because these groups frequently bear the cost of conservation interventions, but have less power to defend their interests.

Self-mobilized conservation initiatives come from groups which are usually highly motivated and organized with strong local leadership, and promise to be socially sustainable in the long term. While they may not share the same final goal as conservationists, they often share many common interests and often approach agencies for financial and technical assistance. However, self-mobilized groups are not necessarily concerned with equity issues. Support of local elites can influence local economic and political dynamics, with potentially negative impacts on marginal groups.

Such issues raise the important questions of how far conservation agencies should tackle social equity concerns. For example, in a community-based project supported by WWF in the Solomon Islands, financial and technical support for resource management and environmental protection is mainly controlled by men but has implications for women, who find their influence on local decision-making has been further eroded. In acts of resistance, women then tend to flout the rules of the protected area management plans (Adams, 1996).

Some kind of social mapping is just as important as biodiversity mapping, but it needs to include more than just lists of stakeholders, their interests and types of social impact. It should also analyse the *processes* and *means* by which people pursue their interests, the different sources of power, and various strategies to achieve goals.

Coalitions of different actors have enormous political importance in promoting grassroots biodiversity protection and protected area management at both a policy and field level (Silva, 1994). Coalitions and alliances strategi-cally exploit the middle ground of shared interests. Used proactively, coalitions can be responsive to political opportunities at local, national and international levels.

TENURE AND USUFRUCT RIGHTS

It is agreed in some quarters that land rights, security of tenure and usufruct rights are not only human rights, but also prerequisites for biodiversity conser-vation. It is assumed that tenurial security encourages rural people to make investments of labour in land because they can reap the benefits. However, attempts to establish secure tenure can be fraught with difficulties, because they challenge vested interests and control over resources. The renegotiation of property rights is often contested within communities, between communi-ties and the state, and sometimes between conservation agencies and local populations. Securing local tenure is also controversial for conservationists because many fear that local people will exploit lands in the same way as other populations, or lease their land to outsiders. Indeed, local tenurial security does not always protect the environment; for example, some local groups negotiate away their rights for commercial gain (Sekhran, 1996).

Common property regimes (CPRs), where a group of resource users share rights and duties towards a resource, are receiving emphasis as environmentally, socially and economically viable forms of property and management. Conservation projects rarely frame environmental concerns in terms of 'security of tenure', but there are some notable exceptions (for example, support for extractive reserves in Brazil; primary environmental care projects in Indonesia).

Supporting and (re)negotiating local property rights is a complex political and legal process. Property claims often consist of overlapping rights; indigenous concepts of territory do not normally conform to simple property classifications; tenure is dynamic; it may not be in people's best interests to claim land titles; and local claims challenge vested interests and control over resources. Coalitions of local and international groups are usually required to challenge existing power structures, allowing alternative tenure systems to emerge. Legal aid is frequently required. In many cases traditional land rights are honoured only in so far as they do not conflict with national priorities. This presents formidable problems to conservation agencies involved in negotiating secure tenure systems for people and conservation.

For example, there have been many problems in documenting and gaining legal acknowledgement of customary land tenure within the East Kayan Mentarang protected area in Indonesia. Despite the mapping of customary land using oral histories, sketch maps and global positioning systems (GPS) and geographic information systems (GIS) methodologies, it was difficult to capture complex relationships of traditional resource management systems on maps. Property rights and claims are a complex bundle of overlapping and hierarchical rights and claims, distributed among many persons and related to other social relationships. This contradicts the clear boundaries assumed by state title programmes. While some government officials support this local mapping process, others refuse to recognize the maps as having a legal basis (Sirait et al, 1994; Laidlaw, 1996).

LOCAL MANAGEMENT INSTITUTIONS

Local 'sustainable institutions' (including secure *tenure* arrangements and equitable *organizations*) are considered essential for community-based conservation. Institutions may be considered the underlying (formal and informal) rules which influence patterns of behaviour, whereas organizations administer those rules.

Advocates of people-oriented conservation often assume that local people have, or can build, institutions which represent common interests; that these are egalitarian; that they have effective conflict resolution mechanisms and can enforce rules and sanctions; and that they are capable of protecting resources and hence biodiversity. However, there is much evidence to suggest that traditional institutions tend to break down under internal and external pressures, and that new institutions may reinforce existing social inequalities. What lessons are being learned about new organizational forms?

The criteria to assess the robustness of local organizations are well developed. Building new institutions frequently involves changes in the underlying structures of rules that influence behaviour patterns, and in the capacity of local people to represent their interests. There are concerns that some new community-based organizations may be negatively affecting the livelihoods and environmental entitlements of marginal groups. Policy-makers should recognize that marginalized subgroups may seek (and require assistance) to reform them.

Since the mid 1990s, development policy has paid increasing attention to the contribution of social capital to economic and social development. This might be considered local capacity to exert pressure for change, resulting from greater involvement in public affairs – or a greater capacity for marginalized groups to get their voices heard. Investing in social capital involves investments in non-tangible human resource endowments and attention to improving the institutional basis for participation (including decentralization policies). Concepts of capacity-building in conservation programmes need to consider these deeper processes of institution and organization-building for social sustainability in conservation.

Support for the Rondonian rubber tappers in Brazil has emphasized the organization and mobilization of local rubber tapper associations (see Chapter 23). These are a prerequisite for claiming land-use concessions from the government. The formation of an association is usually preceded by group meetings, which involve a mixture of consciousness raising and organizational development. Facilitators explain about extractive reserves and motivate local people to organize themselves into an association. The role of the union of rubber tappers is explained. Rubber tapper associations are encouraged to resist loggers, cattle ranchers and other land grabbers. However, there are several weaknesses in these local-level organizations; they often do not outlive the project cycle, there are difficulties in communication between distant households, and there is a legacy of debt peonage from rubber trading. The success of associations also depends on the recognition of women's roles in production and protest; but while women are frequently involved in tapping rubber and extractive activities, they have generally not had the opportunity to participate in the union or other group activities. (Rosendo, 1996; Campbell, 1997).

PARTICIPATION

It is now widely assumed that participation is required to achieve sustainable and effective conservation, particularly in protected areas; that it can bring economic and social benefits to marginalized groups; and that devolution of decision-making will benefit biodiversity. However, some assumptions about participatory approaches are untenable when unequal power relations and processes at a local level are considered. Do local people have the social autonomy and freedom to participate in decision-making?

Analysts distinguish between participation as a means and an end. In the former sense, participation is seen as a more efficient tool for realizing pre-determined objectives set by outsiders. This tends to view people merely as a tool or resource for conservation. In the latter sense of participation as an end, involvement is seen as a fundamental right of local people to influence the course of events. Here it is viewed as an empowering process, critical to the goal of self-determination. The distinction is thus between a manipulative and facilitative approach. These two perspectives imply entirely different power relationships between actors, and represent a challenge to conservation when defined from above.

Participation also covers a spectrum of meanings from token dialogue to self-mobilization. It is important to understand how participation works in particular cultural and political contexts. Different social institutions affect rules about, for example, the rights to make decisions and to speak in public. Such rules influence participatory rural appraisal (PRA) events, which may become the means through which dominant ideologies are reproduced.

The cultural contexts of decision-making raise some key questions in participatory development and conservation. What is being devolved and to whom? How are decision-making and rights over resources actually distributed? What is the relation between spokespersons and those they speak for? (Peters, 1996).

In Latvia, the legacy of Soviet rule can pose major cultural and political obstacles to participatory development and conservation. Soviet totalitarianism produced a culture where it was not safe to talk to anybody. Latvians were recruited to inform on neighbours, colleagues and even relatives. Today, people still commonly express the view that 'you do not share problems'. They are unclear about who to talk to, when to talk to them, or even why and how to talk to them. This is not to say that Latvian people have no interpersonal skills, but that communication in the workplace or within institutions often appears to be just 'going through the motions'. This cultural context has made people very wary about prospects of, for example, forming cooperatives for forest management (Buhler, 1997).

When we talk about participation, we often assume that it is the project's job to encourage local people to participate. However, we can turn the concept around and ask: how does a conservation organization participate in local people's projects? In many cases people collaborate with outside actors to fulfil a variety of private aspirations (for example, to secure land titles and maintain traditional power relationships). PRA methods may therefore yield little social change without sustained political support at local and national levels. There is a danger that PRA exercises can just be fleeting events in the lives of communities which raise expectations but may not bring long-term change. Some literature tends to make implicit (if not explicit) links between PRA and empowerment, popularly conceptualized as influencing decision-making. While PRA is important in facilitating communication, it is increasingly recognized that empowerment involves deeper institutional reorientation and transformation. For many grassroots groups, empowerment means more than just influencing decision-making but includes, for example, access to skills, a view also shared by more progressive PRA practitioners.

LIVELIHOODS

It is generally agreed that sustaining or providing alternative livelihoods is important to stop the exploitation of protected areas; that livelihood opportunities can be integrated with nature conservation objectives; and, for example, that extractive reserves and multiple-use forestry can provide benefits to people and biodiversity.

However, recent research exposes some contradictions between livelihood–conservation objectives of local people and conservation projects (Freese, 1996; Peters, 1996). Conservation approaches, which link livelihoods to biodiversity conservation, are raising some serious social and ecological questions.

Many studies, for example, have outlined the key role of forest products in the livelihoods of rural groups (particularly poorer subgroups), and have assessed the economic valuation of non-timber forest products (NTFPs) and environmental values. Such arguments have generated conservation programmes on protective enterprises, ecotourism and marketing of NTFPs. However, forest-based enterprises pose several dilemmas. For example, there are ecological concerns about the implications of extraction of NTFPs over long periods; social and equity concerns related to multiple use and protection; economic concerns about marketing; and political concerns. As a result, emphasis on livelihoods, NTFPs and extractive reserves diverts attention away from land reform needs. Livelihood and conservation dilemmas should be addressed at an institutional, as well as at economic, levels – for example, through the promotion of land reform as well as finding marketing solutions for NTFPs.

Conservation projects often have negative impacts on local livelihoods and welfare. These effects are well documented in the case of traditional protected-area programmes, but less well known in community-based conservation projects. Projects should seek to mitigate the negative effects of conservation on the livelihoods of local people – particularly poorer subgroups. Livelihood issues should be addressed not only as an environmental imperative but also as an issue of social justice.

THE ENABLING POLICY ENVIRONMENT

It is often assumed that policy and legislation supporting decentralization are required to enable local groups to initiate, manage and protect community-conservation initiatives; that the existence of policy and legal documents are assumed to protect local groups against inside and outside threats; that decentralization helps promote more sustainable land use and biodiversity conservation in the long term; that decentralization policy and implementation are 'rational' processes (Lutz and Caldecott, 1996).

A close look at examples of promoting an enabling policy environment reveals the political nature of policy change and implementation. Rather than assuming lack of political will, policy outcomes and implementation are best considered the outcomes of power processes and negotiations of many different actors. Analyses of successful policy changes reveal the key role of coalitions of local and non-local groups. Political pressure resulting from coalitions is also crucial for sustaining implementation. Although local people and traditional conservationists may share intersecting interests, they do not necessarily have the same goal. This means that conservation organizations have to recognize that their priorities may differ from local priorities and be prepared to negotiate interests fairly. This can be helped by encouraging openness and transparency in decision-making, particularly concerning who bears the costs of particular decisions, and by acknowledging accountability to many stakeholders in addition to governments and donors.

CONCLUSIONS

Conservation policy and practice should embrace progressive social agendas (processes fostering self-determination, and human rights and equity concerns), as well as biological and ecological ones. Environmental and social concerns are inextricably woven together. By integrating progressive social agendas within conservation programmes, environmental organizations align themselves with the broad democratic principles of open rather than totalitarian society.

Conservation organizations should seek greater participation from wider civil society if the trade-offs between conservation and human welfare are to be minimized. Conservation organizations need to consider systems of environmental brokerage, in which diverse values and interests are negotiated. By supporting wider participation, conservation organizations thus defend the right of people to determine their own conservation objectives and practices.

Conservation organizations should also be prepared to accept nature and conservation as defined from below, as well as from above. In entering wider negotiations with greater numbers of actors, conservation organizations should be prepared to accept new definitions of nature. This implies acceptance of a plurality of interpretations, meanings and approaches. This may well challenge older conservation objectives, but can serve to enrich a wider understanding of humanity's relationship with nature.

REFERENCES

Adams, L (1996) *A Gender Analysis of Community Resource Conservation and Development Institutions: The Case of Marovo Lagoon, Solomon Islands*, WWF Forest Unit, WWF International, Gland

Agrawal, A (1997) *Community in Conservation: Beyond Enchantment and Disenchantment*, CDF Discussion Paper, Conservation and Development Forum, University of Florida

Anderson, B (1983) *Imagined Communities*, Verso, London

Blaikie, P and Jeanrenaud, S (1996) *Biodiversity and Human Welfare*, URISD Discussion Paper No 72, United Nations Research Institute for Development, Geneva

Borrini-Feyerabend, G (ed) (1997a) *Beyond Fences: Seeking Social Sustainability in Conservation*, vol 1 A Process Companion, IUCN, Gland

Borrini-Feyerabend, G (ed) (1997b) *Beyond Fences: Seeking Social Sustainability in Conservation*, vol 2 A Resource Book, IUCN, Gland

Buhler, W (1997) *Latvia, Forests and People*, WWF Forest Unit, WWF International, Gland

Campbell, C E (1997) 'On the front lines but struggling for a voice: Women in the rubber tapper's defence of the Amazon Forest', *The Ecologist* 27(2): 46–54

Freese, C (1996) *The Commercial, Consumptive Use of Wild Species: Managing it for the Benefit of Biodiversity*, WWF-US and WWF International Discussion Paper, WWF, Gland

Hobley, M (1996) *Participatory Forestry: The Process of Change in India and Nepal*, ODI Rural Development Forestry Study Guide 3, Overseas Development Institute, London

Laidlaw, M (1996) *People-Oriented Forest Conservation: Kayan Mentarang, Indonesia*, WWF Forest Unit, WWF International, Gland

Lutz, E and Caldecott, J (1996) *Decentralization and Biodiversity Conservation*, The World Bank, Washington, DC

Peters, C (1996) 'Observations on the Sustainable Exploitation of Non-Timber Tropical Forest Products: An Ecologist's Perspective', in Ruiz Perez, M and Arnold, J (1996) (eds) *Current Issues in Non-Timber Forest Products Research*, Proceedings of the Workshop Research on NTFP, Hot Springs, Zimbabwe, 28 August–2 September 1995, Centre for International Forestry Research, Jakarta

Peters, P (1996) 'Who's Local Here? The Politics of Participation in Development', *Cultural Survival* 20(3): 22–25

Pimbert, M and Pretty, J (1995) *Parks, People and Professionals: Putting Participation into Protected Area Management*, UNRISD Discussion Paper No 57, UNRISD, IIED,WWF, Geneva

Rosendo, S (1996) *Social and Environmental Support for Rondonian Rubber Tappers*, WWF Forest Unit, WWF International, Gland

Sekhran, N (1996) *Pursuing the 'D' in Integrated Conservation and Development Projects (ICADPs): Issues and Challenges for Papua New Guinea*, ODI Rural Development Forestry Network Papers 19b, Overseas Development Institute, London

Silva, E (1994) 'Thinking Politically about Sustainable Development in the Tropical Forests in Latin America', *Development and Change* 25(4): 699–721

Sirait, M, Prasodjo, S, Podger, N, Flavelle, A and Fox, J (1994) 'Mapping Customary Land in East Kalimantan, Indonesia: A Tool for Forest Management', *Ambio* 23(7): 411–417

Western, D, Wright, R W and Strum, S (eds) (1994) *Natural Connections: Perspectives in Community-Based Conservation*, Island Press: Washington DC

A house of spirits of the Mijikenda elders, Kenya

Protected areas protect more than just biodiversity. Many have important environmental, economic, cultural and even spiritual benefits. In Kenya, kaya forests are important religious and ceremonial sites that also harbour unique forest ecosystems.

PART IV

SEEKING A WIDER RANGE OF PARTNERS AND VALUES

Although protected areas are intended to protect biodiversity, many have a range of other values. These are beneficial in that they provide additional incentives for protection, but also sometimes carry a cost in terms of implications for the quality of the resulting protected area. In Part IV authors look at the role of protected areas in protecting spiritual values, providing recreational benefits and in safeguarding water and fisheries resources.

Recognition of these wider values also opens up the possibility of working with a range of partners to secure protection. This is particularly important at a time when many governments are finding it hard to secure the funds for long-term management of protected areas. The section therefore ends by looking at some examples of partnerships for protection, including both NGOs and private initiatives in Latin America and commercial companies in Scandinavia.

15 LIFE RESERVES: OPPORTUNITIES TO USE SPIRITUAL VALUES AND PARTNERSHIPS IN FOREST CONSERVATION

Paul Sochaczewski

INTRODUCTION

The concept of 'life reserves' describes areas which are important to local communities because the site provides spiritual, cultural or religious comfort as well as ecological benefits. The individual's relationship with nature and forests is complex and has several facets:

- *The practical/pragmatic:* we all have to eat, breathe, earn a living and so on, and our connection with nature in this context is direct, Cartesian and can often be defined by economic valuations, science and laws.
- *The spiritual/emotional/religious:* these non-pragmatic factors are difficult to quantify but nevertheless affect us deeply. Why do we need living green in our lives? What is our emotional love–fear relationship with wilderness? Why do we need birdsong?
- *Cultural context:* a mix of pragmatic and spiritual factors exists in specific cultural contexts – different tribes, different expectations, different connections.

Many (mostly Northern-influenced) conservation programmes emphasize the practical and pragmatic approach. Although this is important, organizations could also approach conservation holistically by incorporating both pragmatic and spiritual motivations where appropriate. By recognizing this human complexity, programmes have an opportunity to build significant partnerships for conservation. Many conservation initiatives reflect well-intentioned arrogance: 'We know what's best for you.' However, organizations should be prepared to accept that projects may not develop according to standard dogma. As James Swan (1990) writes:

When you go to the top of the mountain seeking guidance, you have to be prepared to follow through with what comes to you, if you want to have the power of that place working in you and through you – and what comes to you is what you need, not necessarily what you want...There is a danger in trying to explain sacred places in terms of modern science, because modern science may not be able to allow them to exist. The problem is with the scientific model. There is no Newtonian–Cartesian explanation for why shamanism works, but it does, which is much more important...The 'new science' which will guide humanity into the 21st century must be able to account for and work with such conditions as spiritual states of consciousness and the things which occur as a result of such states, because they are an integral and extremely important component of human existence.

EXAMPLES OF HOW CONSERVATIONISTS WORK WITH OR FOR LIFE RESERVES

Around the world, the Earth's surface is sprinkled with places whose names alone stir deep feelings in us: Mount Fuji, Lascaux, Jerusalem, Delphi, Denali, the Great Pyramids, Stonehenge, Haleakala Crater, Mount Kailas, the Ganges River, Machu Picchu and countless others. Many sacred places lack the widespread recognition of, say, Mount Kilimanjaro, but are nevertheless important to local communities. In the oldest epic poem known, which can be traced back to Sumeria some 5000 years ago, the hero Gilgamesh and his cohorts are described as approaching a sacred stand of cedar trees.

SACRED GROVES

A sacred forest can be described as any stand of forest that is considered valuable by a local community and which is protected by that community for reasons that include the spiritual. In general, they are separate and inviolable. Sacred groves are found worldwide, particularly in developing countries.

Much has been written, some of it unbearably romantic, about how a simple, rural, poor, developing-world life style is sustainable and enriching. In some cases it is true, though, and Marglin (undated) wrote about the successful and satisfying life style of the people of Orissa, India, whose life includes respect for a sacred forest:

The sacred grove is the keystone in a way of life that has maintained such astounding sustainability. Far from being a mini-nature preserve, the sacred grove is both locus and sign of the regeneration of body, land and community. It stands for the integration of the human community in nature.

UNESCO (1996b) takes a more pragmatic approach:

Sacred groves have served as important reservoirs of biodiversity, preserving unique species of plants, insects and animals. Sacred and taboo associations attached to particular species of tree, forest groves, mountains, rivers, caves and temple sites should therefore continue to play an important role in the protection of particular ecosystems by local people. Particular plant species are often used by traditional healers and priests who have a strong interest in the preservation of such sites and ecosystems. In some regions of the world, beliefs that spirits inhabit relict areas have served to quickly regenerate abandoned swidden plots into mature forest. In other areas, sacred places play a major part in safeguarding critical sites in the hydrological cycle of watershed areas. Furthermore, in a number of instances sacred sites have also been instrumental in preserving the ecological integrity of entire landscapes. For these reasons, sacred sites can help in assessing the potential natural vegetation of degraded ecosystems or ecosystems modified by humans.

Gadgil and Vartak (1996), experts on Indian sacred groves, have catalogued more than 400 sacred groves in Maharashtra state alone. They believe that sacred groves had their origins 'in the hunting–gathering stage of society, where they served to create the proper setting for cult rites, including human sacrifices'. They see a parallel between sacred groves and the way in which ancient Greeks worshipped the goddess Diana and her forests. They also acknowledge secular reasons for establishing sacred groves, such as the preservation of a valuable tree which was relatively rare in the locality. They point out that a sacred grove of the water deities, Sati Asara, harboured a solitary but thriving specimen of the liana known as *gaidhari* (*Entada phaseolides*), used in treating cattle for snakebite. This was the only specimen of this species within a radius of 40 kilometres, and people came from considerable distances to this grove to ask the priest for the medicinal bark.

Sacred sites are often overlooked when planning conservation projects. In the extreme south of China's Yunnan Province (the world's most northern tropical rainforest), some 400 'dragon hills' or *lung shan*, provide for people's spiritual and physical well-being (Pei, 1985; Sochaczewski, 1996). However, when it came to the management of several large nature reserves in the province, neither the Chinese, nor WWF, who were the project planners, thought to include the dragon hills in their efforts, preferring to focus on centrally gazetted and managed chunks of real estate that had only peripheral value to local communities. They missed a major opportunity to achieve conservation and relate conservation to the needs and spiritual lives of local people.

Though poorly studied, the sacred groves of Xishuangbanna may contain important new natural pharmaceuticals. Dr Pei Sheng Ji, director of the Kunming Botanical Institute and one of China's leading ethnobotanists, has listed some 25 new drugs that have been developed from Chinese traditional medicines used by national minorities. About a third of the medicines have been developed from *lung shan* plants by minorities in Xishuangbanna. From

Tripterygium hypoglaucum, a plant used by the predominant Dai tribe, Chinese researchers have extracted a compound called triptotide hypolide, which is now prescribed by doctors throughout the country to treat rheumatism and arthritis. The *lung shan* forest also harbours wildlife, including many bird species which eat insects that would otherwise eat the villagers' rice crops. The forest also acts as a watershed, ensuring a regular flow of clean water throughout the year. Dr Pei notes: 'The holy hill is a kind of natural conservation area founded with the help of the gods, and all animals, plants, land and sources of water within it are inviolable' (quoted in Sochaczewski, 1996).

Sacred forests generally harbour important reservoirs of biodiversity which may have disappeared elsewhere. In Ghana, for example, UNESCO worked with local communities to protect a sacred forest which contained endemic tree species which had been wiped out elsewhere. With the encouragement of local priests, the 'sacred' trees were used as breeding stock to grow saplings used in a successful regreening project in neighbouring areas. Links could be established with forestry, agriculture and community development groups to acknowledge sacred forests as reservoirs of valuable plants and, with the permission of the caretakers, extract plants for regeneration elsewhere. (Some sacred forests face a variety of threats, and in certain circumstances a detailed biological inventory can help guardians generate outside support for the preservation of the sites.)

Tree planting is a particularly powerful way to heal the land and heal the spirit. 'Planting a tree is a symbol of a looking-forward kind of action; looking forward, yet not too distantly', observed Richard St Barbe Baker, a patron saint of tree planters who led a movement he called Men of the Trees. Buddhist 'forest' monks in Thailand, for example, were increasingly frustrated because the forests by which they defined their calling were being destroyed. Recognizing their obligation to society, several monks began energetic land-restoration programmes. The monks won support of local people and of some officials, but several monks were attacked by thugs hired by timber operators and other influential people who feared that their lucrative operations would be curtailed. One well-publicized highlight of the forest monks' efforts is an ongoing ordination of old-growth trees. In this ritual a monk wraps a saffron-coloured sash around a tree, thereby giving the tree the rank of monk and protecting it from harm, just as a monk is (theoretically at least) himself protected.

In India, Swami Vankhandi (literally Sage of the Forest), a Hindu hermit, has single handedly been saving the Himalayan foothills Sattal Reserve Forest since 1978. The site is in a transition zone of tropical and temperate biomes and is therefore rich in biodiversity. The entire region in the state of Uttar Pradesh is a land of spiritual penance and worship. Hindu, Buddhist, Sikh and some Christian pilgrims consider these as sacred mountains and as places of pilgrimage, spiritual retreat and learning. It also lies at the start of the strenuous and important Himalayan pilgrimage to Mount Kailasa. Swami Vandkhandi has sought to reestablish links between nature and man's sacred belief and traditional values, and has devoted his life to creating within the forest environs a spiritual centre dedicated to the worship, study, protection and regeneration of forests and nature. For the past 18 years, Vankhandi has banned tree felling, foraging for fuelwood and fodder and hunting in the surrounding reserve area. He has planted local and endangered species, and encouraged surrounding villages to do the same. In the reserve forest he has himself planted more than

3000 trees, and re-established herbs used in traditional ayurvedic and ethno-medicinal practices. He has also built water tanks for collecting rain and spring water for wildlife.

LINKS WITH FRESHWATER INITIATIVES

One of the most universal connections between sacred forests and people is water. Many sacred forests are catchment forests, and local people well recognize the importance of maintaining the forest if they want to maintain their water supplies. In the Indian subcontinent, for example, it is common to see a *naga* (dragon, based on the king cobra) shrine at water sources, streams and river crossings. The logic is that in order to provide a regular supply of clean water it is essential to protect the water catchment area.

MANAGEMENT OPTIONS

Life reserves may not easily fit into commonly used protected area categories. In addition, life reserves may not flourish under a standard protected-area approach, and their very existence may challenge conceptions of what is meant by a protected area.

In Asia, sacred groves reflect some of the most successful conservation programmes simply because they ignore the middleman – in this case, the government. Some people who live close to life reserves may be wary of any outside intervention, regardless of how well intentioned. To these life-reserve guardians, simply respecting a sacred site might be reward enough, and legal gazettement would be irrelevant at best or unwanted at worst. Nevertheless, some situations will call for some form of formal gazettement. Several options exist.

IUCN Categories

None of the six IUCN protected area categories relate directly to life reserves. The closest category is Category V, the definition being broad enough to include cultural, religious and spiritual forests. The guidelines say little about how these areas should be managed, but the implication is that there should be an element of external planning or control, which might conflict with the communal nature of the sites. The guidelines also suggest that the area 'should provide opportunities for public enjoyment through recreation and tourism' which also might conflict with traditional management systems. Life reserves might also fall under Category VI, although caretakers of many sacred forests actively discourage the kind of resource use (sustainable or otherwise) that this category promotes.

UNESCO categories

The World Heritage Convention offers another option for providing recognition and protection of sacred forests. UNESCO (UNESCO, 1996a) recognizes a type of site in which cultural landscapes represent the 'combined works of nature and of man... they are illustrative of the evolution of human society and settlement over time, under the influence of the physical constraints and/or opportunities presented by their natural environment and of successive social, economic and cultural forces, both external and internal.' UNESCO adds: 'The nominations should be prepared in collaboration with and the full approval of local communities.' UNESCO also provides a useful management tool in the 'man and biosphere' categories.

Other options

There may be scope for lateral thinking. For example, the elders who were responsible for maintaining the sacred *kaya* forests of the Kenya coast wanted some form of legal protection but did not trust the forest department, and hence decided not to request that the *kayas* be designated as nature reserves. A more appropriate legislative home for these areas, they felt, was to put the 40 or so forests under the auspices of the national museums of Kenya, with the designation of national monuments. It may be possible in some countries to develop special categories of protected areas which are sacred and natural. And IUCN might be encouraged to revise their guidelines specifically to recognize life reserves. Another option is to deliberately not lock sacred forests into existing Western moulds but simply encourage communities to protect and manage these sites, and give these communities sufficient resources and visibility so that power brokers leave them alone.

RECOMMENDATIONS

Partnerships–local

Opportunities to use spiritual liaisons should be examined. For example, the Siberian forests of the Russian Republic of Sakha (also called Yakutia) have gained considerable publicity from the fact that the government has pledged to protect by the year 2000 an area twice the size of Germany (700,000 square kilometres). The publicity for this achievement was generated from the WWF Forest for Life campaign which encourages countries to protected representative samples of forest ecosystems; but the campaign barely mentions the role of local people. The Yakutia, however, is a land of traditions and strong spiritual and cultural beliefs, and perhaps significant areas of forests (both within and outside the formal nature reserves) are considered sacred and might benefit from a life reserve approach.

Partnerships–global

Organized groups representing single religions and approximately six major international interfaith groups, play an important but often unheralded role in developing soft-law treaties, such as various declarations on human rights.

Often these groups are eager to become more involved in environmental issues and could become conservation policy partners. There are basically two reasons why religious groups increasingly focus on the environment. The first is that caring for nature is often integral to their dogma and belief systems. The second is that an environmental orientation gives the religion something useful to do, which religious leaders hope will make the faith increasingly relevant and attract or maintain believers.

CONCLUSION

The ideas proposed here should be seen as one part of a conservation programme, complementing and supporting agreed geographic and biological priorities. For life reserves to become a useful part of the protected area network, however, it is vital that conservation organizations accept that 'spiritual' partners may not have the same outlook on life or the same reporting, documentation or planning sophistication as the people who run other projects.

REFERENCES

Gadgil, M and Vartak, V D (1976) 'The sacred groves of Western Ghats in India', *Economic Botany* 30(2): 160

Marglin, F A and Mishra P C (undated) 'Sacred Groves: Regenerating the Body, the Land, the Community', *Ecology from Below*

Pei S (1985) 'Some effects of the Dai people's cultural beliefs and practices upon the plant environment in Xishuangbanna', *University of Michigan Annals of Botany* 27, 321–339

Sochaczewski, P S (1996) 'God's Own Pharmacies', *BBC Wildlife*, January

Swan, J A (1994) 'Sacred Places of the Bay Area', in Singh, R (ed) *National Geographical Journal of India*, vol 40: 123–130

UNESCO (1996) *Operational Guidelines for the Implementation of the World Heritage Convention*, paras 35–42, Paris

UNESCO (1996b) *Sacred Sites-Cultural Integrity, Biological Diversity*, Programme Proposal, 19 November 1996, Paris

16 NATURE-BASED TOURISM IN TERRESTRIAL PROTECTED AREAS

Paul F J Eagles

INTRODUCTION

Since the last century, tourism use of protected areas has changed from a few hundred hardy travellers to hundreds of millions, due to expanding affluence, cheaper travel costs and increasing interest in the environment. The rapid worldwide growth in tourism reveals both strengths and deficiencies in the existing management structure of nature-based tourism in protected areas. This chapter discusses the most important of these issues, reviews current literature and suggests practical policy measures to ensure that both tourists and ecosystems maximize the benefits.

DEFINING NATURE-BASED TOURISM

Nature-based tourism is based upon the desire of people to experience nature in their leisure time. The growing levels of participation have led to the recognition of at least four submarkets (Figure 16.1), differentiated according to the travel motives of the travellers (Eagles, 1995a).

Ecotourism involves travel for the discovery of, and information on, wild natural environments and may be the fastest growing tourism submarket.

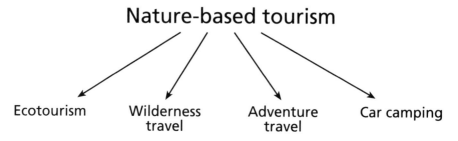

Figure 16.1 *Nature-based tourism*

Wilderness travel involves personal recreation through primitive travel in natural environments that are devoid of human disturbance. Adventure travel is personal accomplishment through the thrills of dominating dangerous environments. Car camping is safe family travel in the interface between the wild and the civilized.

Kenya and Tanzania are well-documented examples of the growth of nature-based tourism. Starting with only a few thousand tourists in the early 1950s, Tanzania's tourism increased to 350,000 visitors in 1995 and Kenya to 865,300 visitors in 1994. In both countries the tourism industry is closely tied to the world-class system of national parks and game reserves. The foreign exchange earnings from tourism rival, and sometimes exceed, those of agriculture, the other important export. However, nature-based tourism is only a small part of the overall tourism industry, possibly 7 per cent.

The link between environmental protection, international tourism and economic development became widely recognized in Eastern Africa in the early 1970s. Filani (1975) and Western and Henry (1979) proposed the development of national tourism policies, closely linked to national development strategies. Kenya and Tanzania have been successful leaders in the development of ecotourism industries based upon a comprehensive structure of national legislation, policy planning and site management. However, not all tourism development efforts in sub-Saharan Africa have been successful. Ankomah and Crompton (1990) identified five factors inhibiting these development efforts as: negative market image, lack of foreign exchange for capital development, lack of trained personnel for tourism, weak institutional frameworks for planning, and management and political instability.

MANAGING PARKS AND TOURISTS

Despite the clear growth in nature-based tourism, both the mainstream tourism industry and protected area management have a blind spot for this emerging phenomenon. Therefore, some of the key issues to be considered in managing nature-based tourism are examined and priorities are highlighted below.

Tourist travel motives, marketing and management

Ecotourists' motives can be different from the motives of typical travellers. As a result, the ecotourism travel industry must be designed differently from the standard travel approach. Research suggests that the key concepts underlying ecotourist travel motivations are wilderness, wildlife, parks, learning, nature and physical activity. In order to satisfy ecotourists, these ideas should underlie both the management of natural resources and the provision of tourist services.

Many park agencies are reluctant participants in the tourism business. Most managers are trained in resource management and few have professional education in tourism, finance or marketing. As a result, the development of tourism policy is often reactive, with a weak conceptual and policy basis. The complexity of tourism management in parks is often underestimated. They must balance environmental protection and visitor use of the resource. They must deal with the demands of visitors, local residents, regional interests, the national government and the private tourism industry. Usually the park is managed as a public good, owned by government, and financed from tax revenues with all tourism products sold at an operating loss. It is critical to recognize that tourism management in protected areas requires a sophisticated management structure.

Management of environmental quality

Ecotourists seek high levels of environmental quality. Most ecotourism is concentrated in national parks, wildlife reserves and similar types of protected areas. Each of these protected area systems has environmental integrity goals. Therefore, the ecotourist's travel motives and the management philosophy of the parks' agencies are similar. However, tourist use has the potential to degrade environmental quality through overuse, damaging behaviours, unplanned access to sensitive sites and inappropriate use levels. Recreation in parks sometimes leads to soil erosion and compaction, vegetation damage, water pollution, changes in fire regimes, vandalism and noise. However, Pigram (1980) recognized, in a landmark paper, that whereas tourism can lead to environmental degradation and therefore be self-destructive, it can also contribute to substantial enhancement of the environment with proper management. Management of natural resources and visitor use should aim to maintain ecological integrity, with the allied concepts of ecological sustainability and preservation of biodiversity as the policy focus.

Limits of acceptable change

All human actions in natural areas cause some impact. This can be positive or negative and can vary in scale. How much impact, therefore, is acceptable? Determining impact, assessing acceptability, managing and monitoring must all be carried out (Stankey et al, 1985; Prosser, 1986). The amount of environmental and social impact allowed is a management decision. The decision involves the legal and policy environment of the protected areas, the existing use levels, the desires of the tourists and the larger political environment. Given the complexity of these decisions, an open decision structure that allows for input from all interested parties is essential. No one group, such as entrenched tourist operators or environmental groups, can be allowed to dominate other, equally legitimate, interests. Increased levels of public policy discussion, with concerned action by environmental groups, is necessary if protected area managers are to withstand the strong pressure from self-serving tourism interests who wish to maximize their financial return through minimal investment in environmental management. Gakahu (1992) provides a useful and thorough review of the interrelationships between wildlife tourists, reserve management and policy for the Maasai Mara National Reserve in Kenya.

A beneficial tool for management is zoning within a park. Sensitive sites are zoned for low levels of use, while more hardy areas are zoned for intensive uses. A similar approach can be used to separate incompatible recreational activities.

Management of tourist use

Canada, the United States, New Zealand, Australia and most European countries have more than a century of experience in developing approaches for the management of tourists in natural areas. The use is often high, and it is not uncommon for national parks to be visited by millions of visitors each year with generally acceptable levels of impact.

Research shows that park visitors' satisfaction with their visit is not directly correlated with use density or gross numbers. Satisfaction is more closely correlated with environmental quality, the adequacy of facilities and programmes and the accuracy of expectations (Graefe et al, 1984). Therefore, to maintain visitor satisfaction in crowded locales, protection of natural features must be assured, facilities must be capable of handling the numbers, services must be of high quality, and visitors' expectations must be appropriate. Approaches to managing large numbers of visitors include: abundant pre-trip information, quality transportation networks, scheduling of access, use limits, hardening of facilities in sensitive areas, visitor education, and law enforcement.

In countries with a history of park use, repeat consumers become familiar with the expected behaviour during park visitation. This provides for visitor management that operates relatively smoothly. A major challenge for the future is the education of international tourists who come from cultures where significant natural sites are not present or are given low value. Higher levels of pre-trip information, visit monitoring and enforcement may be required with these visitors.

A comparison of the management of park tourism in Western Africa to that of Eastern Africa, shows that even with Western Africa's significant natural resources, the tourism levels are well below those of Eastern Africa. The reasons for the lower levels of use include: less visible wildlife concentrations, weak national transportation networks, inefficient hotel facilities, poorly trained tourism staff, weak marketing, and a lack of tourism infrastructure in the parks. Drawing on the success displayed in eastern Africa, the basic needs for ecotourism development can be summarized as (Sournia, 1996):

* good basic information within and outside the country;
* good technical information available for trip planning and during the trip;
* good tourist reception achieved through training of hotel and park staff and guides;
* good accommodation and transport to ensure adequate levels of safety, comfort and medical attention; and
* Good facilities adapted to local conditions and to the types of visitors targeted.

ALLOCATION OF ACCESS

Sensitive environments are easily damaged by open tourism access, and some argue that protected areas are only suitable for low-impact recreation, such as wilderness travel or natural history tours. Allocation of access is therefore a major policy issue.

There are several alternative management options for sensitive area allocation. A typical approach is first come, first served. The rationale is that this gives equal access to all, an important fairness issue on public land. In high demand areas, a system of registration, which can occur months or even years ahead of the visit, may be used. For example, regulation of white-water raft trips on the Colorado River through the Grand Canyon National Park in the US results in registration up to 18 months in advance. Such an approach can, however, be unfair for international tourists who may be unfamiliar with the timing and means of registration.

The private sector uses market demand and price to allocate access – higher demand translating into higher prices. This approach is acceptable on private land but has severe implications for publicly owned resources since it discriminates against those with lower incomes. Lotteries are sometimes used where demand is much higher than supply. This provides equal access to all, but is difficult to manage for international visitation. The use of qualifications to allocate access occurs infrequently, although some sensitive environments are only accessible to people who undertake scientific research and have the associated qualifications. Dangerous environments can be restricted only to those with specialized training. A typical example is the requirement of individual training before scuba diving is allowed in marine national parks. Finally, political power is sometimes used to gain preferential access, both by individuals and groups, and bribery of bureaucrats or politicians can take place.

Most sites use a combination of allocation approaches. Many parks have a proportion of their recreation facilities allocated to advance registration systems and a portion to first-come, first-served access on site. As use levels increase, it is necessary to continue to develop fair and open use–allocation procedures. Such policies must be fair to all potential users, balance individual and group access, recognize the special needs of international visitors, and be cost efficient.

Market specialization

The large size and increasing sophistication of the tourism market is resulting in more specialization of services, with four identifiable tourist products associated with protected area use (see Figure 16.1). Each product has specialized equipment, information needs, environmental impacts and consumer demands. Furthermore, the different areas of specialization may well be at different levels of maturity – an area which needs wider consideration (Eagles, 1995a).

Many park managers do not discriminate amongst tourist products, despite the fact that within each niche market there are identifiable needs for various levels of involvement and expertise. As increased market specialization continues, the factors defining ecotourism specialization, such as quality and availability of information, environmental quality, programme and facility design, and uniqueness of the local environment, all need to be addressed.

Managing recreation conflict

High levels of use, varying recreation goals and finite resources lead to conflict amongst recreational groups. Competition for access to resources, disputes over activities at a site, and use density are pivotal issues. It is essential that such conflict is kept to a minimum in order to avoid tourist dissatisfaction. Recreation managers need to understand the diversity of visitors' motives, the outcomes necessary to attain the tourists' goals, and the consequences of people interacting with others with different agendas.

Enforcement and monitoring

Tourism is very sensitive to social issues. Tourists do not have to travel and will quickly avoid an area if there are safety, behaviourial or deprecative concerns. Proper regulation development and enforcement are essential to sustain tourism. The lack of enforcing environmental rules results in environmental degradation, removing the key travel-motive factor for the ecotourist. Some countries in South America, Central America and Africa have difficulty in enforcing resource and visitor management regulations. This is due to under-funded park agencies, political corruption and bribery. As a result, their park systems and ecotourism industries do not reach market potential.

Consumer assurance of quality

The last 20 years have seen a dramatic rise in consumer awareness of the concept of product quality. The private sector has found that high-quality products are demanded by consumers and are an important component of market advantage. The public sector has lagged behind in this area. Most park managers give scant attention to visitor-use quality; the prevailing attitude is that the consumer can take or leave what is provided. This approach is faltering as sophisticated ecotourists show preferences for areas providing a better quality product (Eagles, 1995b).

Consumers with advanced environmental preservation attitudes expect certain levels of environmental impact and service quality related to their travel experience. The idea that ecotourism must practice what it preaches – environmental sensitivity – is powerful and persuasive. This has led to the development of guidelines to govern all aspects of the ecotourism experience. For example, the Ecotourism Society (1993) and the ecotourism industry in Ecuador are working on a countrywide evaluation effort. Key to the programme is a set of operational standards. The degree of implementing these standards is being monitored by ongoing surveys of ecotourists. Similarly, Australia is leading the world in the development of an ecotourism accreditation scheme for tour operators, accommodations and attractions.

Facility design

Ecotourist use involves the development of a wide range of equipment and facilities. Sensitive facility design has become widespread in Central American destinations serving the North American and European markets. Within Canada and the US such design is common within parks, but is rare in the private sector developments. The US and Australia have comprehensive guidelines for designing sustainable facilities and programmes (NPS, 1994).

Community development

Most natural areas are located in rural terrain. The development of tourism in such areas can have considerable impact on the local people (Lindberg and Enriquez, 1994). Sensitive-use policies are required that cause minimum negative social impacts but allow high levels of local involvement. Jobs for local people are a high priority, but are often difficult to provide in a sophisticated knowledge-based industry, such as ecotourism or adventure tourism.

The development of tourism policies which are sensitive to local concerns is essential for obtaining community support. In Belize, for example, local economic and social benefits caused an increase in support for ecological conservation (Lindberg and Enriquez, 1994). Often the special concerns of indigenous people need to be taken into account. This can involve the assurance of positive economic impact to local communities, the closure of culturally sensitive sites to tourism, and involvement in management. Both public-sector landowners and private-sector service providers have responsibility to guide community development in positive directions.

Financial viability

Tourism is considered to be an export industry because of its ability to earn foreign currency. It is this feature that makes the industry so attractive to the economic sectors of society. Nature-based tourism is the most important foreign currency earner for some countries who lack industrial, financial or resource-extraction industries.

The rapid expansion of facilities, programmes and operators illustrates that the nature-based tourist industry is financially viable. Thresher (1981) found that a lion in Amboseli National Park in Kenya is worth much more as an object for viewing, than as an object for hunting. This logic is now commonly accepted in Eastern and Southern Africa. However, the flow of economic benefits from tourism is not necessarily as advantageous for the ecosystems on which tourism depends. The majority of park programmes in the world are underfunded. Typically, sufficient funds are only available for a minimum of resource protection. In these cases, tourism can be destructive because of the inability to provide sufficient visitor management structures.

Resource protection in protected areas should be paid from government taxes because all people benefit (Eagles, 1995b). Nevertheless, recreation primarily benefits the users and, therefore, should be paid from user fees. Increasing reliance on user fees is a trend in many countries, both rich and poor. Tanzania, Kenya, Costa Rica and Canada are all experimenting with innovative fee and management structures in order to raise management funds.

Driml and Common (1995) showed that the economic benefits of nature-based tourism in selected Australian locales far exceed government expenditures. Their research estimated the value of tourism in five Australian World Heritage areas (Great Barrier Reef, Wet Tropics, Uluru National Park, Kakadu National Park and Tasmanian Wilderness). Tourism expenditures in these areas in 1991 to 1992 was Australian$1,372,000,000; the total management budgets were Australian $48,700,000; and the user fee income to the management agencies was Australian $4,160,000 – in other words, the management budgets were only 3.5 per cent of the tourist expenditure. The report also noted that tourism research expenditures in Australia were very low compared to other economic generators such as agriculture and mining, both of which have a smaller economic impact. This is a common problem. Most governments do not recognize the significance of the economic value of nature-based tourism and, as a result, underfund its development.

Public and private sector cooperation

The long-term success of protected area tourism requires cooperation between the public and private sectors. Typically, the private sector provides most of the services and consumer products, such as accommodation, food, transport, media and advertising, associated with tourism. Thus, the public sector relies upon the private sector for handling the day-to-day activities of the visitors, while the private sector relies upon the public sector for resource protection, infrastructure and security services.

The operation of an ecotourism industry requires the cooperation of both sectors. This situation is not always appreciated and much time and effort are wasted in conflict situations, where none fundamentally exist.

CONCLUSIONS

Protected area management in many countries has well-developed resource management policies. However, the visitor management sector is often weakly developed. As a result, the management structures are sometimes severely challenged. Environmental damage, visitor satisfaction problems, group conflicts and funding problems are symptomatic.

Park-related tourism can be sustained indefinitely, as long as management structures ensure the protection of natural environments and provide high-quality travel experiences. A summary of the principles of ecotourism management include the following.

- Ecotourism should lead to both nature conservation and local economic benefit.
- Well-educated management staff are essential.
- All public and private ecotour businesses should have an environmental strategy and an environmental officer.
- Tour operators and tourists should demand high environmental standards from their associates, hotels, transportation providers and destinations.
- Culturally and economically sensitive community development is necessary.
- Ecotourism should be designed to benefit local communities, socially, economically and ecologically.
- High-quality information, service delivery and well-educated guides are essential.
- Planning and management capabilities are key for long-term success.
- Environmental protection is based upon the fiscal viability of management, both public and private.

- Ecotourism and environmental protection require the development of management structures to handle use of sensitive environments.

REFERENCES

Driml, S and Common, M (1995) 'Economic and Financial Benefits of Tourism in Major Protected Areas', *Australian Journal of Environmental Management* 2(2): 19–39

Eagles, Paul F J (1995a) 'Understanding the Market for Sustainable Tourism', in McCool, S F and Watson, A E (eds) *Linking tourism, the environment and sustainability*, Proceedings of a special session of the annual meeting of the National Recreation and Parks Association, 1994, Department of Agriculture, Forest Service, Intermountain Research Station, (republished at http://www.ecotourism.org/datafr.html.)

Eagles, P F J (1995b) 'Tourism and Canadian Parks: fiscal relationships', *Managing Leisure* 1(1): 16–27

The Ecotourism Society (1993) *Ecotourism Guidelines for Nature Tour Operators*, North Bennington, Vermont

Filani, M O (1975) 'The Role of National Tourist Associations in the Preserving of the Environment in Africa', *Journal of Travel Research* 13(4): 7–12

Gakahu, C G (1992) *Tourist Attitudes and Use Impacts in Maasai Mara National Reserve*, Wildlife Conservation International, Nairobi

Graefe, A R, Vaske, J J and Kuss, F R (1984) 'Social carrying capacity: An integration and synthesis of twenty years of research', *Leisure Sciences* 6(4): 395–431

Lindberg, K and Enriquez, J (1994) *An Analysis of Ecotourism's Economic Contribution to Conservation and Development in Belize*, World Wildlife Fund, Washington DC

National Park Service (1994) *Guiding Principles for Sustainable Design*, United States National Park Service, Denver Service Center, Denver, Colorado (republished at http://www.nps.gov/dsc/dsgncnstrl/grpsd)

Pigram, J J (1980) 'Environmental Implications of Tourism Development', *Annals of Tourism Research* VII(4): 554–583

Prosser, G (1986) 'The Limits of Acceptable Change: An Introduction to a Framework for Natural Area Planning', *Australian Parks & Recreation* 22(2): 5–10

Stankey, G H, Cole, D N, Lucas, R C, Peterson, M E and Frisell, S S (1985) *The Limits of Acceptable Change (LAC) System for Wilderness Planning*, USDA Forest Service General Technical Report INT–176, Ogden, Utah

Sournia, G (1996) 'Wildlife Tourism in West and Central Africa', *Ecodecision* 52–54

Thresher, P (1981) 'The Present Value of an Amboseli Lion', *World Animal Review* 40: 30–33

Western, D and Henry, W (1979) 'Economics and Conservation in Third World National Parks', *BioScience* 29(7): 414–418

17 WETLAND CONSERVATION: CHALLENGES AND OPPORTUNITIES IN THE NEXT MILLENNIUM

Biksham Gujja

INTRODUCTION

As we approach the next millennium, it is an opportune time to reflect and examine what challenges lie ahead in terms of conservation and management of key natural resources such as freshwater. Management of freshwater has direct implications for wetland ecosystems. Already in the past few hundred years, untold damage has been done to wetland ecosystems. Although our perception of wetlands has changed from one of wastelands or dirty places to a recognition that they are some of the most productive ecosystems in the world (Maltby, 1986), much remains to be accomplished if we are to manage these vital resources in a manner which will benefit future generations. Worldwide, wetlands face an uncertain future. Human attitudes must change; new wetland management tools and practices must be set in place. These are major challenges for the next millennium. It remains to be seen whether we can meet these challenges.

WHAT ARE WETLANDS?

The term wetland covers a broad scale of ecosystems; the Ramsar Convention defines wetlands as: 'areas of marsh, fen, peatland or water, whether natural or artificial, permanent or temporary, with water that is static or flowing, fresh, brackish or salt, including areas of marine water the depth of which at low tide does not exceed six metres'. If the Ramsar definition is strictly applied, most of the Earth's mass, apart from deserts, can be categorized as wetlands. Definitions of certain ecosystems are further complicated by the fact that definitions may vary between developed and developing countries.

Wetlands account for approximately 6 per cent of the global land area and estimates of the area of global wetlands vary from 5.57 to 8.56 million square kilometres. However, there are many uncertainties regarding their extent: even within a country, estimates of wetland areas vary significantly. For example, in

India some estimates suggest there are about 58 million hectares of wetlands (17 per cent of the land area), including all rice fields, while other sources suggest the area only covers 4.1 million hectares about 1.2 per cent of the total area (WWF and AWB, 1993). Therefore, due to the rate of destruction, and the wide range of definitions and discrepancies in current evaluations, the global wetland area may be overestimated.

WETLAND FUNCTIONS, VALUES AND PERCEPTIONS

Scientific perceptions of wetlands have recently been revised. Even though it has been widely documented that wetlands were considered as wastelands, there is no evidence of such perceptions in many developing countries, particularly in Asia. On the contrary, many swamps, ponds and lakes are considered as sacred. Similarly, in many native North American cultures, ponds are sacred.

Wetlands are probably the most threatened ecosystems in the world. In developed countries, most wetlands have already been drained and converted to other uses. In the US, more than 118 million acres (about 48 million hectares) of wetlands have been lost: more than 22 states have lost over 50 per cent of their wetlands. In California, this figure reaches 91 per cent. Surveys conducted from the mid 1970s to the mid 1980s indicate that 2.6 million acres (more than one million hectares) were lost in just nine years (Dahl and Johnson, 1991). Similarly, two-thirds of the wetlands in Europe existing at the beginning of this century have been lost. In South Africa, although data are scarce, wetland loss in certain catchments ranges from 48 to 90 per cent.

To put these figures in perceptive, the total area irrigated in China is 47 million hectares. The per capita wetland *degradation* in the US is around 0.25 hectares – five times more than the per capita area of irrigated land (0.045 hectares) in China. The loss of wetlands continued in developed countries until the 1980s. In North America, federal efforts to restore wetlands have significantly increased since this period. About 50,000 hectares of wetlands have been restored from 1987 to 1990 (Dahl and Allord). Wetland restoration is currently a major business. Many private companies now promote restoration and have become highly proactive in promoting the conservation and creation of these vital ecosystems.

There are many contrasts in the manner in which wetlands have been used and appreciated between developed and developing countries. In India, for example, many wetlands were created to provide irrigation. India has 65,253 artificial wetlands with an area of 2.6 million hectares. This compares with an area of 1.4 million hectares of natural wetlands (WWF and AWB, 1993). In many countries wetlands are part of the rural culture and economy. Most of the wetlands in Asia are used for a wide range of purposes. In many instances, it should be noted that people are using wetland resources even without ownership of the area.

Wetland degradation, alteration or conversion to other uses is currently taking place in many developing countries as they switch to *modern* irrigation methods, expansion of agriculture, cash cropping, water extraction, industrialization and urban growth. As a result, there is considerable pressure on these ecosystems and a need to find alternative ways to manage remaining wetlands, both for conservation purposes and to ensure the livelihoods of local communities.

NEW CHALLENGES LOOKING TO THE FUTURE

Existing strategies to conserve wetlands need to adopt a radically different approach, both at policy and programme levels. The much-publicized emerging freshwater *crisis* could be an opportunity to save many wetlands from further degradation. The international community generally agrees that, in the coming decades, water and not oil will influence the political, economic and conservation agendas of many countries. There is an urgent and legitimate need to deliver more freshwater to communities in many countries. At the same time, however, there is an overwhelming need to protect and maintain existing freshwater ecosystems.

THE RAMSAR CONVENTION: ACHIEVEMENTS AND CONSTRAINTS

The first significant effort to conserve wetlands may be traced to an international meeting of experts, held at Espoo, Finland, in March 1970. This initiative produced a draft paper for a meeting at Ramsar (Iran) in 1971 where the treaty was signed by 18 countries. Although the convention came into existence primarily to protect waterfowl, it also recognized the importance of wetlands as 'resources of great economic, cultural, scientific and recreational value' (Ramsar Convention Bureau, 1997).

The Convention on Wetlands of International Importance especially as Waterfowl Habitat (usually referred to as the Ramsar Convention) is a somewhat broad framework adopted by contracting parties. Particular emphasis is given to conservation, management and the wise use of resources. Under the convention, contracting parties identify wetlands of international importance and designate such sites for protection. The convention also urges contracting parties 'as far as possible to compensate for any loss of wetland resources' if a listed site has been deleted or restricted due to some 'urgent national interest'. Countries have to inform the convention of changes or likely changes of ecological character of wetlands 'as a result of technological developments'.

The convention does not advocate strict protection comparable to categories I and II of IUCN's protected area categories. Listed Ramsar sites are probably comparable to Categories III to VI of IUCN's framework. *Wise use* has become a central concept to wetland conservation worldwide. This is probably because many such wetlands were primarily maintained and used by local and international elites as hunting grounds, long before the Ramsar Convention came into existence. Many examples exist where wetlands were designed and managed for attracting migratory birds so that hunting could be sustained. But recently, many such wetlands were declared as national parks, and stricter management and protection rules have applied. In some situations, walls were built to separate communities from the park's resources, resulting in violent conflicts, massive damage to the ecosystem, as well as serious hardships imposed upon local communities.

ACHIEVEMENTS OF THE RAMSAR CONVENTION

To date, 111 countries have joined the convention – Belize and Luxembourg are the latest members. Together, these countries have listed 907 sites with an area of 68 million hectares, an area the size of France and Switzerland together, or about 10 per cent of the estimated global wetland area. While this has been a major achievement, it must still be viewed in perspective so that further advances can be made.

- The convention is not globally representative. The convention was intended to conserve sites of international importance. Out of 950 sites listed under the convention, more than 400 are in western Europe. The UK alone has 106 sites whereas only 70 sites have been listed for Asia (Frazier, 1996). Although criteria and guidelines exist to help identify and govern sites to be included in the list, not all Ramsar sites have the same level of international importance. In addition, there are still a fair number of internationally important sites that have not been listed under the convention.
- There are significant differences in the size of wetlands listed under the convention – from just 0.1 hectare (Hosbie's Spring, Christmas Island, Australia) to 6,278,200 hectares (Queen Maud Gulf, Canada) (Frazier, 1996). The current system does not differentiate between the relative importance of different sites. In terms of size alone, at 800,000 hectares the Parc National de Virunga in the Democratic Republic of Congo is almost twice as large as the combined area of the 106 Ramsar sites of the UK. The average size of Ramsar sites in Western Europe, 12,400 hectares, is six times less than the global average, 75,000 hectares.
- Ramsar contracting parties have not yet listed all important wetland sites. Gaps in the current coverage of sites need to be addressed.
- Many of the listed sites have not been properly maintained. The Montreux Record was established in 1990 to identify Ramsar sites 'where changes in ecological character had occurred, were occurring or were likely to occur as result of technological development'. In practice the listed sites have degraded considerably and need considerable improvement. To date, more than 62 sites in 28 countries have been placed under the record (some 3.8 million hectares), about 46 per cent of the area of all the Ramsar sites in these 28 countries. At the global level, the area covered by the Montreux Record sites is only 5.6 per cent, but many other sites may have to be listed if the guidelines are to be truly effective. So far only four sites have been removed from the Montreux Record, which indicates that countries are doing little to improve the ecological character of those wetlands.
- The importance of wetlands is gaining increased recognition. The Ramsar Convention meets every three years – the Conference of the Parties (COP) – to review progress. In 1980, around 100 people participated at COP1; by 1996, the attendance was almost 1000. The past six conferences have adopted more than 120 recommendations and resolutions. Unfortunately, the growing level of participation and number of adopted recommendations and resolutions has not been reflected in conservation achievements and substantial resources are diverted to organizing such meetings.

While considerable achievements have been made by the Ramsar Convention over the past 25 years, there is now a major need to translate all of this planning into concrete actions which will benefit wetland ecosystems at the local and national levels. For this to happen, current approaches may have to be revised and modified to suit the times.

PRESENT UNDERSTANDINGS AND CONSERVATION ACTIONS

National and international conservation efforts to conserve and manage wetlands are broadly based on the following assumptions.

Information on wetlands is vital

Information on wetlands has been compiled and published by various organizations. Most regions of the world now have national and/or regional directories that provide basic information on the character and specifications of wetlands. However, there are still many gaps in the literature, particularly on wetlands in developing countries. Further studies are therefore still required. Information also needs to be orientated more towards wetland managers.

There is often no information available on the manner in which communities living around wetlands interact with these habitats. Based on the population density of each country and the area of the wetlands described in the regional and national wetland directories, a rough estimate indicates that some 300 to 400 million people live in close proximity to wetlands. Such figures should, however, be viewed as an underestimate of the real situation since communities tend to concentrate around freshwater sources.

Wetlands are valuable

Many wetlands have already been converted and subsequently degraded during the process of change from wastelands to more productive lands. Wetlands are now viewed as one of the most valuable ecosystems, with a range of functions that include supporting the livelihoods of people, to providing revenue from tourism. Recent studies support the economic value of wetlands (some US$14,785 per hectare, per year) as seven times higher than that of tropical forests. Compared with the value of crop lands (US$92 per hectare), wetlands are 160 times more valuable. It should, however, be recognized that such figures are only indicative since the final figures will depend upon adopted methodologies. However, financial arguments should not be overlooked as they are possibly the most persuasive means of convincing governments to protect and conserve wetlands.

Conservation organizations are increasingly using the value of wetland ecosystems as a prime tool in convincing governments and people to take appropriate protection and management measures. Taking the above values into consideration, the total annual value of all Ramsar sites would be around US$1,005 billion. Examining this more closely, it is clear that the potential value generated by a country's Ramsar sites, which may be only a small fraction of the total wetland area, is much higher than the gross national product of many countries.

It is essential that any such valuations are not taken out of context, where they may become counterproductive to the purpose of convincing governments. Many countries who have valuable wetlands already experience problems with paying their annual dues to the Ramsar Convention (a few hundred dollars). Payment of dues is a recurrent agenda item of the Ramsar standing committee.

There is clearly considerable scope and need for conducting economic assessments of wetlands in developing countries. Such studies have to primarily include the local communities who are interacting with and *benefiting* from the ecosystems. One study from the Koi Nature Reserve, a Ramsar site in South Africa, records a commercial value of R395,673 in 1992, a value of R36 per hectare. This is meagre in terms of money. To this value, however, must be added the value of the wetland to the 130 families living in the region through fisheries and similar benefits.

Such valuation has not yet convinced countries to conserve their national wetlands. Many resources have been diverted to compile information on the economic value of wetlands. However, these valuations have not significantly influenced government policies. Such highly exaggerated and unrealistic figures will not appeal to governments or the people. Different methods of valuing wetlands must therefore be found.

PEOPLE AND WETLANDS

There is a clear need to involve people and local communities in wetland management. The understanding for this approach is that traditional *conservation* is not only expensive but is unsustainable if local people are not convinced of the importance of wetlands. In many countries people depend upon wetlands for their day-to-day needs. In some situations, people may appear to be part of the problem, but they could well become part of the solution. This understanding has led to the promotion of participatory implementation and management approaches with local communities and stakeholders. Threats of conflict between local people and conservation authorities can create a context in which consultation with local communities, government departments and conservation organizations may be necessary (Pimbert and Gujja, 1997). In such instances, tools such as participatory rural appraisal (PRA) can be used to:

- assess the social and economic impact of wetland management on local people;
- revise wetland management plans, taking people's views and aspirations into consideration; and
- initiate a dialogue on required policy reforms.

In examples from India and Pakistan (Pimbert and Gujja, 1997), some of the PRA exercise provided useful information and insights. It was also demonstrated that unless local people were involved, it would not only be difficult to conserve wetlands but probably impossible. While these initiatives proposed corrective measures, again it is difficult to put such measures into practice within existing structures and constraints. There are obviously limitations to these approaches, and the involvement of local people in projects should not be viewed as an easy solution to saving wetlands.

WETLANDS AND TOURISM

Some wetlands, particularly Ramsar sites, are major attractions for national and international tourism (see Chapter 16). Many studies are underway to quantify the benefits of tourism to a particular country and to the local people. In reality, ecotourism not only brings financial benefits but also net losses to local communities, while governments may also end up subsidizing the tourists. Apart from management problems such as violation of land rights, it may be difficult to convince local people of the need to conserve wetlands unless they themselves will benefit in some way from the presence of tourists.

THE EMERGING FRESHWATER CRISIS: A NEW OPPORTUNITY?

The emerging freshwater crisis (see Box 17.1) may provide an opportunity to promote global wetland conservation, restoration and protection. The situation is complex: many countries are still not using a fraction of their renewable freshwater resources, but these same countries are often facing dual problems: degradation of wetlands and rivers and severe scarcity of water for basic human needs. The challenge is simple and straightforward – find ways and means within the present economic realities to improve water use (both in quantitative and qualitative terms), while improving, or at least not causing further damage to, freshwater ecosystems.

Many opportunities exist to improve water availability for human use by traditional methods, as well as modern technological methods and waste water conservation (Nigam et al, 1998). In many parts of the world, the freshwater crisis will be a major opportunity for conservation organizations to act, if they follow innovative options to address recognized needs, while improving ecosystem management. Solutions, such as those based on reducing global water usage, will need to be developed if countries and communities are encouraged to apply them.

Economic globalization has created a rapid demand for energy. This may lead to the construction of dams in many countries that are economically poor but rich in biodiversity. These countries need assistance and support to conserve their freshwater ecosystems while pursuing their energy needs.

Conservation of freshwater ecosystems in general, and wetlands in particular, poses a great challenge for the coming decades. At the same time, the growing realization of the importance of these ecosystems for economic

---

BOX 17.1 FRESHWATER USE

At the global level, freshwater use has increased 650 per cent from 579 cubic kilometres to 3580 cubic kilometres in this century (1900–1990). This is about 54 per cent of the total renewable water. It is predicted that usage will continue to increase by 40 per cent by the year 2020, to reach 5187 cubic kilometres. At the country level, the situation is somewhat different. For example, more than 30 countries use less than 1 per cent of the annually renewable freshwater. Some of these countries are the sites of nationally and internationally important wetlands. Population growth is also accelerating in many of these countries, a great proportion of which need to use more water for human consumption and other needs. The challenge remains to increase water use without causing any further damage to the ecosystems in general and wetlands in particular.

---

prosperity and basic human needs is a major opportunity for intervention and action. Future efforts to save wetland ecosystems have to take the following factors into consideration and deal with them accordingly:

- Population growth will continue and there will be additional pressure on freshwater resources. This is a reality and additional debate will not change the situation dramatically. There is no need to prove the obvious, unnecessarily spending additional resources and time.
- The aspirations of people in developing countries are changing rapidly. Providing water for basic needs is a political issue and many governments cannot avoid this.
- Many countries have a legitimate need to increase their energy supply. This supply should be expected to grow in future years.

Taking the above into consideration, policies and programmes to conserve freshwater ecosystems should address the following challenges.

Challenge 1: increase the number of Ramsar sites

The present selection of Ramsar sites does not represent global realities. There is a great disparity in the current listing of sites. Many developing countries have not included internationally important sites in their selection. They need to be convinced that such listings are beneficial to the country as well as to local communities. Local people often resist having wetlands listed due to land claims and restrictions on the use of resources. Conservation organizations have to work with governments and local communities to identify the most suitable Ramsar sites and, equally important, to find mutually agreeable solutions and opportunities to ensure that communities will support any such designations. It is likely that there are, at least, an additional 1000 sites of international importance which are in need of improved management. Conservation of such sites may be essential for maintaining the hydrological cycle.

Challenge 2: managing wetlands sites

Listing of Ramsar sites is relatively easy. Improving the ecological quality of wetlands after designation poses a major challenge. There are instances where, once the site has been designated, degradation continues to take place. Since the Ramsar sites are internationally important, some countries can not alone bare the cost or burden of conserving these wetlands. Many parties to the convention need international assistance, particularly technical support, in order to manage these sites. Such support has to be more directly visible in future if the international community wants to conserve some of the last remaining large wetland ecosystems.

Challenge 3: people as part of the solution

To some extent, many conservation efforts have directly or indirectly restricted the control of wetland resources by local communities. Most often, such controls were set in place with good intentions but without consulting the people. It is clear that this process will not work and any pressure to restrict the local people is counterproductive. Involving people in conservation and management of local resources is not a question to be considered: it is the only option for conserving wetlands in the long term. Ample evidence exists to demonstrate that if this option is not taken up, remedial measures are not only expensive but may result in further degradation of wetlands. Future policies have to work so that involving people is not seen as part of crisis management, but as an essential component in conserving wetlands and other aquatic ecosystems.

Challenge 4: catchment and watershed approaches

Future threats to wetlands originate mostly from outside the wetlands themselves. Any interventions must be integrated at the catchment and/or watershed level. This approach needs a totally different management system as well as different actors. Maintaining the quality of the ecosystem should become a major requirement of future conservation programmes. Combatting water pollution is already a major issue that needs to be addressed.

The challenge is certainly very big and requires a coordinated approach. At the same time, there are opportunities for change as the global awareness of the freshwater situation and its direct link with the wetland ecosystems increases. The future of wetlands can certainly be more assured provided the right steps are taken.

REFERENCES

Dahl, T E and Allord, G J (undated) 'History of Wetlands in the Conterminous United States. Technical Aspects of Wetlands', *National Water Summary on Wetland Resources*: US Geological Survey Water Supply, Paper 2425, 19–26

Dahl, T E and Johnson, G E (1991) *Status and Trends of Wetlands in the Conterminous United States: Mid-1970s to Mid-1980s. Report to Congress*, US Department of the Interior, Fish and Wildlife Service, Washington DC

Commission of the European Communities (1995) *Wise Use and Conservation of Wetlands*, Communication from the Commission to the Council and the European Parliament, COM(95) 189 final, Brussels

Convention on Wetlands of International Importance especially as Waterfowl Habitat (2 February 1971) Ramsar, Iran

Frazier, S (1996) *An Overview of the World's Ramsar Sites*, Wetlands International, UK

Gujja, B and Perrin, M (1999) *A Place for Dams in the 21st Century*, WWF International Discussion Paper, Gland

Maltby, E (1986) *Waterlogged Wealth. Why waste the world's wet places?* Earthscan, London

Nigam, A, Gujja, B, Bandyopadhyay, J and Talbot, R (1998) *Freshwater for India's Children and Nature*, report by WWF and UNICEF, Gland

Pimbert, M P and Gujja, B (1997) 'Village voices challenging wetland management policies: experiences in participatory rural appraisal from India and Pakistan', *Nature & Resources*, 33(1): 34–42

Ramsar Convention Bureau (1997) *The Ramsar Convention Manual. A Guide to the Convention on Wetlands* (Ramsar, Iran, 1971), 2nd edition, Gland

WWF-India with Asian Wetland Bureau (1993) *Directory of Indian Wetlands 1993*, WWF, New Delhi

18 THE ROLE OF NGOS IN PROMOTING ALLIANCES FOR BIODIVERSITY CONSERVATION

Gustavo Suárez de Freitas

INTRODUCTION

Peru is internationally recognized as a megadiversity country. Its territory extends from the Pacific Ocean to the rainforests of the Amazon River basin, passing through the coastal deserts and the valleys, plateaux and snow covered peaks of the Andean mountain range. This geographical and physical diversity is reflected in the fact that Peru contains 84 different life zones: a huge range of ecosystems which together provide a home to approximately 19 per cent of the world's bird species, 10 per cent of mammals, 21 per cent of diurnal butter-flies, 18 per cent of bats, and 13 per cent of freshwater fish. It is evident that a series of different measures are required to ensure conservation of such a wide spectrum of biological diversity. Among these, the establishment of protected areas is a fundamental element within the overall conservation strategy.

Peru also has a high level of cultural diversity. There is an important Quechua population, mainly in the Andean region, which, together with the Aymaras in the south of the country, provides a link with the culture of the Inca and pre-Inca periods. In the Amazon region there are more than 60 ethno-linguistic groups, many of whom preserve their traditional ways of life and age-old systems of knowledge. More than one third of the Peruvian population lives in rural areas, and there are now few areas of Peru that could really be described as uninhabited. Moreover, many rural populations legally occupy territories that are much larger than the areas where they live and cultivate the land. Given the need for an extensive system of protected areas which is repre-sentative of the country's biodiversity, it is easy to understand that protected areas and the rural population are profoundly interrelated and mutually affect each other in many different ways. It is undeniable that the establishment of a protected area system is beneficial for a country, but there is also an opportu-nity cost involved arising from the prohibitions or limitations imposed on the direct use of the natural resources they contain. Those most affected are the rural populations living in or around the protected areas.

THE PERUVIAN PROTECTED AREA SYSTEM

The first Peruvian national park was declared in 1961, and the second in 1965. However, it was some time before a systematic approach to protected area planning was adopted. The Forest and Wild Fauna Law of 1975 defined and established four protected area categories: national parks (equivalent to Category II), national reserves (Category VI), national sanctuaries (Category III) and historical sanctuaries (Category III), which together made up the National System of Conservation Units (SINUC). Responsibility for the management of these areas was vested with the General Directorate of Forestry and Fauna (DGFF) within the Ministry of Agriculture.

By the early 1980s the SINUC included 21 protected areas within these four management categories. In 1990, four new management categories (reserved zone, protected forest, hunting reserves and communal reserves) were added to the old protected areas system to create the present Peruvian National System of Natural Protected Areas (SINANPE), and 20 new areas were incorporated within the system. By 1997 the SINANPE incorporated a total of 46 areas within the eight different management categories. These areas cover a total of 8.44 per cent of the national territory, although coverage of many important ecosystems is still insufficient. In 1992, responsibility for the management of protected areas was transferred to the General Directorate of Protected Areas and Wild Fauna (DGAPFS), a department of the National Institute of Natural Resources (INRENA), a new semi-autonomous agency created within the Ministry of Agriculture.

NGO INVOLVEMENT IN PROTECTED AREA MANAGEMENT

International support for Peruvian protected areas dates back to the late 1960s, when WWF began providing support for the management of the newly created Manu National Park. From the early 1980s onwards, the DGFF made a concentrated effort to increase the level of support from international conservation agencies and to involve private national organizations. In 1983 a committee was created, involving representatives from government departments, universities and international conservation organizations, to coordinate conservation projects in Peru. This organization, known as the Conservation Projects Support Committee (CAPC), mobilized resources from an existing joint IUCN and WWF project unit, working in the Manu National Park, the Paracas National Reserve and the Lagunas de Mejia National Sanctuary. To formalize this cooperation mechanism, the Peruvian Foundation for the Conservation of Nature (FPCN) (now named Pro Naturaleza) was set up. In 1985, this institution assumed responsibility for the project management responsibilities previously handled by CAPC.

Strengthening the protected area system was, and has remained, a central component of Pro Naturaleza's institutional mission. Most of this chapter concentrates on the activities of Pro Naturaleza, which remains the largest Peruvian non-governmental organization (NGO) involved in this kind of work. However, this is not intended to belittle the vital role played by other Peruvian NGOs, such as APECO (the Peruvian Association for the Conservation of

Nature), and international organizations with a strong presence in Peru, such as Conservation International.

Initially, NGOs' involvement in protected areas focused around obtaining and channelling donations of money and goods, in most cases from overseas, for use by the national protected area authority. These funds were used to provide direct support for area protection and management, through infrastructure development, donations of equipment, staff training, boundary demarcation and other related activities. However, the need for a more direct contribution to managing protected areas was soon identified. NGOs became involved in training (in collaboration with the La Molina National Agrarian University) and the provision of technical support for resource management and public use of the protected areas. Most importantly, they began to get involved in protected area planning. Therefore, over the years, a broader vision of protected area management has developed. Pro Naturaleza's support to the protected area system now encompasses three principal areas of activity:

- direct management support;
- support for protected area design, planning and policy-making initiatives, emphasizing the participation of different stakeholders; and
- integrated conservation and development activities with populations living in and around protected areas.

As our knowledge of the protected area system has increased, Pro Naturaleza has become better able to identify needs, to define conservation priorities, and to formulate new project proposals. An important element of the overall experience, although difficult to quantify, has been the joint learning process that has evolved between NGOs and the government, leading to the development of improved approaches to protected area management, at both a technical and conceptual level. Such cooperation is particularly important in developing countries such as Peru, where there is a great need to pool scarce resources and develop a common approach in the face of economic and social problems.

Many positive results have been achieved by NGO-government cooperation in Peru. These include advances in planning the protected area system, promoting new forms of organization and cooperation mechanisms, obtaining Global Environment Fund (GEF) support for the protected areas system, and, most recently, drafting new laws for protected areas. The ongoing relationship between the parks administration and private organizations has been particularly valuable at a time when the director of INRENA has changed no less than 15 times in 12 years. Thus, the participation of the private sector has not only contributed to the efficient implementation of projects in key protected areas, but has also helped in providing continuity for the long-term management of the system.

DIRECT SUPPORT FOR PROTECTED AREA MANAGEMENT

When the Peruvian Foundation for Nature Conservation was founded in 1984, of the existing 21 protected areas in the system, only 11 were being managed, and even this involved only minimum numbers of personnel who were employed directly by the national park authority or other government agencies. Moreover, about this time, the governmental budget for protected areas began to decline just when it was recognized that the national system of protected areas needed to expand, both in terms of number of areas and management capacity.

The foundation's initial portfolio of projects addressed the needs of those key protected areas identified by a report drawn up by the Peruvian Conservation Data Centre (CDC) in 1986. These projects provided equipment, infrastructure development, training and technical support for protected area planning and management. The number of areas supported in this way has grown over the years, and this has made a significant contribution to improvements in the management of the protected area system.

Between 1984 and 1998, management support has been provided to a total of 16 protected areas, covering 5,437,682 hectares, representing 90 per cent of the former System of Conservation Units (SINUC), and 57 per cent of the present SINANPE. Pro Naturaleza has made a vital contribution towards preserving the integrity of the protected area system during a period of economic and social crisis, when internal security conditions have made field work extremely difficult at times. Some of the most important results of our work include: joint funding of 80 park rangers with INRENA (representing 60 per cent of total field staff of the protected area system); organizing training courses for park rangers and protected areas managers; undertaking community planning consultations; construction of control posts, administrative buildings and conservation and development centres; the provision of infrastructure and equipment; and the preparation of technical reports. Furthermore, the boundaries of four protected areas have been demarcated in their entirety, as well as critical sections of the boundaries of four other areas.

Although Pro Naturaleza continues to provide direct management support of this kind, in recent years a more integrated approach has been adopted which addresses a wider range of management issues. This change of emphasis also reflects the improved capacity of the official authorities to assume direct responsibility for protected area management – as a result of increased finance made available from state funds, grants by international cooperation agencies and the new National Protected Area Fund (FONANPE) set up with funds from the GEF.

LIMITATIONS OF STATE-DIRECTED MANAGEMENT

When Pro Naturaleza began to provide support to the protected area system in the middle of the 1980s, the prevailing vision was one of a society dominated by a powerful state with direct responsibility for managing almost all the nation's resources, as well as for key economic activities. Reflecting this view, the development of the Peruvian protected area system was based on the work of government and universities, with occasional support from international technical agencies. It should be stressed that, despite its limitations, this approach put in place strong foundations for the system. Substantial progress was made in designing a system representative of the country's biodiversity, and important technical work was undertaken. These were the priority tasks and less emphasis was placed on local participation in managing protected areas.

During the 1970s, the Forest and Wild Fauna Law incorporated the concept of participation within the management of protected areas – for example, by providing for the formation of local support committees. Additional categories of protected areas were created, such as the communal reserves, to attend to the needs of the rural populations. Protected area law also recognized the rights of ancestral populations to remain within the protected areas and use the resources they contain. However, there were few examples of participation being achieved on the ground. This provoked tensions and in a number of cases generated conflicts between local people and the protected area authority.

Therefore, although the FPCN initially encountered a variable situation with respect to the relationship between local populations and the protected area authority in different parts of the country, there were a number of common features, which by the mid 1980s were preventing progress towards adopting more efficient models of protected area management.

- The authorities had a vertical mentality and an authoritarian attitude towards the local population.
- The role of park guards was to control infractions by the local population, which was seen principally as an actual or potential problem.
- No mechanisms existed for the participation of local people and other interested parties in the decision-making process; nor was the legitimacy of participation recognized. Thus, work with the surrounding populations was limited to publicizing the importance of the protected areas; and only in a few cases were the first steps taken towards opening up the planning process to include participation by local people.
- The concept of protected area management and administration referred exclusively to land contained within the protected area boundary. Protected area planning was also largely restricted to the interior of the protected area. No account was taken of the impact of the protected areas on the surrounding terrain, and no attention was paid to their development needs.
- There was a limited understanding of the system of protected area categories and, as a result, protected areas were often assigned to inappropriate categories.
- There was also insufficient technical knowledge of the management options available. Priority was given to managing strictly protected areas, such as national parks and national sanctuaries, and to a lesser extent national reserves. In the latter case these often ended up being treated as national parks under a different name, with the emphasis on protection, rather than on the sustainable use of natural resources for the benefit of the local population, which is the principal objective of this category of protected area.
- Priority was given to pure scientific research, without taking account of the possibility of undertaking research which could provide direct benefits to local people, and without involving them in the work.
- The local population was viewed as being homogenous; there were no strategies to respond to the needs of different sectors of the population, and there was a very limited sociological knowledge of the issues involved. In particular, there was an inability to identify conflicts and to resolve them in an appropriate manner.

- There was confusion regarding who the protected areas belonged to; the predominant view was to regard them as government property.

It should be pointed out that the above list of problems is by no means exhaustive. Moreover, it is a generalization that does not do justice to particular cases and to individuals who were already beginning to develop a broader and more integrated vision of protected area management in collaboration with the local populations. However, it gives a generally correct and valid overview of the prevailing situation that provided the starting point for the work of the Pro Naturaleza.

THE NGOS' CONTRIBUTION TO THE DEVELOPMENT OF A NEW PERSPECTIVE

The receipt of technical and economic support from WWF–US marked the introduction of the concept of participatory protected area planning to Peru. Strategic planning and other modern managerial concepts were transmitted to NGOs through their links with the progressive business sector in Peru, as well as the influence of international NGOs such as WWF and the Nature Conservancy (TNC). Relations established between Peruvian NGOs and IUCN, and participation in the CNPPA and national parks congresses, provided a channel for the reception of conceptual tools, such as the World Conservation Strategy, which were interpreted or adapted to Peruvian circumstances and applied with increasing success.

Strategic planning, with its critical analysis of context and existing management frameworks, together with the results of appraisals carried out using participatory methodologies, identified the obstacles to achieving protected area conservation objectives. This provided the basis for the collaboration between NGOs and government agencies in designing projects of the type known today as integrated conservation and development projects (ICDPs). Today there are a number of Peruvian NGOs, working together with international NGOs or financially supported by them, as well as some international NGOs with a direct presence in Peru, providing support for the protected area system; all of them are applying, in one form or another, similar concepts and practices. These NGOs act as intermediaries, interpreters, or – to use the terminology of systems theory – interfaces between the national protected area authority and the local populations.

Pro Naturaleza has been able to make contacts, build bridges and form alliances with local populations, with benefits in the form of a more positive and harmonious relationship between the protected areas and local people, using tools such as participatory protected area planning, participatory rural appraisal, and stakeholder analysis. The results of applied research have been incorporated within programmes of sustainable resource management, and a multidisciplinary approach has been adopted for analysing and resolving problems.

Evidently this kind of work is highly complex and often of a delicate nature. It requires not only an intense effort on the part of individuals and institutions, but also the existence of flexible and agile organizations which have

---

BOX 18.1 THE PACAYA SAMIRIA NATIONAL RESERVE

The Pacaya Samiria National Reserve is the largest protected area in Peru, and the most important area of seasonally flooded tropical forest within the protected area system. When Pro Naturaleza and the Nature Conservancy (TNC) began to work in the Pacaya Samiria National Reserve in 1992, with the support of US–AID, they found that there was an important local population of more than 30,000 people living on the borders of the reserve (both within and outside the protected area), who were considered by the authorities to be 'trespassers'. It was a situation of total hostility, with uncontrolled exploitation of the natural resources of the area, both by local people and outsiders. After four years of field work, involving participatory planning, pure and applied research, and the training and motivation of protected area personnel, relations between park wardens and local people have improved, projects for the sustainable use of natural resources (legally permitted in national reserves) are being carried out, and work is underway to prepare a new zoning plan for the reserve. This plan, together with appropriate mechanisms for local control over natural resources, will ensure compatibility between the need to protect the biodiversity of the reserve and its sustainable use by both local people and resource users from other areas. The infrastructure and capacity of the authority to control the reserve have been improved; but at the same time, the reserve can now count on the support of local populations who benefit from its existence.

---

adopted modern management practices and are prepared to adapt and discard paradigms which have become a hindrance to progress, and – in a word – are orientated towards the future.

WHAT HAS BEEN ACHIEVED?

Efforts are now being made to move beyond participatory protected area planning towards effective models of participatory management by stakeholders, amongst which the local populations are the most prominent group. However, this represents the next step and is still at a preparatory stage. Progress to date has resulted in significant improvements in relation to the initial situation described above:

- The attitude of protected area personnel towards local populations is less top-down and more orientated towards collaboration.
- In their relations with local people, the park wardens see themselves as leaders in promoting change and progress, rather than as militarized guards.
- The legitimacy of participation by local populations in planning and in developing projects is recognized, although there are still no officially recognized mechanisms for achieving this aim.
- The concept of participatory planning and management of protected areas increasingly takes full account of the wider context and the need to extend the influence of protected areas in order to promote the sustainable development of the surrounding areas.

BOX 18.2 THE MANU BIOSPHERE RESERVE

The Manu Biosphere Reserve is outstanding in terms of both biological and cultural diversity. Its core area, the Manu National Park, presents an almost unbroken sequence of unaltered natural habitats, ranging from high Andean grasslands more than 4000 metres above sea level down to extensive areas of lowland tropical rainforest. The biosphere reserve was established in 1977, but it was not until the end of the 1980s that, with the participation of NGOs such as APECO and Pro Naturaleza, and with the support of WWF, progress was made towards applying this form of protected area management. Working together with local people, indigenous organizations, local authorities and government agencies, progress has been made towards defining a common vision of the biosphere reserve and agreeing on management objectives. Actions have included participatory planning processes, conservation and development projects, conservation education and applied research undertaken with the participation of local people. Communities in the high Andean sector, which were traditionally hostile towards the protected area on account of land tenancy disputes, have completely changed their attitude as a result of Pro Naturaleza's support for the improvement of agricultural productivity and its help in obtaining land titles. Proposals drawn up by NGOs have also helped to resolve a number of other specific problems, converting enemies into collaborators. The formation of a Manu Biosphere Reserve management committee, made up of representatives of local people and key stakeholder groups, represents an important step forward.

- There is a better understanding and application of the concepts of protected area categories and zoning, as well as of the techniques available for the appropriate management of the protected area system.
- Attempts are being made to manage direct use areas as well as indirect use areas.
- Applied research into managing resources in and around the protected areas is being carried out with the participation of local people.
- Incorporating social sciences and more detailed appraisals within planning and management processes has permitted an understanding of the characteristics of different sectors of the population and different user groups. This in turn has enabled interests and areas of conflict to be identified and solutions to be proposed.
- There is an increased awareness that protected areas belong to the nation and all its citizens, and that protected area authorities should be accountable to Peruvian society as a whole.

It should be stressed that the above is valid as an overall vision of the trends in protected area management in Peru, even though, in some cases, it does not have the full support of government agencies and their personnel. But it is true to say that this vision is being applied at a local level in all projects that are successfully carried out in Peruvian protected areas.

LESSON LEARNED

From the experience of Pro Naturaleza and other NGOs in working collaboratively with the government, some of the more relevant lessons learned are as follows.

- Protected areas and people are not necessarily in opposition. Most of the problems between protected areas and local inhabitants are caused by misunderstandings arising from the absence or inadequacy of communication processes, or by the poor technical and managerial skills of protected areas personnel.
- Local people accept the existence of protected areas when they are given information about what a protected area is, and receive some kind of benefit from the protected areas.
- Local people and other stakeholders can provide strong support for protected area conservation if they are given the opportunity to participate fully in planning and managing the area.
- The biosphere reserve concept is an excellent approach to protected area management because it provides strong links between the needs of people and protected areas.
- Integrated conservation and development programmes (ICDPs) are good tools for linking protected area management with buffer zone management. These projects are also an excellent way to promote local participation and to raise support for protected areas.
- International and national NGOs can play an important role in linking protected areas with people – for example, in the design and implementation of comanagement schemes.
- Protected areas in Categories V (protected landscapes) and VI (resource management areas), provide great opportunities and options to link people with protected areas. These categories allow the more biologically or ecologically important and/or fragile zones of the protected area to be strictly safeguarded, while providing regulations for varying degrees of sustainable use of renewable natural resources. Moreover, Categories V and VI provide the best opportunities for directly involving local people and other stakeholders in protected area management.

RECOMMENDATIONS

Governments, especially in developing countries, should:

- Recognize the collaborative management of protected areas as an appropriate tool for simultaneously fulfilling the objectives of biodiversity conservation and sustainable development. This includes the participation of the social groups involved in protected area planning and management, as well as sharing responsibilities with different types of institutions.
- Make wider and more frequent use of Categories V and VI of the IUCN's protected area classification system, since these provide excellent opportunities for achieving compatibility between environmental protection and

sustainable resource use, and for developing positive linkages between people and protected areas.

- Apply the concept of the biosphere reserve as a means of integrating protected areas with development actions at a local level, and on a larger scale as well.

Donor agencies, intergovernment organizations and financial bodies should:

- Support projects which strengthen the comanagement of protected areas and promote the adoption of the biosphere reserve concept, including projects designed and carried out in collaboration with NGOs, and especially those which integrate conservation and development objectives.
- Support applied scientific research and training in order to increase our knowledge of the issues involved in moving towards the collaborative management of protected areas, and prepare personnel to meet the challenges involved.

International agencies should:

- Provide more assistance to national NGOs to help them support and reinforce the move towards participatory management of protected areas.

CONCLUSION

The experience in Peru clearly shows that partnerships between private and government conservation organizations can achieve significant results for managing the national system of protected areas in a developing country. One of the most important aspects of this partnership has been the continuing joint learning process that has led to the adoption of new, improved approaches to protected area management.

The experience of Pro Naturaleza and the Peruvian protected area authorities, which started out with small projects and modest funding, has grown to the point where Pro Naturaleza now has the capacity to undertake complex conservation projects with budgets between US$0.5 million and $1 million. It would have been unthinkable to undertake projects of this magnitude and technical complexity only a few years ago!

REFERENCES

Fundación Peruana para la Conservación de la Naturaleza (1994) *Una de cada de cooperación para la gestión de las áreas naturales protegidas en el Perú*, FPCN, Lima, Peru

Centro de Datos para la Conservación (1986) *Ecosistemas Críticos en el Perú*, Informe al WRI, Washington DC

19 Private Initiatives for Protected Areas in South America[*]

Jessica Brown and Brent Mitchell

Introduction

In Latin America, as in other regions, conservation strategies are becoming increasingly bioregional, operating on the scale of ecosystems and the wider landscape to conserve biological and cultural diversity. There is growing recognition that protected areas can no longer be treated as islands, but must be seen in the context of overall land use, with an emphasis on compatible management of surrounding lands and creating linkages among reserves (IUCN, 1997). The region's experience with 'paper parks' – protected areas in name only – has demonstrated forcefully that approaches that rely solely on regulation and enforcement are costly and too often meet with failure. Conservationists are finding they must adopt inclusive approaches that encourage local participation.

These new directions in conservation will rely on engaging local residents and communities in protecting and managing areas, which increasingly, as countries in the region consider new types of land tenure mechanisms, are privately or communally owned. Throughout the region, local and indigenous people have a tremendous stake in, and much to contribute to, the stewardship of their land and resources.

The stewardship approach offers a means of cultivating local involvement and reaching beyond the boundaries of conventional protected areas. Stewardship means, simply, people taking care of the Earth. It is defined here as efforts to create, nurture and enable responsibility in landowners and resource users to manage and protect land and natural resources. By fostering individual and community responsibility, the stewardship approach puts conservation in the hands of the people most affected by it.

The stewardship concept draws on an array of tools to conserve natural and cultural values. These tools include education, voluntary management

[*] The authors gratefully acknowledge the contributions of several people who provided information for this chapter, including Mary Lou Higgins, Olga Alicia Nieto, Heman Verscheure, Sonia Wiedmann and Oswaldo Baez.

agreements, the use of deed restrictions (such as conservation easements and covenants), public or private partnerships in protected areas management, and outright acquisition of property by private organizations (Mitchell and Brown, 1998; Diehl and Barrett, 1998; Endicott, 1993).

The emergence of networks of private reserves in many Latin American countries is one important way in which the stewardship approach is being applied. While relatively recent in their inception, private reserves are already making significant contributions to conserving natural and cultural heritage, and the movement is gaining momentum. While networks of private protected areas are emerging in Central America, this chapter reviews experience from four countries: Ecuador, Brazil, Colombia and Chile. It discusses the contributions of private reserve programmes, the challenges and pitfalls of this approach and offers recommendations for research and practice to advance private land conservation in the region.

EXPERIENCE FROM SOUTH AMERICA

Ecuador

In Ecuador a growing network of small private natural areas is playing an important role in conserving the country's rich biological diversity. Although the national system of protected areas covers almost 20 per cent of the country, its ability to conserve representative biodiversity is still limited, due to Ecuador's varied topography and accompanying diversity of microregions and life zones. Conservation of small natural areas is therefore an important conservation strategy in a country with Ecuador's unique ecological characteristics (Baez, 1997).

Ecuador's first private reserve, Río Palenque (200 hectares) was created in the early 1970s. In 1992, Fundación Natura provided initial support for creating several private protected areas in the western part of the country. The initiative was launched as part of the organization's Bosques Occidentales (Western Forests) project, with funding from a debt-for-nature swap and support from WWF and the Nature Conservancy. During this period, a number of other NGOs were creating private reserves, including Fundación Maquipucuna (with a 4500 hectare reserve) and Fundación Jatun-Sacha (with three reserves totalling 6500 hectares). As interest increased, the network quickly grew from a regional organization to a national one as landowners of private natural areas in the Sierra and Amazon regions expressed their interest in being included.

The national network of private reserves, Corporación Red Nacional de Bosques Privados del Ecuador, received legal recognition in 1996. Its objectives include: to promote models of combined production and conservation; encourage research and environmental education; and foster an exchange of management experience. Individuals wishing to join the network must own or administer a property that has a native forest remnant and/or is in the process of restoration. Members are expected to: 'conserve, protect and restore an environment which contributes to the maintenance of biodiversity and/or of natural and genetic resources'; participate in activities of the network; pay annual dues; be willing to adopt programmes of environmental education and sustainable management; and demonstrate their commitment to the conservation of the native forest (Fundación Natura, 1995).

Today there are 41 members of the Corporación Nacional, including landowners and administrators of private natural areas. Additionally, there are a number of private reserves which are not part of the national network. Ecuador's private forest reserves range in size from ten hectares to 19,000 hectares, covering a total area of more than 70,000 hectares (Anon, 1998). Most of the reserves in the national network are small parcels of forest averaging 100 hectares in size and are typically located far from state-protected areas, thereby contributing significantly to the diversity of microregions and species protected nationally (Dodson, 1995).

There is considerable potential for the future development of private protected areas in Ecuador. These reserves present opportunities to develop diverse models for management that combine production, multiple use and strict conservation for example, through the use of forest products for artisanal and medicinal purposes, and other low-impact activities such as tourism, recreation, environmental education, training and agroforestry. Several private reserves are increasingly active in community outreach, providing support in areas such as agriculture and rural development.

Brazil

The Reserva Particular do Patrimônio Natural, or Private Reserves of Natural Heritage (RPPN), programme in Brazil is an example of the role of national legislation in encouraging private initiative in conservation, and ensuring the standards and permanence of these initiatives. Eight years after the enactment of legislation, there are 185 private reserves covering 370,850 hectares, with representation in every region of Brazil.

The RPPN programme was created by a 1990 decree, two years after Brazil adopted its new constitution. Updated in 1996 to address the directives of the Convention on Biological Diversity, the enabling legislation defines a private reserve as an:

> ...*area of private property designated for special protection at the initiative of the landowner, based on the recognition of the public authorities of its important character from the point of view of biodiversity or landscape, or based on environmental characteristics which justify restoration activities.*
> Wiedmann, 1998

The objective of the RPPN programme is to protect representative natural resources in the region through private reserves in which scientific, cultural, educational, recreational and leisure activities are permitted but do not compromise the integrity of the natural resources intended to be protected. The RPPN programme seeks to augment the number of private reserves of flora and fauna by establishing a regulatory framework, a guarantee of permanence (often termed 'conservation in perpetuity'), and incentives for their creation through tax exemptions, priority in environmental financing and the creation of a network of private reserves.

The current legislation enabling private reserves has its roots in the country's 1934 Forest Code, which allowed for nature protection on private property and provided certain tax exemptions. The 1988 Brazilian constitution stated that environmental protection is the responsibility of the state, as well as of citizens. Subsequent legislation, such as the RPPN legislation, has provided Brazilian citizens with the legal and technical means to participate, voluntarily, in the protection of Brazilian ecosystems (Wiedmann, 1998).

Participation in the RPPN programme is entirely voluntary, and a reserve is created at the initiation of the landowner. Designation is made following a technical visit to evaluate resources on the property. Priority is given to the recognition of contiguous reserves, in order to create ecological corridors, and to wetlands. The landowner must register the reserve's creation on property maps and put up signs indicating the area and prohibited activities. Hunting, fishing, trapping, logging, fires and any other environmentally damaging activities are not permitted. The landowner must also survey his property, develop a management plan and present periodic reports, all with the help of IBAMA (the Brazilian federal environment agency), NGOs and nature protection associations. In return, the landowner is totally exempt from local taxes. He has priority in financing environmental projects, and his land is officially recognized as a reserve.

The RPPN programme has demonstrated that many Brazilian citizens are willing to participate in biodiversity conservation on their own properties. Brazilian and international NGOs (including Funatura, Fundacão Boticario and the Nature Conservancy), along with landowners and a growing number of businesses, are creating and managing private reserves. Future legal mechanisms are needed to ensure that the tax-exempt privileges of the RPPN programme are not abused.

Colombia

Despite many challenges, a network of private protected areas is growing in Colombia. The Red de Reservas Naturales de la Sociedad Civil, or Civil Society Natural Reserves Network (RRNSC), works with landowners to improve or secure management of important natural areas. The network of private reserves offers the potential to improve buffer zone management of state-protected areas, and to help resolve conflicts with residents living near protected areas.

The national system of state-protected areas in Colombia covers approximately 10 per cent of the land area of the country. Almost all of these areas can be characterized by human settlements and conflicts over tenure and property. The management of these areas has generally been to control and remove human populations, but this has not been fully effective or possible, given the constraints of political, social and fiscal realities in the country. The network of private protected areas offers opportunities for enlisting local populations in natural area management.

Private land conservation was granted full legal recognition in 1993 under Law 99, the new law creating the Colombian Ministry for the Environment.

Under this law, it became possible to recognize the conservation efforts of NGOs and communities, and the traditional uses of natural resources that protect and enhance biological diversity. Colombia's regulatory framework for private reserves addresses criteria and management objectives similar to those for IUCN categories V and VI (Higgins and Nieto, 1996).

In 1996 there were over 100 private reserves forming the network, which was established with the support of the WWF Colombia programme. Approximately 70, totalling almost 13,000 hectares, have been surveyed (Higgins and Nieto, 1996). The majority of the reserves are in the Andean region, reflecting the population concentration, but the network has reserves in all regions of the country, representing a range of ecosystems and vegetation types. As of yet, there is no mechanism to prioritize, according to conservation importance, which areas are protected.

Examples of economic incentives provided by certain municipalities for conservation on private lands include: discount of property taxes for landowners protecting water sources; reductions of property taxes based on forest cover; and incentives for reforestation and conservation of native forests. The Fundación Herencia Verde, in cooperation with the WWF Colombia programme, is using geographic information systems (GIS) to quantify water regulation capabilities of a watershed in the Central Andes; this information will be used to compensate landowners who provide environmental services in the form of water regulation (Higgins and Nieto, 1996). Certificates of forest incentives provide subsidies for up to 75 per cent of the costs of production in plantations and compensate for the direct and indirect costs of maintaining natural forest ecosystems (WWF, 1998).

Conservation services provided by the network of private reserves include: fauna and flora conservation; genetic resource banking; pollination; production of seeds, flowers and fruits; production of thatch; production, regulation and natural purification of water; carbon sequestration; soil conservation and erosion prevention; demonstration of agroforestry and silviculture systems; organic food production; education and the development of an environmental culture; research; and ecotourism (Nieto, 1997).

In Colombia, small private reserve lands can represent an important source of income for families and smallfarmers. Working at this scale may also be important for conservation, given the high degree of fragmentation of habitats, especially in the Andean region. Incentives for managing these areas may be more effective than restrictions.

Efforts to maintain and enhance traditional, harmonious land uses are difficult given the current social and economic conditions in the country. Violence and intimidation by guerrillas, and the paramilitary and military forces affect all aspects of life, including conservation, especially in rural areas. The government has limited capacity to work effectively with communities and NGOs under these conditions (WWF, 1998). Nevertheless, the network of private protected areas continues to grow, with NGOs, various municipalities and departments of Colombia emerging as partners in creating incentives and mechanisms for recognizing and rewarding environmental services provided by the sound management of private lands.

Chile

Chile is a country rich in biodiversity and species endemism, owing to its biogeographical insularity, its length and its altitudinal gradients. Yet much of this biodiversity is threatened by legal and illegal forestry and agricultural practices. The government estimates that 120,000 hectares of native forest is affected each year by these activities (Verscheure, 1998). At least 45 per cent of the mountainous country has serious erosion problems.

Government efforts to protect natural areas began over a century ago, and the first nature reserve was established in 1907. Today the national protected areas system (SNASPE) includes over 14 million hectares in 92 units, representing nearly 19 per cent of the land area of the country. This large area is difficult to manage, however, and conservation objectives are compromised by ineffective legislation and illegal extractive activities such as logging and cattle ranching inside protected areas.

Private citizens have helped to support the national protected areas system by securing funding allocations for management, defending state-protected areas against damaging activities, supporting new protected area designations, and sponsoring environmental education. However, seeing profound changes in areas outside of the national system, they are now doing more: buying land to create private protected areas.

The movement began with the 1990 purchase of 500 hectares of forest to protect habitat of the endangered Chilean *huemul* (the South Andean deer, *Hippocamelus bisulcus*) by the National Committee for the Defense of Fauna and Flora (CODEFF). In 1991 a North American citizen acquired 275,000 hectares to create Pumalín Park. Following negotiations with the government, this private reserve has recently been given to Chile as Pumalín National Park, to be managed in a public–private partnership. Another NGO, Lahuen Foundation, purchased 500 hectares of Araucaria forest. In the coastal range a forestry company set aside 754 hectares as Oncol Park. Beyond these, there are a number of initiatives of private owners who have dedicated part of their properties for conservation, and others that protect land for tourism purposes.

In 1997, with the assistance of WWF International, a network of private protected areas (RAPP) was established to facilitate exchange, provide training and informational services, advise on new legislation, and guide other individuals and groups wishing to protect land. The network also hopes to direct conservation efforts to areas of high conservation priority, to identify opportunities for adding new areas, and to generally promote the use of private approaches to protecting natural areas.

Today the network links 50 owners and 59 properties, covering 295,630 hectares (Verscheure, 1998). Though it currently protects less than 0.5 per cent of the total land area of the country (and this figure is dominated by one property), the network is an important step in private land conservation and is working to develop new laws and incentives for conservation. Distributed across half the country, Chile's emerging system of private protected areas is spreading the message of conservation to communities and local authorities.

CONTRIBUTIONS OF PRIVATE RESERVES

In each of the countries described above, and elsewhere in Latin America, private reserve programmes are playing a significant and growing role in meeting in situ biodiversity conservation objectives. Their contributions include, among others:

- *Increasing protected area coverage nationally and complementing state-protected area systems:* for example, in Ecuador small private reserves, typically located far from state-protected areas, are ensuring protection of a greater diversity of microregions and species nationally. In Brazil, on the other hand, priority is given to contiguous reserves and to the creation of biological corridors among protected areas.
- *Sustaining traditional land and resource uses*, including traditional hunting and fishing practices and sustainable harvest of forest products; some private reserves in the region are maintaining, or reviving, traditional forestry and agricultural practices. These models of sustainable use have an important demonstration value.
- *Providing social and environmental services*, such as protection of user resources, conservation of genetic resources, and environmental education.
- *Linking conservation with income-generating activities*, such as ecotourism, recreation and agroforestry.
- *Enhancing protected area management capacity* through partnerships between public agencies and NGOs; joint management agreements with landowners and other groups; and the provision of advice and, in some cases, financial assistance for private reserve management.

Equally significant is the contribution of these first private reserve programmes towards creating the social, institutional and legal conditions for future partnerships to flourish in the region. To this end, they are:

- *Demonstrating success in diverse settings*, introducing the approach to diverse actors, and enlisting new partners at the local, national and regional levels.
- *Creating the legal basis for private land stewardship* through the establishment of legal precedents and the enactment of legislation.
- *Establishing incentives for conservation on private land*, including tax advantages as well as non-financial incentives, such as public recognition.
- *Strengthening the role of NGOs in protected areas management* and demonstrating productive public and private partnerships.
- *Building networks of private reserves* and creating linkages among diverse actors.

Finally, as the above points illustrate, by strengthening local institutions, fostering citizen participation in conservation, and bringing together diverse stakeholders, these initiatives are making a valuable contribution to building civil society in the region.

CHALLENGES AND POTENTIAL PITFALLS

As the establishment of private reserves gathers momentum in Latin America, a number of issues emerge which must be addressed if this approach is to succeed in the long term. Some of these considerations are operational. The definition of what actually constitutes a private reserve must be clarified and management guidelines developed further. Ultimately, it will be important to ensure some degree of consistency of standards among countries in the region while, of course, taking into account the unique priorities and circumstances of each setting. Legal and institutional mechanisms must be in place to ensure 'conservation in perpetuity'. Long-term provision for management and monitoring will be essential to ensure adherence to agreements, as well as to evaluate the effectiveness of different approaches.

The complexity of land use, tenure and institutional roles in many Latin American countries pose major challenges to conservation at the level of landscapes (Higgins and Nieto, 1996). Mechanisms are needed to accommodate people with unclear land titles in order to encourage sustainable practices on these lands (WWF, 1998). Other potential pitfalls of private land conservation which must be avoided include: lack of coordination among key institutions and sectors; divestment of management responsibility by public agencies without sufficient support; and a tendency to react to specific conservation opportunities and threats rather than set strategic priorities.

More broadly, and of critical importance, Latin American private reserves must not be established in a vacuum, ignoring the overall context of surrounding land uses and social issues. Private reserves are as vulnerable to the 'park as island' problem as are conventional protected areas. As with system planning of state-protected areas, the design of private protected areas must take into account a variety of social issues which include: land-use patterns inside and outside of protected areas; local people's livelihood requirements; local patterns of access to resources; human population trends; cultural aspects; equity issues; and existing pressures and likely future threats to the landscape as a whole.

Private protected areas must recognize the land and resource rights of local and indigenous people. In this respect, NGOs and other agencies must take care to ensure that private land protection does not reinforce the interests of powerful private landowners at the expense of landless or other marginalized groups.

RECOMMENDATIONS FOR RESEARCH AND PRACTICE

To advance private land conservation in Latin America, further research and opportunities to exchange experience are needed in the following areas.

Legislation and policy

There is need for a regional review of existing legislation supporting conservation on private and communal land (including traditional and customary laws as appropriate). This information must be made available to other Latin

BOX 19.1 CHALLENGES TO DEVELOPING STEWARDSHIP

Stewardship techniques offer great potential to strengthen and extend the impact of conventional protected areas in conserving natural and cultural heritage. Challenges to developing stewardship initiatives in any context include the following (Mitchell and Brown, 1998).

Creating a legal framework conducive to private initiatives

Incentives (such as tax advantages) for conservation and best management practices on private lands must be incorporated within national legislation. Even voluntary and non-binding tools often benefit from governmental recognition. As key actors in stewardship, NGOs require a stable legal basis for establishment and legitimacy as an important sector in any civil society.

Creating the climate for productive, enduring partnerships among sectors

Government agencies charged with protected areas management must have the flexibility to develop appropriate partnerships with NGOs and other private interests. To create an atmosphere of trust and cooperation, the government must view these NGOs as true partners, rather than subcontractors. NGOs must be willing to engage in non-adversarial relationships with government; all parties must be committed to ongoing communication and coordination of efforts.

Integration within land-use planning and protected areas management

Private stewardship efforts, however extensive, are no substitute for a strong government role in land-use planning and protection of natural areas. These efforts should reinforce land-use planning and policy at all levels. At the same time, private initiatives should be viewed not as an afterthought, but as central to meeting protection and management objectives. To this end, coordination among private and public actors is essential.

Ensuring participation by all interested parties

Stewardship relies on public support and participation. Whether through landowner contact or public fora, opportunities must be created for those most affected by land-use decisions to voice their concerns. Value must be placed on local knowledge and traditional resource management systems. Opportunities for collaborative management should be explored.

Marshalling the necessary resources

Funding is necessary for land acquisition and compensation for certain development rights or uses. Often NGOs are in a strong position to raise private funds for these purposes. Fiscal incentives, such as reduced property taxes, may carry a cost in terms of lost revenues to municipalities.

Striking a balance between responding to opportunities and taking a strategic approach

To maintain the ecological integrity of landscapes and to protect representative ecosystems requires strategic approaches. A key challenge lies in coordinating the efforts of diverse actors, all using different mechanisms, to achieve biodiversity conservation goals at the scale of bioregions. While responding to protection opportunities as they arise, local stewardship initiatives must also be proactive, addressing emerging trends in land use, such as reprivatization or increased development pressure.

American countries who are now in the process of developing legislation and economic incentives for land stewardship. At the same time, there is a need to review how perverse incentives (such as taxes and subsidies) are working against the stewardship concept.

Institutional arrangements

There is a need for further documentation of innovative management options for protected areas, such as collaborative management agreements and NGO–government partnerships. Research should explore the conditions contributing to the success of these emerging institutional arrangements.

Cultivating a stewardship ethic

Stewardship on privately and communally owned land relies on voluntary engagement in conservation, which may or may not respond to financial incentives. Preliminary research and a great deal of experience from the field indicates that value-based motivations, such as pride in the land, a desire to maintain traditional uses, and a sense of responsibility to future generations, are important factors. There is a need for further research in this area in the Latin American context .

Documentation of current examples

A comprehensive review of the coverage of private protected areas and their contributions to biodiversity conservation in Latin America is needed, and should be incorporated within existing protected areas data bases. Further documentation of case studies should be made widely available through publications and other fora, so that practitioners can learn from successes and failures in implementing stewardship strategies worldwide.

Training and exchange of experience

As Latin American NGOs play an increasingly important role in private reserve establishment and management, they will need support and training in techniques of private land stewardship, including negotiation, conservation planning and monitoring. Conservationists, landowners and resource users involved with private reserves need opportunities to exchange experience.

CONCLUSIONS

The growing networks of private reserves in Latin America are already making a significant contribution to conservation in the region. For the stewardship approach to be effective in the long term, further progress must be made in developing appropriate legal and institutional mechanisms, and creating the conditions for partnerships among diverse actors. Care must be taken to ensure that private reserves, like other types of protected areas, are not created as islands but rather are managed in the context of surrounding land uses, with respect for the land and resource rights, and the livelihoods of local people. With greater integration into local and regional planning, these local stewardship initiatives will be in a strong position to contribute to broader conservation strategies.

Developing conservation strategies on a bioregional scale in Latin America will require tools that can be applied across a mosaic of land ownership and use patterns. This will rely on approaches that engage local residents and communities in the stewardship of their natural and cultural heritage. Private reserves, along with other private land stewardship techniques, are emerging as an important element of this new approach in Latin America.

References

Anon (1998) *Perfil Institucional de la Corporación Nacional de Bosques Privados del Ecuador*, Corporación Nacional de Bosques Privados del Ecuador, Quito

Baez, O (1997) 'Conservación de Areas Naturales Privadas en Ecuador', in *Ponencias I Congreso Latinoamericano de Parques Nacionales y otras Areas Protegidas*, Santa Marta, Colombia

Diehl, J and Barrett, T S (1988) *The Conservation Easement Handbook*, Trust for Public Land, San Francisco, CA, and Land Trust Exchange, Alexandria, VA

Dodson, C (1995) *Editorial de Boletín Informativo de la Red de Bosques Privados del Ecuador, 1*, Fundación Natura, Quito, Ecuador

Endicott, E (1993) *Land Conservation through Public–Private Partnerships*, Lincoln Land Institute and Island Press, Covelo, CA

Fundación Natura (1995) *Boletín Informativo de la Red de Bosques Privados del Ecuador, 1*, Fundación Natura, Quito, Ecuador

Higgins, M L and Nieto, O A (1996) *Private Protected Areas Network of Colombia: New Management Alternatives*, WWF–Colombia

IUCN (1997) *Statement adopted by the IUCN World Commission on Protected Areas (WCPA) Symposium on 'Protected Areas in the 21st Century: From Islands to Networks'*, November 1997, Albany, Australia

Mitchell, B A and Brown, J L (1998) 'Stewardship: A Working Definition', *Environments*, 26(1): Special Issue on Stewardship: An International Perspective, Heritage Resources Centre, University of Waterloo, Ontario

Nieto, O A (1997) 'Red de Reservas Naturales de la Sociedad Civil', in *Ponencias I Congreso Latinoamericano de Parques Nacionales y otras Áreas Protegidas*, Santa Marta, Colombia

Verscheure, H (1998) *Report to WWF in support of the Network of Private Protected Areas in Chile*, WWF International, Gland

Wiedmann, S M P (1998) 'Les réserves privées du patrimoine naturel au Brésil', *Environments*, 26(1): Special Issue on Stewardship: An International Perspective, Heritage Resources Centre, University of Waterloo, Ontario

WWF (1998) *From Theory to Practice: Incentive Measures in Developing Countries*, WWF International Discussion Paper, Gland

20 The Role of Large Companies in Forest Protection in Sweden[*]

Sue Stolton, Nigel Dudley and Karin Beland-Lindahl

INTRODUCTION

As the role of the state declines in many countries, the importance of conservation initiatives by the private sector continues to increase. One important aspect of this is the growing role that commercial companies play in protected area management. While the trend towards the greening of commerce is seen most strongly in some of the developed countries, examples can be found all over the world. The link between industry and environmental management can include involvement in protected-area establishment and management. Companies can provide support to national protected-area networks in a number of ways, ranging from providing financial, logistic or technical support for existing protected areas, to sympathetic management of buffer zones or even putting aside some of their own land into protection (McNeely, 1998). To date, these opportunities have only been partially explored and few examples have been documented. This chapter examines how some large forest management companies are becoming involved in forest protected area management in Sweden.

SWEDISH FOREST INDUSTRY: THE BACKBONE OF THE ECONOMY

Over the past 1000 years, Swedish forests have played a central role in the development from an agrarian to an industrial society. The forest industry is often perceived as the 'engine' of the Swedish economy and the basis of past and future development. Sweden is one of the leading exporters of pulp, paper

[*] The authors are very grateful to the following for information on company policy: Olof Johansson (AssiDomän), Erik Normark (MoDo), Per Simonsson (SCA) and Borje Petterson (Stora). They would also like to thank Per Larsson of WWF–Sweden and Erik Sollander of WWF International for commenting on and discussing the text. Any remaining mistakes in fact or interpretation are our own responsibility.

and wood on the world market. The export value of Swedish forest products was 90 billion SEK in 1997 and those employed in forestry and forest-related activities numbered 200,000 people out of a population of eight million. The forest industry is the largest consumer of transportation in the country; every third export ship carries wood products and these also account for 35 per cent of rail freight. Over half the country's 420,000 kilometres of roads are logging roads (Lindahl, 1998).

Half of Sweden's forests are owned by family forest owners, with the rest split between the corporate sector and state and public bodies. Forest companies own 37 per cent of forested land in Sweden (some 8.6 million hectares), of which five companies – AssiDomän, Svenska Cellulosa AB (SCA), the newly merged Stora-Enso, Mo & Domsjö (MoDo) and Korsnäs – own 8.2 million hectares. AssiDomän is the largest single forest owner, with 3.4 million hectares of forested land (National Board of Forestry, 1997). The company has until now been partly state owned, but is currently being restructured as 900,000 hectares of productive forest land is split off to create a new state-controlled company.

THE DEBATE ABOUT FOREST MANAGEMENT

Forestry has been at the centre of public debate since the early 1970s, when citizens' groups occupied logging sites to stop aerial spraying of chemical herbicides. By the end of the 1980s, the dynamic of the debate had changed towards conservation of biodiversity and, as a result, protection of remaining old-growth forests, particularly in the far north. Scientists entered the scene with figures and graphs that illustrated the biodiversity 'crisis' of the Swedish forests. All the actors, including industry, acknowledged the importance and the main causes of the problem, although disagreements remained about how these could be resolved.

A second shift in the debate came when consumers and buyers, primarily from Germany and the UK, began to take an interest in Swedish forest politics in the early 1990s. Rather than being simply a national issue, industry was forced to listen to the concerns of an international audience. Various market-orientated initiatives and events have dominated the forestry debate of the 1990s: boycotts or threats of boycotts, conflicts, dialogues, negotiations and, lately, efforts to introduce independent certification of forest management (Lindahl, 1998).

Central to this debate is the question of how much forest should be set aside in protected areas. During the preparation for the 1994 Forestry Act, three respected ecologists (one of whom now works for the Swedish forest company Stora) produced an estimate that 5 to 15 per cent of the productive forest land below the mountain range needed to be set aside to provide effective biodiversity conservation. The higher figure assumed that forest management remained unchanged – with 5 per cent acceptable if management was changed to more closely mimic natural-disturbance patterns. Although the government body subscribed to the 5 per cent figure below the mountains, this goal was never included in the final biodiversity action plan. It was replaced by a more general acknowledgement that a target might be set once experience of the new forestry laws had been built up.

In 1994, a new Swedish forestry act was passed. The new forest policy enshrined in this act has (at least in theory) equally ranking environmental and production goals. The environmental goal states:

> *The productivity of forest land shall be preserved. Biodiversity and genetic variation in forests shall be secured. Forests must be managed so that plant and animal species which exist naturally in forest ecosystems can survive under natural conditions in vigorous populations. Endangered species and vegetation types shall be protected. The forest's historical, aesthetic and social values must be defended.*

> National Swedish Board of Forestry and
> Swedish Environmental Protection Agency, 1997

In the last few years, the debate about protection has intensified. In 1996, 88 Swedish ecologists and biodiversity specialists signed an appeal to Sweden's forest industry to refrain from logging the remaining old-growth forest (Naturskyddsföreningen, 1996). Furthermore, according to most specialists, there is not enough old-growth forests below the mountains to achieve a theoretical 5 per cent target anyway, and restoration will have to be built into the development of any protected areas network.

SWEDISH FORESTS: STATUS

Forests cover around 60 per cent of Sweden's land area (24,425,000 hectares out of a total of 40,700,000 hectares according to the Food and Agriculture Organization – FAO – although forest land defined by the Swedish forest act covers only 22,900,000 hectares). Of this total, only a relatively small amount is protected. According to statistics from the Swedish Environment Protection Board, 832,000 hectares of productive forest are protected in the form of national parks, nature reserves or domän (Swedish Forest Service) reserves. This area is equivalent to 3.8 per cent of Sweden's total forest land, although distribution is uneven. Only 0.1 per cent is protected in the southernmost counties; and although some 43 per cent of low-productive mountain forests are protected, outside these areas the level of protection falls to between 2.4 to 0.1 per cent. In recent years there has been an increased focus on conservation of southern forests; however, some researchers fear that a disproportionately narrow focus on southern forests will result in ecologically important northern forests being ignored.

Table 20.1 *Protected productive forest land (1000 ha)*

National Park	36
Nature Reserve	553
Domän Reserve	243

The low level of protection is particularly relevant since about 40 per cent of red-listed, at threat according to IUCN categories, vertebrates and half the other red-listed species in Sweden are found in forest habitats. (Naturvårdsverket, 1997).

THE ROLE OF PRIVATE COMPANIES IN PROTECTION

Although the need for more protection of biologically important forest areas is now generally recognized, the Swedish authorities have decided to put the emphasis on voluntary policies which work with forest owners in increasing protected area networks rather than on relying upon new legislation. As the National Board of Forestry states:

> ...there is a need for more nature reserves to be designated, especially in the southern and central parts of the country. However, the government has not yet been prepared to define the total size of such areas. This will depend on how well biodiversity can be encouraged and protected, under guidelines created through the new forest and environmental policies, and how far reaching the voluntary environmental measures taken by the forestry sector will be.
>
> National Swedish Board of Forestry, 1997

Partly as a result of the Swedish forest policy, three complementary strategies have evolved to expand the network of forest reserves. These are presented below.

Habitat protection through compensation

Some small but important habitats can be protected under the auspices of the 1991 Nature Conservation Act. By 1996, some 500 sites had been protected covering 1100 hectares. Limited resources mean that the county forestry boards tend to ask forest owners to defer from felling, rather than coming to a permanent arrangement. Habitat protection has generally been carried out on privately owned lands, since the larger companies have so far voluntarily agreed to refrain from felling such areas. Most companies will, however, ask for compensation if, or when, habitat protection is authorized under the 1991 Nature Conservation Act (National Swedish Board of Forestry and Swedish Environmental Protection Agency, 1997).

Reserves created by purchase through the use of government funds

The protection of valuable natural forests has only been financed with public funds in Sweden since the 1980s. From 1992 to 1996, a total of 290 natural forest sites were bought, covering 46,000 hectares and equalling 0.2 per cent of Sweden's forest land. Half are montane forests; a quarter are natural coniferous forests in other areas; and the rest are deciduous forests and other important forests in south Sweden. This policy has given forest companies the opportunity to sell forested land to the government to create nature reserves. SCA, for example, has sold 30,037 hectares of forest areas since 1989 to be established as nature reserves. Although government purchases of land have been important in increasing the protected areas network, the insufficient level of funding available has made it a very slow process. Although there is now political agreement about substantially increasing the available funds (see below), this will still only provide a partial solution to the conservation of forest areas in Sweden.

The establishment of voluntary reserves by forest owners

This can be achieved either through internal decisions (which can be changed at any time) or through conservation contracts with third parties – *naturvård-savtal* (where the landowner receives financial compensation). According to a survey of voluntary protected areas in January 1996, a fifth of all the private forest owners and all large companies have established voluntary reserves (only sites greater than 0.5 hectares were included). An analysis of the report by the Swedish National Board of Forestry and the Environmental Protection Agency (1997) suggested that:

> *These [voluntary reserves] are expected to reach a figure of between 500,000 and 800,000 hectares below montane forests...equivalent to between 2 to 4 per cent of the total area of forest land [but that] information on voluntary reserves is, in many ways, unreliable and preliminary. Therefore, it is important to study them more closely to find out about their extent and their environmental values.*

The ability to identify key habitats is a prerequisite of protection. Since the 1980s Sweden has had a nationwide inventory of so-called virgin forests, although the narrow definition of virgin forests has in the opinion of some scientists led to many valuable old-growth forests being excluded from the inventory.

An inventory of all private forest land was completed during 1998. All other forest owners who are completing the forest inventory have to be finished by 2003 at the latest; however, several large companies have already completed most of the inventory process. The intention is to map all key habitats, but it possible that up to 20 or 30 per cent could be missed since they are hard to identify (Sollander, 1998).

THE ROLE OF FOREST CERTIFICATION IN PRIVATE CONSERVATION INITIATIVES

The voluntary nature of company protection has been further refined by another development – initially driven by non-governmental organizations – towards independent certification of forest management. This has been achieved through liaison with the Forest Stewardship Council (FSC), an independent international organization for certification of forest management through accredited certifiers to meet agreed environmental and social standards.

In 1995, the Swedish Society for Nature Conservation and WWF–Sweden launched 'preliminary' criteria for the certification of forest management in Sweden as a starting point for FSC certification. In developing the criteria, scientists, forest owners' associations, unions, *Sámi* organizations, forest companies and environmental NGOs were consulted. A formal FSC working group, with a balanced composition of stakeholders, was formed in February 1996 with the aim of developing a national FSC standard. Subgroups focused on forest management standards and chain of custody issues, which are of great importance in a country with many small land holdings. The process involved a long series of debates and some conflict, with the forest owners' association and Greenpeace Sweden withdrawing. However, the standard was eventually endorsed in 1997 – the first national FSC standards in the world.

The standard addresses a broad range of issues relevant to forest management in Sweden. Some important environmental components include protection for so-called key habitats and old-growth forests (including restoration incentives), protection of mountain forests from further fragmentation, and modified management and restoration of deciduous forest types. The 'social' part of the standard addresses working conditions, long-term employment and training, as well as indigenous rights including traditional reindeer grazing on forest land. The suggested standard prescribes certification of entire landholdings only, although step-by-step implementation will be allowed.

The Swedish standard states that FSC certified management units must include protection for a range of important forest habitat sites within commercial holdings. At least 5 per cent of certified land (excluding very small areas and areas already legally protected and compensated for by the state) must be exempt from forest management – thus standardizing the earlier proposals for protected area targets (Swedish FSC Working Group, 1997). It may be that perceived government weakness with respect to forest protected areas has meant that the Swedish FSC standard has put extra emphasis on protection, compared with management. This is highly significant because certification to this standard will add an important additional guarantee that protected areas established by companies might have a long-term future.

THE FOREST COMPANIES: WHAT HAVE THEY PROTECTED?

In the following section, company literature is analysed to see how well major landowners are meeting the aims of the Swedish government in terms of voluntary protection of forests. (Many NGOs believe that these aims are not high enough to maintain biodiversity.) All the companies responded to a questionnaire, distributed as part of the research for this chapter, and are either FSC certified or in the process of certification. This means that they are all bound to protect at least 5 per cent of their productive forest (only those areas above 0.5 hectares) under certification rules. All also called for further government funds to be made available for protection, particularly for the compensation of owners of small forest holdings. Costs of nature conservation were quoted in terms of extra costs of buying timber from other sources.

AssiDomän

AssiDomän is the largest landowning forestry company in Sweden, with 3.3 million hectares of forest. All of its forest holdings are now certified according to FSC standards. This has included protection at a range of scales, from landscape planning to considerations at a stand level. Currently, 1.1 per cent of the productive forest holdings are protected by legislation, but further land are protected under an 'internal commitment' to meet the FSC standards, reaching a total of slightly over 5 per cent. In addition, smaller areas are excluded during the planning of forest operations, adding approximately another 10 per cent of the total. The sum effect is that 15 to 20 per cent of the productive forest land is excluded from management. In addition, non-productive forests (defined in Sweden as areas producing less than one cubic metre annually) should be left untouched according to the FSC standards, which adds a further 15 per cent of the company's total land. The company calculates that forest protection on productive land is equivalent to around 12 per cent of a potential annual income without any conservation requirements (interpreting these figures is difficult without more information).

Svenska Cellulosa AB (SCA)

SCA owns 1.8 million hectares of productive forest in Sweden. The company is currently in the process of FSC certification. Very little SCA land is formally protected under the Nature Conservation Act, although since 1989 some 30,000 hectares (1.3 per cent of the company's total landholdings) have been sold to the government as nature reserves. Under FSC agreements, the company reports that about 25 per cent of the tree-covered area (including non-productive forests) will be untouched by active forestry or managed to conserve biodiversity. On average, 5 per cent of total forest land will be protected.

Stora

Following its recent merger with the Finnish Enso company, Stora-Enso is the largest forest products company in the world. It has around two million hectares of land in central Sweden, of which 1.6 million hectares are productive forest. Stora adopted a forest management and nature conservation strategy in 1993, that excludes key biotopes, old-growth forest and habitats for endangered species from forestry on company land. Stora has set aside 22,421 hectares of productive land as legally protected nature reserves. The company is also signing up to the Swedish FSC process and thus will adhere to putting aside 5 per cent of its productive land for nature conservation. However, Stora believes that FSC certification will only necessitate minor changes to these principles, mainly in terms of mapping additional small conservation areas. In terms of reliability and permanency, verifying these efforts by a certification contract does, however, make a difference. The total level of protection will only be affected to a minor degree. Stora believes that some management interventions will be needed in order to maintain biodiversity in some of the areas that have been set aside. The company has estimated that nature protection will cost an additional 80 million SEK per year.

MoDo

MoDo has 1.03 million hectares of productive forest. In its *Guidelines for Sustainable Forestry*, the company states that it excludes 10 per cent of its forest from commercial management for environmental reasons, although it does not state how much of this is productive land. MoDo aims to achieve FSC certification by 1999. It is currently identifying and mapping areas of special value for nature conservation that should be part of the 5 per cent set-aside under FSC rules, in a survey to be completed by 2000. In some cases, modified management will be needed to maintain biodiversity values in protected forests.

CONCLUSIONS

It is clear that substantial areas of forest are being, and are likely to continue to be, protected on company land in Sweden. The extent of this protection must be virtually unique (although similar changes are taking place in neighbouring Finland). However, 'voluntary' reserves are often small, between 0.5 and 30 hectares, in part due to the high number of small forest owners. There is therefore a need to create larger protected areas.

The role of the FSC is particularly interesting. Certification has come to Sweden at the end of 20 years of debate about forest management. Many of the changes necessary for FSC certification have already taken place; the result is that certification has pushed the process of change further forward and, crucially, provided some level of verification, rather than creating a revolution overnight. In time, certification may be most important in terms of holding companies to their commitments, even if chief executive officers (CEOs) change or financial times become more difficult. However, the strength of the FSC commitment remains untested and will depend eventually upon the extent to which certification becomes an accepted part of standard business practice, as well as upon consumer demand for FSC-certified products.

It is also clear that this process has taken place through necessity, at least in part because of a failure to address protection needs in other ways and the lack of a comprehensive conservation strategy on the part of the government. It may be an illustration that the market, through consumer demand, is more responsive to conservation needs than are Swedish politicians or the government. Many of those involved say that further government funding is needed alongside voluntary or market-driven measures. An evaluation of the government's policy of voluntary protection concluded that the lack of resources for forest protection and the lack of information on the policy, in particular for landowners, were important reasons why the policy has yet to show major advances in forest protection in Sweden (Naturvårdsverket & Skogsstyrelsen, 1998). It should also be noted that in 1998 the Swedish government presented plans to more than double the spending on new protected areas in the coming years. This will probably enable the legal protection of 250,000 hectares of productive forest land in the coming ten years and could mean that the legally protected forest land outside the mountain regions will be doubled.

How possible is it to draw general lessons from the Swedish experience? It seems that, in places where there is a vocal public support for conservation issues, companies may well respond more quickly than governments to the demand for more protected areas. When companies decide to set up protected areas, they can also often move more quickly than the cumbersome bureaucracy of government. On the other hand, there is as yet little proof that such protected areas will be as reliable or as permanent as those on state land. Protected areas established in connection with FSC certification may be more secure, but the FSC itself is a voluntary process and is dependent upon continued support from consumers and companies.

More fundamentally, there may be questions about how appropriate companies are, as *institutions*, in identifying and managing protected areas. The emphasis of much of the rest of this book has been on widening approaches to protected areas, bringing local people within management and so on. Companies, as single owners, may take a very different approach. Although Swedish law provides a relatively high level of protection of social rights (access, fruit and berry collection, etc) this will not be the case in many other countries. While company reserves look set to be increasingly important elements in protected area networks, it is likely that more work will be needed to see how they fit into the general conservation framework. The issue of transparency is also important. Experience from around the world shows that commercial companies have sometimes been less than candid about the conservation implications of their work; institutions such as the FSC can help address this by formalizing the need for a certain amount of transparency.

REFERENCES

Lindahl, K B (1998) Forests *and Forestry in Jokkmokk Municipality*, Discussion paper for the European regional meeting on the Underlying Causes of Deforestation and Forest Degradation in Europe, Bonn, 28–29 October 1998

McNeely, J A (1998) *Mobilizing Broader Support for Asia's Biodiversity: How civil society can contribute to protected area management*, Asian Development Bank, The Philippines

National Board of Forestry (1996) *The Swedish Forest*, Jönköping, Sweden

National Board of Forestry (1997) *Development of the Swedish Forests and Forest Policy During the Last 100 Years*, National Swedish Board of Forestry, Jönköping

National Swedish Board of Forestry and Swedish Environmental Protection Agency (1997) *Nature Protection and Nature Conservation in Forests*, National Swedish Board of Forestry, Jönköping, and Swedish Environmental Protection Agency, Stockholm

Naturskyddsförenningen (1996) *Stop logging Sweden's last old-growth now!*, pamphlet from the Swedish Society for Nature Conservation, Stockholm

Naturvårdsverket & Skogsstyrelsen (1998) *Den nya skogspolitikens effekter på biologisk mångfald – Utvärdering*, Naturvårdsverket Rapport 4844

Naturvårdsverket (1997) *Skogsreservat i Sverige*, Rapport om skogsreservatens utveckling och omfattning efter den nya skogspolitiken, Naturvårdsverket Rapport 4707

Sollander, E (1998) *European Forest Scorecards*, WWF International, Gland

Swedish FSC Working Group (1997) *Endorsed Swedish FSC Standard for Forest Certification*, Swedish FSC Working Group, Stockholm

Photo: WWF-Canon/Juan Pratginestos

Extractive reserve in Amapá, Brazil

Diversity of functions also implies a diversity of management approaches. In Brazil, rubber tappers have established extractive reserves, where biodiversity conservation goes hand-in-hand with traditional livelihoods.

PART V

DEVELOPING NEW MODELS FOR PROTECTED AREAS MANAGEMENT

New opportunities, perspectives and partnerships also imply changes in the ways that protected areas are managed. In broad terms, these involve replacing remote, top-down management styles with more participatory and comanagement approaches. They imply that those responsible for protected areas need to gain the confidence to release some of their control (and, in some cases, all control) to local communities. Comanagement systems are inevitably more complicated but experience suggests that they have a greater chance of long-term success. The chapters in Part V look at the institutions involved in protected areas management, at collaborative management models and at the options and challenges posed by transboundary reserves. The question of how working landscapes can fit into protected areas is also tackled from European, Latin American and Pacific Islands perspectives. Lastly, the issue of how management effectiveness can be verified is also discussed.

21 PROTECTED AREA INSTITUTIONS*

Jeffrey A McNeely

INTRODUCTION

Institutions and individuals having a direct, significant and specific stake in a protected area may originate from geographical proximity, historical association, dependence for livelihood, institutional mandate, economic interest, or a variety of other concerns. However, these 'stakeholders' are united in being aware of their own interests in managing the protected area, possessing specific capacities or comparative advantages for such management, and having a willingness to invest specific resources – such as time, money or political authority – for such management (Borrini-Feyerabend, 1997). The different stakeholders generally have different interests, ways of perceiving problems and opportunities about the protected area, and varying approaches to protected area management. Their interests all need to be appropriately represented if the protected area system is to be effectively managed.

The key words here are 'appropriately represented', for not all stakeholders necessarily have equal legitimacy in making their views heard. An important role of government is to establish criteria for determining the relative importance of the various stakeholders (see Box 21.1).

In seeking to ensure that the interests of these various stakeholders are fairly represented, governments have devised a wide range of institutional approaches for protected area management.

INSTITUTIONAL ARRANGEMENTS FOR PROTECTED AREA MANAGEMENT

Institutional options for managing protected areas can be based on land ownership, legal framework, management responsibility, decision-making or financial support (Barborak, 1995). Eight general categories of institutional options for management are discussed briefly below, with examples from around the world.

---

* A fuller discussion of the issues raised in this chapter, with particular reference to Asia, can be found in McNeely, J A (1998).

BOX 21.1 CRITERIA FOR IDENTIFYING STAKEHOLDERS IN PROTECTED AREA MANAGEMENT

Many stakeholders might claim a legitimate voice in determining how a protected area is established and managed. To determine the relative importance of the various claimant stakeholders, the following criteria might be useful:

- the capacity to contribute to protected area management;
- existing rights to land or natural resources;
- continuity of relationship (for example, residents versus visitors);
- unique knowledge and skills for managing the resources at stake;
- potential losses and damage incurred in the management process (opportunity costs);
- historical and cultural relations with the resources at stake;
- degree of economic and social reliance on such resources;
- degree of effort and interest in management;
- equity in the access to resources and the distribution of benefits from their use;
- compatibility of the interests and activities of stakeholders with the national protected area system plan; and
- present or potential impact of stakeholder activities on the resource base.

Consideration of these criteria can help determine which are primary stakeholders and which are secondary, leading to different voices in decision-making and different roles, rights and responsibilities in protected area management. Such decisions often are best taken at the individual protected-area level rather than attempting to provide the same criteria across an entire system (Borrini-Feyerabend and Brown, 1997).

Owned by and at least partially managed by a national protected area agency

This is the dominant institutional arrangement in most parts of the world. Individual sites within such a system can vary in management style, degree of privatization of services and the role of local communities in management.

In Asia, for example, since most protected areas have been established in forested areas, it is perhaps understandable that the great proportion of protected area agencies are part of ministries or departments of forestry. This has also facilitated the allocation of forest land to protected status, as in India, Indonesia, Lao PDR, Myanmar, Nepal and Thailand. However, this link has been criticized because forestry departments have tended to give higher priority to the exploitation of timber than to protected areas. Furthermore, legislation for protected areas has sometimes been incorporated in more comprehensive forestry protection laws, which may weaken implementation and enforcement.

A few countries have assigned management responsibility for protected areas to other ministries such as the environment (Bangladesh, India, Pakistan and The Philippines) or the interior (US and Sudan), while others have tried a different arrangement such as a special board (Singapore) or have linked protected areas more to tourism and recreation (Malaysia).

Clear government agency responsibility for protected area management does not necessarily mean that all agencies within a government respect the protected area. In Indonesia, for example, the department of agriculture may provide various forms of subsidies to illegal enclaves within protected areas. Departments of transport may see protected areas as ideal for the development of roads, since no private landowners need to be bought out. Ministries of energy may see protected areas as ideal places to build dams, thereby avoiding expensive resettlement of local communities. In many parts of the world, government protected area management authorities are beleaguered even within their own government structures. For example, in India, many mining concessions have been granted in protected areas, even though the protected area regulations forbid such land use. Some forestry departments still grant timber concessions within protected areas, even when the protected area agency is also within the ministry of forests.

Institutional weakness may mean that government protected-area agencies are unable to spend the budgets allocated to them by government, much less additional funds from external sources. For example, in 1993, the Sri Lankan Department of Wildlife Conservation used only 56 per cent of its budget, primarily because the department was (and remains) seriously under-staffed. Ironically, revenue from Sri Lanka's protected areas in 1993 amounted to US$850,000 – roughly equivalent to recurrent expenditure. The trends in visitor numbers continue to rise in Sri Lanka, especially from domestic sources, indicating that the protected areas – at least conceptually – could be self-financing. However, as in many countries, the revenue earned is returned to the national treasury. If given the incentive and means of becoming self-financing, the Sri Lankan Department of Wildlife Conservation could increase its revenue and apply the funds to the institutional development required to enable the protected areas to carry out their functions (Government of Sri Lanka, 1994). The Sri Lankan experience may be typical for many protected area agencies whose budget is provided by the national treasury; the lack of market incentives may serve as an institutional constraint to innovation.

The institutional management of coastal and marine protected areas by governments remains a significant problem – sometimes in the hands of protected area agencies within forest departments having little experience in marine conservation, or managed under fisheries departments that are interested primarily in productive harvests.

Owned and managed by parastatal conservation trusts

This model incorporates the comparative benefits of both public-sector oversight and autonomous, private-like administration. By allowing parastatals to retain revenues from the protected areas, governments create incentives to maximize the earning potential of natural areas. One example is the Sabah Foundation, a Malaysian parastatal operating under the umbrella of a state-level management committee on which all the relevant stakeholder agencies sit. It holds a timber concession of almost one million hectares, within which two important lots of lowland and hill forests are designated as conservation areas that will remain intact while the rest of the concession is worked. While Danum Valley (43,800 hectares) and Maliau Basin (39,000 hectares) are not legally established as protected areas, they serve virtually all of the functions of legally established sites, including tourism.

The parastatal approach has been reasonably successful in East Africa and the Caribbean, where management of protected areas has been turned over to parastatal organizations which are closely regulated by government and usually include at least a portion of government ownership, but enjoy management and financial independence. The Kenya Wildlife Service is a government-owned company rather than a trust (Poole and Leakey, 1996). Both East Africa and the Caribbean have economies that are heavily based on tourism, and the parastatal protected-area management agencies have successfully managed their protected areas for high-volume tourism, reinvesting their protected areas network at a significantly higher rate than the government agencies of roughly comparable countries. WCMC data indicate that investments in protected areas owned and managed by governments are much lower than investments by parastatal protected-area agencies (see Table 21.1). This disparity is explained largely by the fact that parastatals are able to retain their revenues and are run on a more businesslike basis; they often are also more effective at attracting additional revenues from other sources, including foreign assistance and various forms of local fund-raising. Furthermore, the feedback between the management effectiveness of a protected area and its attractiveness to tourism encourages parastatals to invest appropriately in maintaining the ecological quality of protected areas.

Table 21.1 *Investment in protected areas: parastatal and governmental agencies compared*

| | Level of investment (US\$ per km²) | |
	Parastatal	Governmental
Africa	570	51
Caribbean	1379	510

Owned and managed by provincial or state authorities

Particularly in large countries with federal systems of government, such as India, Pakistan, Malaysia, Australia, Brazil, Germany, Canada and China, protected areas at the provincial or state level are often very large and better managed than national parks. Countries such as these typically also have a national level of recognition for sites of particular importance, such as world heritage sites, biosphere reserves, national parks or tiger reserves (in the case of India).

Owned and/or managed by local governments such as counties or municipalities

With the trend toward decentralization, the role of local-level government agencies in protected area management may be expected to grow in the coming years. The role of local government is usually limited to managing small areas of local importance for recreation, watershed protection and similar services. In Brazil, the municipal government of São Paulo province has created numerous protected areas, with at least one site in each of its 583 municipalities. The areas to be conserved were selected by local communities as part of their cultural and natural patrimony and they have actively participated in the effort from conception through to implementation. Each municipality decides where and how to manage its protected areas, with each area reflecting the needs and aspirations of the local population rather than following any particular model (Barzetti, 1993). In Asia, most municipal-level protected areas are managed for recreational objectives.

Sometimes the local government has a perspective that is different from that of the central government; the conflicts between the federal government and the individual states of Australia are well known in conservation literature. Since the local, or even state or provincial, government cannot be held accountable by the international community because it has not signed or ratified international conventions, a conflict of interest can be created with the national government.

Owned or controlled by private individuals or corporations

In some parts of the world – such as Latin America and parts of Africa – large landholders allocate at least part of their property for conservation purposes, sometimes incorporating tourism. For example, in Natal Province, South Africa, some 8 per cent of the land is in protected areas, but an additional 14 per cent is under conservation management by private landowners.

Colwell (1997) suggests that 'entrepreneurial marine protected areas' can protect discrete areas that serve as refuges for threatened marine life, build local capacity in protected area management, act as test cases for management techniques, build public awareness and support, and provide core areas for larger marine protected areas that may require more time to develop. Such entrepreneurial protected areas use existing commercial infrastructure (such as boats, lodgings, communications equipment and so forth), making it possible for such areas to be quickly established, based on the principle that tourism and other commercial support can achieve long-term economic and environmental sustainability.

While commercial entities may abuse their power over a protected area they control, the commercial approach can still make an important contribution to a framework where the management potential of commercial partners is utilized. Furthermore, the commercial approach works only in areas that have sufficient attractions – such as coral reefs or visible wildlife – to ensure a steady-paying clientele to offset the costs of managing the area. For entrepreneurial protected areas to be truly successful, they need to be part of an integrated national system that includes traditional managers as well as professionals from the national protected-area agency.

Large corporations control millions of hectares of forested lands as timber concessions or mineral concessions, and in some cases this land is better managed than similar areas in government hands. Governments can employ land-use restrictions, easements and other mechanisms to restrict development options over large areas of predominantly private land that maintain important conservation values, in this way contributing to national systems of protected areas.

Managed or owned by NGOs

Increasingly, local, regional, national and international NGOs are being entrusted with overall management of at least some protected areas or some management responsibilities in protected areas owned by government. In the Seychelles, Cousin Island Special Nature Reserve (1500 hectares) has been established as a privately owned protected area, with management responsibility resting with BirdLife International; this area was legally gazetted as a special reserve in 1975.

In the Netherlands Antilles, a non-governmental organization, the Netherlands Antilles National Park Foundation (STINAPA) was created in 1963 to manage the protected areas of Bonaire, Curaço, Saba, St Maarten and St Eustatius. The government of the Netherlands Antilles retains authority over the protected areas and subsidizes STINAPA, but the NGO actually manages the protected areas. In an interesting urban innovation, in September 1997, New York City entered into a contract with an NGO, the Central Park Conservancy, to manage Central Park, with the NGO providing an annual operating budget of US$15.9 million. In Nepal, the King Mahendra Trust runs the Annapurna Conservation Area and helps to ensure that the park is a centre of socioeconomic development and increased environment awareness.

In the US, the Nature Conservancy owns and manages some 1300 sites covering over 500,000 hectares, making a significant contribution to national conservation objectives (Murray, 1995). It has also provided technical advice to NGOs managing protected areas in Belize, Guatemala, Panama, Bolivia, Ecuador and Paraguay (Redford and Ostria, 1995).

Owned and/or run by universities

Universities frequently have responsibility for operating research stations or programmes in government-owned protected areas, and some universities and research institutions also own and manage their own individual protected areas that may be adjacent to the much larger government-owned protected areas. An excellent example is the Natural Land and Water Reserve System, owned and operated by the University of California. This system consists of 26 sites totalling 33,865 hectares, used especially for teaching and research (Kennedy, 1984).

Owned by indigenous peoples or local communities

Indigenous peoples typically have cultural values and institutions that differ from those of the dominant culture within which they are found. They often claim property rights to ancestral lands and waters, and claim the right to retain their own customary laws, traditions, languages and institutions, as well as the right to represent themselves through their own institutions. Furthermore, indigenous peoples living in areas important for conservation are closely linked to their local resource base and have frequently developed resource management systems and social institutions that are responsive to environmental feedback. Thus, their local knowledge has a particular contribution to make to protected area management. However, the primary reason why protected area managers should recognize the decision-making authority of indigenous peoples is that they have prior rights over the land and water where protected areas are being established, and many individuals would assert that such people have the right to make decisions about how to manage their ancestral lands.

When areas within the traditional territories of indigenous peoples are managed as limited-access extractive reserves, they may well be considered as legitimate protected areas worthy of international recognition. In Australia, 'indigenous protected areas' have been developed as IUCN Category VI protected areas; land tenure is vested with the indigenous people, but management is usually carried out by the national conservation agency under a leasing arrangement (see Chapter 8). Other examples of protected areas managed by indigenous peoples are found in Nicaragua, where the Miskito people have formed their own NGO, known as Mikupia, to manage the Miskito Coast Protected Area, overseen by a commission including four national government representatives, a regional government representative, a Mikupia person and two people from the Miskito communities (Barzetti, 1993).

In The Philippines, the Kalahan Education Foundation, a local NGO established by the Ikalahan tribe, is implementing an integrated programme of community forest management and the extraction of non-timber forest products, leading to the production of jams and jellies from forest fruits, the extraction of essential oils, the collection and cultivation of flowers and mushrooms, and the manufacture of furniture. It is based on the Kalahan reserve in Luesan, which supports about 550 Ikalahan families who live within the 14,730 hectare reserve of ancestral land. In eastern Indonesia, many fishing villages have established a form of marine protected area called *petuanang* as part of a body of traditional resource management practices known as *sasi*. The *petuanang* has certain closed seasons, is carefully managed in terms of permitted fishing techniques, and only certain types of fishing gear are allowed (Spiller, 1997). However, in more recent times, the demand for increased production of fish for trade and exports has weakened the control of village leaders in managing traditional resource-management systems, though modern approaches to participatory planning could help resurrect the traditional management systems which worked well for many generations. Such local marine protected areas should be seen as contributing to the national protected area system.

TRENDS IN PROTECTED AREA INSTITUTIONS

Clearly, these different types of management are not exclusive, and with the trend toward bioregional approaches, it is possible for many of these management approaches to exist side by side, with the various management authorities working together toward common objectives that can be agreed through a broadly consultative process of preparing a national system plan or a bioregional plan (see Chapters 10 and 5). A significant challenge in such situations is resolving interinstitutional conflict over how different parts of the system or bioregion will be managed.

Barborak (1995) sees several widespread trends in institutional arrangements for protected area management:

- greater diversity of institutional arrangements, at both the national level and for individual protected areas;
- greater involvement of local communities in planning and managing nearby protected areas;
- a greater role for NGOs and the private sector in managing protected areas or some aspects of them, often in partnership with various levels of government;
- more administrative and financial autonomy for individual protected areas, and more regionalization and decentralization in protected-area system management; and
- greater roles for local and regional governments.

The need to explore the full range of institutional options available is especially acute in the marine environment. For example, the South-East Asia Regional Workshop on Marine Biodiversity and the Convention on Biological Diversity, held in October 1996 in Subic Bay, The Philippines, found that most coastal and marine protected areas have been established by unilateral legal declaration of one government agency with inadequate consultation and support from other sector agencies, such as fisheries or tourism. One result is that the objectives of many coastal and marine protected areas are compromised by the policies and actions of other agencies which are more powerful.

The workshop concluded that the foundation for effective management of coastal and marine resources is 'a sincere and comprehensive commitment by the region's governments to promoting community-based coastal resources management'. It recognized that local communities are often ill equipped to carry out some coastal management responsibilities that may be handed to them in the name of 'decentralization'. On the other hand, many coastal communities have been managing their resources sustainably for generations, while other coastal communities are poor, unorganized and composed of a heterogeneous mix of migrants with few traditional management approaches upon which to fall back. Governments need to create a supportive policy environment, working together with local communities in a form of comanagement that includes recognizing the importance of community participation, at the policy level; legal recognition of community resource rights in exchange for commitments to conserve and manage sustainably; close cooperation with NGOs who are often best equipped to carry out community organization and training activities; and protection against external forces that local communities are unable to fend off on the own, such as commercial trawlers and coastal developers who often have political connections.

CONCLUSIONS

A balanced approach to protected area management will encourage many institutional players to participate in strengthening the national network of protected areas. Dangers to be avoided include governments abandoning their responsibility for the system's management under the guise of privatization; reduced protection of core areas in the forlorn hope that buffer-zone management and local development will reduce threats to strictly protected core zones; excessive local control over nationally or internationally important resources; and excessive privatization to the detriment of public support for protected areas.

A protected area system needs wide diversity in institutional approaches. Many biological processes operate at small scales that vary dramatically in climate, elevation, structure and importance from one setting to the next. An overemphasis on large-scale institutional arrangements, such as centralized protected-area agencies, can undermine institutional mechanisms at smaller scales, such as traditional approaches to conservation. Local knowledge about specific complex interactions and concerns about natural capital can be applied in daily life, especially at the smaller scales. This clearly is not an either-or situation, but instead calls for creating complex, nested systems of governance for protected areas, with different institutions having different responsibilities at different scales. Simply stated, large-scale, centralized governance units do not, and cannot, have the variety of response capabilities – and the incentives to use them – that complex, polycentric, multilayered governance systems can have (Ostrom, 1998).

Clearly, what institutional arrangement is most logical or successful will vary according to the national objectives that have been established for the protected area system and the specific objectives determined for each individual site. Because protected areas do not come in just one size or habitat, neither should their arrangements for management. A greater diversity of institutional approaches helps to stimulate creativity, enabling different kinds of institutions to take rather different kinds of approaches. No single institution can meet the full range of requirements. However, it is essential that the central government establishes national objectives for the protected area system; ensures that the various approaches to protected area management are contributing to the national system; supports the interests of protected areas in the face of alternative land uses; establishes means for exchanging lessons learned from the various approaches; and provides an appropriate regulatory framework to ensure quality control.

REFERENCES

Aldeman, C L (1994) 'The economics and the role of privately owned lands used for nature, tourism, education and conservation', in Munasinghe, M and McNeely, J A (eds) *Protected Area Economics and Policy: Linking Conservation and Sustainable Development*, World Bank and IUCN, Washington DC

Barborak, J R (1995) 'Institutional options for managed protected areas', in McNeely, J A (ed) *Expanding Partnership in Conservation*, Island Press, Washington DC

Barzetti, V (ed) (1993) *Parks and Progress: Protected Areas and Economic Development in Latin America and the Caribbean*, IUCN and Inter-American Development Bank, Washington DC

Borrini-Feyerabend, G (ed) (1997) *Beyond Fences: Seeking Social Sustainability in Conservation*, IUCN, Gland

Borrini-Feyerabend, G and Brown, M (1997) 'Social actors and stakeholders', in Borrini-Feyerabend, G (ed) *Beyond Fences: Seeking Social Sustainability in Conservation*, IUCN, Gland

Colwell, S (1997) *Entrepreneurial conservation: private sector management of small-scale, coral reef marine protected areas*, Paper presented at 8th Global Biodiversity Forum Workshop on Incentives, Private Sector Partnerships and the Marine and Coastal Environment, Montreal

Government of Sri Lanka (1994) *Sri Lanka Forestry Master Plan*, Ministry of Agriculture, Lands and Forestry, Colombo

Kennedy, J A (1984) 'Protected areas for teaching and research: the University of California experience', in McNeely, J A and Miller, K R (eds) *National Parks, Conservation and Development: The Role of Protected Areas in Sustaining Society*, Smithsonian Institute Press, Washington DC

McNeely, J A (1998) *Mobilizing Broader Support for Asia's Biodiversity: How Civil Society Can Contribute to Protected Area Management*, Asian Development Bank, Manila

Murray, W (1995) 'Lessons from 35 years of private preserve management in the USA: the preserve system of the Nature Conservancy', in McNeely, J A (ed) *Expanding Partnerships in Conservation*, Island Press, Washington DC

Ostrom, E (1998) 'Scales, policentricity, and incentives: designing complexity to govern complexity', in Guruswamy, L and McNeely, J A (eds) *Protection of Global Diversity: Converging Strategies*, Duke University Press, Durham, NC

Poole, J H and Leakey, R E (1996) 'Kenya', in Lutz, E and Caldecott, J (eds) *Decentralization and Biodiversity Conservation*, the World Bank, Washington DC

Redford, K H and Ostria, M (1995) *Parks in Peril Sourcebook*, the Nature Conservancy, Arlington, VA

Spiller, G (1997) 'Community-based coastal resources management in Indonesia', *Sea Wind* 11(2): 13–19

22 Working Landscapes as Protected Areas

Adrian Phillips

Introduction

There is a pressing need to extend the coverage of protected areas, particularly in developing countries, in order to meet the requirements of in situ conservation, and for other social and cultural reasons. But traditional models (such as strict nature reserves and national parks) which focus on natural or near-natural environments are not always well suited to this purpose and many have met with failure. More emphasis needs to be put on protecting 'working landscapes' – places where people live and work, and which are also important for biodiversity conservation and for sustaining livelihoods. These working landscapes can be valuable models of how to integrate biodiversity conservation and sustainable use of natural resources. Many such working landscapes in developing countries are managed sustainably and are important for their biodiversity. But they rarely form part of a nation's protected area system. This may be because there is a general misconception that protected areas are about 'locking up' resources from local people and society.

The IUCN protected areas categories system recognizes that a number of purposes of protected areas relate directly to meeting the needs of resident or neighbouring human populations; indeed, it acknowledges that an appropriate human presence (usually by indigenous peoples) may exist in any of the categories, even in Category I wilderness areas. But in the case of protected area Categories V and VI, human presence and impact go further.

Using IUCN Category V to expand protected area networks

Although Category V, the protected landscape or seascape, first appeared in the 1978 IUCN system of protected area management categories, it was at that time regarded as a European concept and a poor relation beside the more highly protected categories, such as Category II national parks. Gradually, however, IUCN has come to take a greater interest in protected landscapes. This stems from the convergence of two lines of thought: that conservation of species and habitats cannot be achieved in strict nature reserves and national parks alone; and that conservation depends upon the involvement of people. Therefore, places where people coexist with nature are worthy of special attention.

IUCN has identified the *objectives* of management and guidance for *selection and organizational responsibility* for Category V areas (see Box 22.1). The inclusion of phrases such as 'harmonious interaction of nature and culture', supporting 'lifestyles ... in harmony with ... the preservation of the social and cultural fabric of the communities concerned', and 'manifestations of unique or traditional land-use patterns and social organizations as evidenced in human settlements and local customs, livelihoods and beliefs' recognize the value of a positive interaction between humankind and nature. In particular, Category V areas can make a special contribution to biodiversity conservation and the protection of natural values in the environment.

There are some 5578 protected landscapes/seascapes recognized by IUCN in the 1997 *UN List of Protected Areas* (IUCN, 1998). Their distribution between the regions of the world is shown in Table 22.1.

Table 22.1 *Distribution of Category V protected areas*

WCPA Region	Category V Sites:		
	Number	Area (km$^{2)}$	Percentage cover of land
North America	2085	245,301	1.05%
Europe	2654	339,927	6.72%
North Africa and Middle East	125	52,056	0.40%
East Asia	159	60,719	0.51%
North Eurasia	21	482	0.00%
Africa (Western/Central)	1	100	0.00%
Africa (Eastern/Southern)	25	11,883	0.11%
South Asia	9	1,562	0.04%
South-East Asia	109	20,491	0.46%
Pacific	11	46	0.01%
Australia/New Zealand	65	59,856	0.75%
Antarctic	1	10	0.00%
Central America	9	54	0.01%
Caribbean	59	14,823	6.21%
South America	245	250,138	1.39%
Total	5578	1,057,448	0.71%

Source: adapted from IUCN, 1998

As Table 22.1 shows, in the past, category V has not had much impact in many developing countries. One reason for this is that conservation effort in many such countries was often initially driven by expatriate natural scientists who were mainly interested in preserving largely unaltered ecosystems. Until recently, IUCN and international conservation programmes have emphasized the least altered environments; for example, under the World Heritage Convention, 'integrity' (the absence of disturbance) is critical in determining what should be inscribed on the world heritage list as a natural site. Furthermore, many conservation experts have felt most confident with the

BOX 22.1 GUIDANCE ON CATEGORY V PROTECTED AREAS

Objectives of Management
- Maintain the harmonious interaction of nature and culture through the protection of landscape and/or seascape and the continuation of traditional land use, building practices and social and cultural manifestations.
- Support life styles and economic activities which are in harmony with nature and the preservation of the social and cultural fabric of the communities concerned.
- Maintain the diversity of landscape and habitat, and of associated species and ecosystems.
- Eliminate where necessary, and thereafter prevent, land uses and activities which are inappropriate in scale and/or character.
- Provide opportunities for public enjoyment through recreation and tourism appropriate in type and scale to the essential qualities of the area.
- Encourage scientific and educational activities which will contribute to the long-term well-being of resident populations and to the development of public support for the environmental protection of such areas.
- Bring benefits to, and to contribute to the welfare of, the local community through the provision of natural products (such as forest and fisheries products) and services (such as clean water or income derived from sustainable forms of tourism).

Guidance for Selection
- The area should possess landscape and /or coastal and island seascape of high scenic quality, with diverse associated habitats, flora and fauna along with manifestations of unique or traditional land-use patterns, and social organizations as evidenced in human settlements and local customs, livelihoods and beliefs.
- The area should provide opportunities for public enjoyment through recreation and tourism within its normal lifestyle and economic benefits.

Organizational Responsibility
- The area may be owned by a public authority, but is more likely to comprise a mosaic of private and public ownerships operating a variety of management regimes. These regimes should be subject to a degree of planning or other control, and supported, where appropriate, by public funding and other incentives to ensure that the quality of the landscape/seascape and the relevant local customs and beliefs are maintained in the long term.

Source: IUCN, 1994

North American national parks model, but this is less applicable in protecting working landscapes. Finally, the term 'protected landscape' to describe Category V areas perhaps embodies a European aesthetic ideal, and there has been some reluctance to apply it directly to other parts of the world with varying traditions and histories.

There is, however, now growing interest in protecting working landscapes in many regions, as demonstrated by the establishment of conservation areas which are managed according to the principles of Category V, and recent efforts to create provisions for Category V designation in the legislation of several countries. IUCN's World Commission on Protected Areas (WCPA) believes that the potential for applying this approach in the developing world is considerable, especially in those parts – such as South-East Asia – where there is a long history of human settlement and land use. Such protected areas can play an important role in biodiversity conservation.

Moreover, Category V areas can demonstrate durable systems of land use in harmony with nature, thus protecting soils, water and vegetation, while linking cultural traditions to sustainable land management. They can buffer more strictly protected areas (possibly as buffer or support zones to biosphere reserves), therefore promoting linkages in favour of a bioregional planning approach. They may conserve genetic resources in crops and livestock. By conserving human history in structures and land-use patterns, these areas also contribute to cultural coherence and help to increase tourism income. By supporting sound local economies in rural areas and encouraging collaborative management of natural and cultural resources, they can serve to illustrate approaches for application elsewhere.

Terrestrial, coastal and marine areas which might benefit from such an approach are those where farming and land-use systems are important because they support wild biodiversity in the area itself or in nearby more strictly protected areas. Other areas which could benefit are those where traditional forms of use (including farming and fishing) exemplify the sustainable use of natural resources (soil, water and vegetative cover) and have the potential to be applied elsewhere, and those where farming systems are associated with, and help to conserve, a wide range of agribiodiversity in crops and livestock (this is by far the most suitable protected area management category for this purpose). Landscapes which are scenically attractive, important for wildlife or of interest for their historic and cultural qualities and traditions, and which therefore offer the potential to develop environmentally sustainable tourism, are also particularly suited to Category V approaches, as are those where there is potential to restore seminatural ecosystems dependent upon traditional land-use practices. Finally, there is the case of marine and freshwater environments where biodiversity is of value for harvesting and sustaining local economies.

We may call such places *working landscapes*. These areas – rich in biological and cultural diversity and offering important economic, social and scenic values – have not yet been widely included in national protected areas systems. But there is a growing need and potential to do so in many regions of the world.

Legislation may be required to apply the Category V approach more widely, although often it will be better to rely upon, and give recognition to, traditional, community-based ways of managing land and natural resources which meet the Category V criteria, including customary laws. In either case, Category V designation would bring benefits at the *individual* site level by:

- helping to record, recognize and protect biodiversity in areas which have not received attention because they are altered environments;
- helping to bring in professional conservation skills to work alongside traditional land management skills of local people, and thereby developing capacity among local communities to manage their own environments;
- focusing financial and other support for traditional methods of land management (for example, agricultural and marketing advice could

reinforce the competitiveness of traditional agricultural methods by 'niche marketing' for organically produced food);

- helping to reinforce land tenure security by bringing out the links between tenure, land management practices and conservation;
- increasing the area's ecotourism potential by raising its image and capacity to manage an influx of visitors;
- building support for conservation among local communities, indigenous peoples, landowners and resource users through innovative methods of community-based and collaborative management;
- fostering a sense of pride among local communities in their local environment by recognizing cultural values and local heritage; and
- encouraging habitat restoration, especially where this will bring benefits to local communities by strengthening their resource base.

The wider *national and regional* benefits of incorporating Category V areas within protected areas networks would also be significant:

- States could meet their obligations under the Convention on Biological Diversity (CBD) by protecting a higher proportion of a nation's biodiversity, and by linking national programmes for the conservation of wild biodiversity with those for agribiodiversity.
- National networks of protected areas could incorporate a wider range of categories, using Category V areas to buffer more highly protected areas and link them up with corridors of sensitively managed environments.
- States could protect entire eco/bioregions, which can rarely be encompassed within one conventional national park. It would also be possible for neighbouring countries to set up transboundary protected areas systems embracing an entire ecosystem by using Category V, along with other types of protected areas.
- National protected areas systems would be more representative and include cooperative models in a wider range of protected area approaches which promote working with local communities, including indigenous peoples.
- Closer alliances could be forged at the national level between conservation and sustainable rural development interests.

Several examples of potential Category V areas in developing countries are described in Box 22.3.

USING IUCN CATEGORY VI

Category VI has been introduced mainly because of arguments put forward by representatives of developing countries at the World Parks Congress in Caracas (1992) who sought formal recognition of the efforts made to link conservation and sustainable resource use, many of which are based on nationwide systems of resource use. The category allows for the sustainable use of natural ecosystems (managed resource protected areas) – those essentially natural areas where ecosystems or species of wildlife are conserved *in order that they may be used sustainably*. In such cases, control has often been devolved to local

BOX 22.2 GUIDANCE ON CATEGORY VI PROTECTED AREAS

Objectives of Management

- Protect and maintain the biological diversity and other natural values of the area in the long term.
- Promote sound management practices for sustainable production processes.
- Protect the natural resource base from being alienated for other land uses that would be detrimental to the area's biodiversity.
- Contribute to regional and national development.

Guidance for Selection

- The area should be at least two-thirds in a natural condition, although it may also contain limited areas of modified ecosystems; large commercial plantations would not be appropriate for inclusion.
- The area should be large enough to absorb sustainable resource use without detriment to its long-term natural values.

Organisational Responsibility

- Management should be undertaken by public bodies with an unambiguous remit for conservation, and carried out in partnership with the local community; or management may be provided through local custom supported and advised by governmental or non-governmental agencies. Ownership may be by the national or other level of government, the community, private individuals, or a combination of these.

Source: IUCN, 1994

communities: indeed, local people may be better guardians of the areas because economic benefits flow to the local community, thus giving it a strong interest in maintaining the site. Such areas exist in a number of developing countries; for example, within Brazil there are reserves for the extraction of rubber, nuts and other forest products for the sustainable benefit of the human communities living in and around them. Hitherto they would not have been regarded as protected areas in the conventional sense, but they now find recognition within the IUCN category system. Similarly, some of the 'protection forests' under Indonesian law may qualify for recognition in this way. It is to be hoped that the new Category VI will be widely adopted as a means of linking conservation and development, particularly within developing countries.

The addition of Category VI was not without difficulty. Some conservation experts feared that it might open the way to the use of areas which had previously been wholly protected; others feared it might be used to give a stamp of approval to forest management systems which were not sustainable. As a result, the IUCN guidelines make clear that to qualify the 'area must be managed so that the long-term protection and maintenance of its biodiversity is assured' (IUCN, 1994). The guidance also indicates that the following four requirements should be met:

1   The area must be able to fit within the overall definition of a protected area (see Chapter 2).
2   At least two-thirds of the area should be, and should remain, in its natural state (the guidance recognizes however, that 'natural' is a relative term).
3   Large commercial plantations are not to be included.
4   A management authority must be in place.

Box 22.2 sets out the objectives of management, guidance for selection and organizational responsibility for Category VI protected areas.

BOX 22.3 CASE STUDIES

The Philippines rice terraces

In the mountainous area of the northern Philippines island of Luzon, some 20,000 km² of rice terracing is farmed by the Ifugao and related groups. Much of this is to be found at relatively high altitudes, up to 1500 metres, on some of the steepest slopes used for rice production anywhere in the world. The resulting landscape is extraordinarily beautiful. It also has strong cultural associations and traditions (Villalon, 1995) and relatively high biodiversity values within the remaining forests, including the vital watershed forests.

The outstanding universal qualities of The Philippines rice terraces were recognized when the site was designated (under the World Heritage Convention) as a cultural landscape world heritage site, in December 1995. This will help focus greater attention on the importance of the area, both as a model for managing tropical mountainous areas as a whole, and for its intrinsic scenic and cultural values. It should also help to secure international support for the efforts of The Philippines government to protect the area through the newly formed Ifugao Terraces Commission.

The Philippines rice terraces thus demonstrate a number of the key principles of the Category V approach:

•   the harmonious interaction of nature and people which has produced an area of distinct character, with significant aesthetic and other values;
•   the importance of the area as a demonstration of how to manage natural resources in a sustainable way; and
•   the significance of the cultural traditions of the community which provide the framework for sustainable land-use practices ensuring the protection, maintenance and evolution of the area and its landscape (Villalon, 1995).

The traditional coffee-growing areas of Northern Latin America

Coffee grown from Colombia to Mexico accounts for over a third of the world's production. The image, reinforced by much conservation literature, is that growing coffee involves the destruction of the natural forests of the region (which it does) and their replacement by a biological desert. This need not, however, be the case. In particular, traditional methods of coffee growing may not be bad news for conservationists at all: 'Coffee is traditionally grown under a canopy of shade trees. Because of the structural and floristic complexities of shade trees, traditional coffee plantations have relatively high biodiversity' (Perfecto et al, 1996).

For some groups of species, such as birds, these areas 'compare well with other natural forest habitats with which many species are shared' (Perfecto et al, 1996). However, the traditional way of growing coffee is giving way to industrial production with little or no shading. Already 50 per cent of all coffee is grown under these intensive systems, which involves the heavy use of chemicals, exposes soils to runoff and soil loss and results in a huge loss in regional biodiversity.

The economic case for sweeping away traditional coffee-farming systems is not water tight. The older systems are better for smallfarmers who can grow other crops as well. Consumer groups in North America now promote coffee grown in this way as better for the environment and (since chemical use is minimal) safer, too, on the breakfast table (Rice and Ward, 1996). The pressures for further industrialization of the process are still strong, but there are signs of a fight back with greater importance now being attached to the smallfarmers' established ways of coffee farming.

St Lucia, Caribbean

The St Lucia plan for a system of protected areas (Hudson et al, 1992) includes ten protected landscapes (IUCN Category V) covering a total of 3477 hectares (approximately 20 per cent of the total protected area proposed by the plan). The Praslin Protected Landscape (873 hectares), for example, incorporates an existing marine nature reserve and 15 existing or proposed historic sites. The St Lucia National Trust has negotiated management agreements with a private landowner to create the Fregate Islands Nature Reserve within this protected landscape and has launched a community strategic planning process in Praslin village. It promotes heritage tourism to the area, where attractions include traditional boat-building and artisanal fishing practices. Nearby, within the Pointe Sable National Park, a well-established collaborative management arrangement ensures sustainable use of the Mankote mangrove for local charcoal production.

The St Lucia system plan was developed as a result of a four-year participatory planning process, involving considerable public input and collaboration among governmental and non-governmental organizations. As the plan notes, a key challenge in its implementation is that:

> ...most of the management areas consist of both public and private lands, with the majority in private ownership...Therefore, innovative land acquisition arrangements, and similarly innovative management partnerships which respect the rights of individual landowners, will be required.

To address these challenges, the St Lucia National Trust plans to develop a land stewardship programme and, as a first step, is reviewing land acquisition options, new incentives for conservation and the possibility of a landowner contact programme (Romulus, 1996).

South Pacific Conservation Areas

Under the South Pacific Regional Environmental Programme (SPREP), a GEF-funded South Pacific biodiversity conservation project has been developed. Through this project, some 14 countries in the region (Cook Islands, Fiji, Federated States of Micronesia, Kiribati, Marshall Islands, Nauru, Niue, Palau, Solomon Islands, Tokelau, Kingdom of Tonga, Tuvalu, Vanuatu and Western Samoa) have identified a number of conservation areas (Wood et al, 1994).

To be recognized, the sites must satisfy all the following criteria:

- They must be nationally or regionally significant examples of ecosystems of global conservation concern, such as tropical rainforest, mangroves, lagoons and coral reefs, and must be large enough to maintain their viability.
- The project must be achievable and exhibit a high degree of commitment by landowners, residents, resources users and other potential partners in the conservation area project.
- The proposed area must be sufficiently large and complex to encompass a wide range of the interactions among people and natural resources prevailing in the country.

They must also meet one of the following criteria:

- The proposed area should contain high levels of biological diversity and ecological complexity, represented by a number of major environments, diversity of ecosystems, and/or large numbers of genera or plants and animals.
- The proposed area may be important for the survival of endemic species, or of species that are rare or threatened nationally, regionally or globally.
- The proposed area may be threatened by destruction, degradation or conversion.

The distinctive features of the conservation area approach in the South Pacific are as follows:

- It recognizes and builds upon the long tradition of community-based conservation of natural resources in the region.
- It has as an essential element the inclusion of the interaction between people and natural resources.

Thus the South Pacific conservation area concept has much in common with that of Category V.

CONCLUSION

The central role played by protected areas in conservation has long been recognized. What has not been widely appreciated, though, is that the way in which protected areas contribute to biodiversity conservation can vary greatly, and – especially in the case of Categories V and VI – may be achieved *through, with and for* people rather than *against* them. Similarly, the contribution which protected areas of this kind can make to sustainable development has frequently been overlooked. By introducing new strategies for ensuring stewardship of working landscapes, the potential for conservation is increased significantly in many countries and links are built between biodiversity conservation and sustainable rural development.

REFERENCES

Hudson, L and Renard, Y (1992) *A system of protected areas for St. Lucia*, St Lucia National Trust, Castries

IUCN (1994) *Guidelines for Protected Area Management Categories*, IUCN Publications, Cambridge

IUCN (1998) *1997 UN List of Protected Areas*, IUCN Publications, Cambridge

Lucas, P H C (1992) *Protected Landscapes: a Guide to Policy Makers and Planners*, Chapman and Hall, London

Perfecto, I, Rice, R, Greenberg, R and Van der Voort, M (1996) 'Shade Coffee: A disappearing refuge for biodiversity', *BioScience*, 46(8): 598–608

Rice, R and Ward, J (1996) *Coffee, Conservation and Commerce in the Western Hemisphere*, Smithsonian Migratory Bird Center, Natural Resource Defence Council, Washington DC

Romulus, G (1996) 'Moving towards a land stewardship programme: The case of St Lucia National Trust', in *Proceedings of a Caribbean Land Stewardship Workshop*, Gros Islet, St Lucia, 26–30 March 1996, St Lucia National Trust, QLF/ACE, Island Resources Foundation and the Nature Conservancy

Villalon, A (1995) 'The Cultural Landscape of the Rice Terraces of the Philippine Cordilleras' in Droste, von B, Plachter, H and Rossler, M (eds) *Cultural Landscapes of Universal Value*, Gustav Fischer, Stuttgart

Wood, P, Kinstone, F and Tilling, A (1994) *South Pacific Biodiversity Conservation Programme User's Guidelines SREP*, Apia, Western Samoa

23 EXTRACTIVE RESERVES: THE USE OF PROTECTED AREAS TO PROMOTE SUSTAINABLE MANAGEMENT[*]

Rafael Pinzón Rueda and Manoel Lima Feitosa[**]

INTRODUCTION

The tales of tourists and visitors to the Amazon of 30 years ago boil down to a sense of awe at that 'huge green carpet', which was the impression gathered from an aircraft, and a feeling of emptiness and loneliness derived from the stereotyped image of 'being lost in the forest'. Today, anyone flying over the region tends to be appalled at the way the 'huge carpet' has been slashed and burned, particularly in the states of Pará, Maranhão, Mato Grosso, Rondônia and Acre.

No one can help noticing the devastation which has occurred in the forest. International reporters photograph apocalyptic, desolating scenes. The world is appalled. The Northern countries are afraid of the greenhouse effect and everyone is clamouring for the conservation of the environment, for the protection of the 'huge, empty green carpet', the heritage of mankind – a pointer to the ecological equilibrium of the planet. But nobody ever talks about the forest-dwellers – those who live inside the huge carpet. The extractive reserves are the vision of people who actually trod the ground, who stopped looking from a distance, who entered the forest and found a different reality, still ignored by many of those doing research on the Amazon.

It is a mistake to describe the Amazon as a great demographic vacuum. It is preferable to modernize the concepts of human geography and adapt them to ecology as the science of human kind's interaction with nature. It would then be found that the ecological equilibrium and sustainability of the Amazon depend on the spatial distribution of the population, according to the traditional extractive approach – adapted to the spatial distribution of plant and animal species. From there, one moves on to a new concept of human occupation where the 'optimum' index is the one which secures sustainability. In the

---

* This chapter has been adapted from: Julio Ruiz Murrieta and Rafael Pinzón Rueda (1995) *Extractive Reserves*, IUCN Forest Conservation Programme, Gland and Cambridge. The material has been used with the kind permission of IUCN.
** Author of the Alto Juruá case study on pages 218–223.

case of rubber tappers, nut gatherers and fishermen, this works out at 5 km²
per family (or one inhabitant per square kilometre). The conclusion then
becomes that the Amazon is not a vacuum, but is in fact suitably occupied by
about 4.5 million inhabitants in the rural area.

A BRIEF HISTORY OF EXTRACTIVISM

For 20 years, from 1965 to 1985, Brazil's policy was to occupy Amazonia and
to expand its agricultural frontier. The government opened up roads, distributed land, organized settlements and provided countless incentives, especially
subsidized credits, to set up cattle farms and timber companies in the region.
This advance of the agricultural frontier into Amazonia destabilized extractive
activities in several regions, transforming forests into pasturelands for cattle
and extractive workers into agricultural labourers or smallfarmers. Others –
rubber tappers who had been violently expelled from their homes – occupied
abandoned rubber plantations or government land. These rubber tappers
remained 'independent rubber tappers', without employers. The independent
rubber tappers of Rio Branco, Xapuri and Brasiléia were the first to come out
in defence of extractivism, organizing themselves in 1976 to prevent further
deforestation of extractive areas. These movements, which came to be known
as *empates* (stalemates), spread to other areas of Acre and to other states
(Amazonas and Pará).

The conflicts between farmers and rubber tappers impressed public
opinion, especially after the death of the leader of the rural workers' union of
Brasiléia, Wilson de Souza Pinheiro, in 1978. These same conflicts later were
to lead to the assassination by farmers of the leader of the rural workers' union
of Xapurí, Chico Mendes, in 1988.

The *empate* movement against deforestation was to serve as a basis for the
political and social maturing of extractive workers. In view of the need to
maintain unity, the principle of the 'collective concessions' came to be
accepted and developed. It must be admitted, however, that in 1980, perhaps
under the influence of the land distribution policy pursued by the government, the extractive workers showed a preference for individual plots. Even
today there is still a minority which has not fully accepted the idea of not
having an individual title right to a plot of land.

In 1985, the rubber tappers came together in Brasilia for their first national
meeting. They requested the end of the colonization of rubber plantations and
asked for the latter to be allocated to them on a concession basis, as a way of
maintaining extractive activities. The request was also aimed at solving the
land problem and protecting the forest against the threat of deforestation for
the benefit of cattle farming.

This meeting of the rubber workers constitutes the historic point at which
the request to set up the 'extractive reserves' became, for the first time, official.
After that first meeting of the rubber tappers, the Instituto Nacional de
Colonização e Reforma Agrária (INCRA) took up the problem. Its directive of
30 July 1987 proposed the setting up the Projeto de Assentamento Extrativista
or PAE (extractivist settlement project):

> *...for the purpose of exploiting areas containing extractive rubber plantations by means of economically viable and ecologically sustainable activities, to be pursued by the communities who occupy or might come to occupy the aforementioned areas...subject to a concession of use in a communal system, in the form decided by the community of beneficiaries – in association, coownership or cooperative.*

From the beginning, social movements joined in the struggle to defend extractivism and to look for solutions, initially to the land problem. Gradually demands were channelled through the Conselho Nacional dos Seringueiros, the CNS (National Council of Rubber Tappers), set up in 1985. In view of the lack of progress achieved by the extractivist settlement projects (PAE) and of growing domestic and international pressure in favour of the preservation of the forests, the CNS, apart from continuing to advocate the creation of extractive reserves as a means of implementing agrarian reform for extractive workers, started to defend them as 'territorial areas for sustainable use and the conservation of renewable natural resources'.

The federal government also took a step forward by legalizing the creation of extractive reserves as part of the national environmental policy in July 1989. According to those laws, the institution responsible for the reserves became the IBAMA, *Instituto Brasileiro do Meio Ambiente e dos Recursos Naturais* (Brazilian Institute for the Environment and Natural Resources), and the management body responsible for reserve matters is the CNPT, Centro Nacional para o Desenvolvimento Sustentado das Populações Tradicionais (National Centre for the Sustained Development of Traditional Communities).

THE FURURE OF EXTRACTIVISM

In the particular case of Brazil, where the defence of extractive natural resources emerged as a result of the struggle by extractive workers to defend their land, the goal pursued was not just sustainable but 'socially just' development. The extractive reserves must remain a means of putting justice into practice, by attributing land to those who have traditionally dwelt on it and defended it.

The following measures are required:

- a balance between development, environmental conservation and social justice;
- participation by society as an agent and not an object in the process, considering that the reserves are self-managed by residents;
- retrieval and refinement of popular knowledge, since the utilization plan of the reserves is based on the experience and wisdom of dwellers who have coexisted there for many years in harmony with nature; and
- lower cost of protecting forests, once the local residents have taken up their defense.

In the development of extractivism, creating extractive reserves is only one stage. A further effort is needed to implement the reserves and ensure that they are a success. The most urgent measures include:

- strengthening local organizations, especially by training human resources;
- supplying the material conditions and tools needed to implement the cooperative management of resources and extractive activity;
- distribution of power over natural resources (concession of use and utilization plan);
- release from ties of dependency on middlemen (supply of goods, inputs and marketing of production); and
- adding value to extracted products (enhancement or pre-industrialization).

CASE STUDY: THE EXTRACTIVE RESERVE OF ALTO JURUÁ

Geographic and environmental data

The Alto Juruá extractive reserve, set up on 23 January 1990, has an area covering approximately 506,186 hectares located at the western tip of Brazil and of the state of Acre. The area of the extractive reserve is part of a biome which, from a macroecological point of view, includes at least four types of dryland tropical forests which are never flooded. One has dense vegetation cover and another is open. The other two are linked to the hydrographic network: the periodically flooded alluvial tropical forest and the terraced tropical forest.

The lowland forests occur on sedimentary material of the Solimões formation, eroded to produce a low relief with a predominance of hills and crystalline rock formations, rising to altitudes of between 200 and 500 metres. Dry open forests of palm trees and bamboo are to be found in the area. The characteristic forest families are the Sapotaceae, Annonaceae, Leguminosae, Leccthidaceae, Euphorbiaceae and Tiliaceae. The shrub stratum (subforest) varies in density according to the structure of the tree stratum and is denser in areas of bamboo and palm trees, becoming less dense as the upper stratum closes over.

The dense tropical forest appears distributed in patches in the central and eastern region, surrounded by open tropical forest, this latter formation occurring more frequently. The alluvial type of tropical forest of the periodically flooded plain occurs in limited fashion along the Rivers Juruá and Tejo in a band of varying width. The terraced alluvial open tropical forest is the one which occurs least frequently in the area of the reserve and is restricted to two patches at the mouth of the River Tejo.

The ecological rhythms of the region are very much marked by the rainfall, with an annual total exceeding 2200 millimetres; the rainiest quarter is December to February, while the driest is June to August. As an annual average, relative air humidity is above 85 per cent. Average temperatures also decrease between June and August and annual averages are relatively low for the Amazon – below 25° Celcius (C) for the year as a whole, with an absolute maximum of 38°C and an absolute minimum below 8°C.

Historic aspects

The occupation of Acre, as with all the Amazon region, began with the search for forest products which could be sold abroad. In the 19th century, latex began to be extracted by the Indians in the lower Juruá and in the Purus. This rubber was sold to merchants in Manaus and Belem who travelled on the rivers, also buying *erva-doce* (canary grass), cinnamon, turtle oil, *copaiba* oil, cocoa and sarsaparilla.

After the bankruptcy of the rubber barons and the import–export companies of Manaus and Belem, the former employees and managers began to operate an itinerant trade as local bosses, some of them taking up residence in the area where they used to work previously. Food imports were replaced by local production of *farinha* meal and other products. The rubber tappers began to have larger families, taking up hunting, fishing and the gathering of other forest products. These were sold either through local bosses or through the *regatões* (itinerant traders).

At the time of World War II, synthetic rubber made its appearance on the market, partially replacing natural rubber. In Amazonia, between 1943 and 1985, the federal government began directly to support and stimulate the rubber production of native rubber plantations and price controls were introduced. At the same time, the Instituto de Colonização e Reforma Agrária validated land claims in Acre. Federal banks financed the rubber growers with subsidized interest rates. This policy did not benefit the rubber tappers, and instead generated a reaction by the industrial sector against all forms of extractive activity.

In 1985, when monthly inflation rates reached double digits, the government abandoned its policy of supporting the real prices of natural rubber. In 1986, a debt collection expedition was set up with police support, causing a revolt among rubber tappers and residents in the River Tejo and Restauração rubber plantation area; after a demonstration by the local people, the government withdrew the police force. At the same time, the rubber tappers were very apprehensive about research into timber potential and preliminary contacts for installing the necessary infrastructure. This was the immediate background to the project for setting up an extractive reserve in the area, an idea which was suggested for the first time in 1987 in trade union meetings of the Restauração rubber plantation.

In 1988, when the National Council of Rubber Tappers (CNS) began its activities in the local area of the Alto Juruá, a preliminary survey was made in the River Tejo basin and a project was launched to set up the first extractive reserve in Brazil. In 1989, the Procuradoria Geral asked the Empresa Brasileira de Pesquisa Agropecuária (EMBRAPA) (Brazilian Farm Research Enterprise) for an ecological evaluation of the region and, in January 1990, the federal government, established the extractive reserve of Alto Juruá.

Socioeconomic data concerning the reserve

The extractive reserve of Alto Juruá has 865 houses with a population of some 5800 persons, in 325 settlements (Colocações) and ten farms. Most of the residents were born on the rubber plantations and only a few, mainly on the banks of the River Juruá, were born in towns.

1991 socioeconomic survey data indicate that 53 per cent of the reserve territory is appropriated as an extraction area, while 47 per cent serves either as a buffer between settlements or consists of uninhabited areas between rivers. Places with permanent inhabitants are identified by small clearings opened in the forest for the main housing or small cleared fields or pasture lands. The reserve territory is divided into:

- areas with strong human activity;
- degraded areas with pioneer vegetation;
- forest areas with extractive use and regular hunting; and
- areas with very low and irregular human activity.

Migration within the reserve is observed to be very low. Families have been living in the same rubber growing areas for more than 20 years and the same settlements for more than ten years. Moves, when they occur, may be due to a number of causes, such as marriage, pressure on natural resources or the increasing number of houses within a settlement, the wish to live closer to relatives, or the need for schooling or medical support, or even for better transport facilities.

All transport is by boat or canoe. There are no roads, even for pack animals. Communication within the area is by trails which are maintained by the residents themselves. The journey from the most distant points of the reserve to the headquarters of the association might take up to two days by canoe, not counting the stretches which have to be covered on foot.

In the educational sector, the 1991 socioeconomic survey indicates that illiteracy is high, affecting 78 per cent of the population. Illiteracy is greater among men than among women. According to the survey, 19 schools were identified in the reserve area but only about one third of the 2265 children, in the five to fifteen-year-old age bracket, had physical access to schools within a radius of up to a two hours' walk from their homes. The schools are public, with teachers paid by the secretariat of education of the state of Acre, or by the education secretariat of the municipality. Some of the schools cannot open for lack of teachers.

In the area of health, the population lives without any sanitary infrastructure. Public health services are incomplete and infrequent. According to the record, between 1981 and 1990, the SUCAM visited the River Tejo area only once, for malaria prevention, although such visits are supposed to be made each year. Until 1991, the rubber tappers used to buy medicines from bosses and *marreteiros* (itinerant traders), or they would consult quacks or take home remedies.

In 1991, the Association of Rubber Tappers and Farmers of the Extractive Reserve of Alto Juruá signed an agreement with Health Unlimited. Twelve health stations were built to receive residents; 12 health agents were trained and are supervised; two manuals were produced and a programme of regular vaccination was initiated. Facilities for the operation include an equipped boat and a permanent team, including a doctor and a dentist.

Management and social organization of the reserve

The area is managed by the Associação dos Seringueiros e Agricultores da Reserva Extrativista do Alto Juruá, the rubber tappers and farmers association, legally established with a statute and a properly elected executive body, which was founded in 1988 and currently includes 371 members. In 1992, as part of its managerial duties, its general meeting set up river committees to achieve better organization on a local level. In some areas, significant participation of residents was achieved, such as in the Rio Tejo, Rio Bagé and Boca do Rio Tejo areas; elsewhere, such as in River Juruá region, participation has been low or non-existent.

The association's headquarters at Boca do Tejo boasts an infrastructure made up of a 300 metre^2 warehouse, a lodging area, shop, meeting room and office, an electricity generator, and a solar panel and battery to supply the radio transmitter. These radios provide essential support for commercial activities as well as for health and education services.

The activities of the families living in the reserve area consist of the extraction of latex, agriculture, hunting and fishing, handicrafts and services. About 65 per cent of the families exploit the rubber trees and more than 90 per cent have cleared plots where they grow manioc, maize and other products.

Work in the family tends to be divided along gender lines, with the men looking after the extraction of rubber, hunting and fishing, and women working at home and in the vegetable garden. Both take part in agricultural work. With regard to property rights, both women and children may own goods within the home or the rubber plantation.

Utilization plan

It should be emphasized that once an area has been expropriated, it becomes state property and the usufruct thereof is granted to local extractive residents through their associations, which is a way of avoiding fragmentation of the land. The precondition for making the concession effective is approval of the utilization plan.

At present, the Alto Juruá extractive reserve has a proposal, by the community, for the use of the area. The association, which is responsible for administering the reserve's natural resources, has the right to supervise the conservation of the rubber trails, the stock of palm trees and other resources in accordance with the utilization plan previously approved of in a general meeting. The association is also responsible, with the support of the National Council of Rubber Tappers, for planning and implementing development strategies favouring conservation and a strengthening of the association itself, with the help of equipment, infrastructure and the recruitment of technical staff.

Current projects

A number of projects are currently underway to support the extractive reserve of Alto Juruá. The main one is the pilot programme for the protection of

Brazilian tropical forests (extractive reserves project), the general objective of which is to test appropriate models of economic, social and environmental management, with a view to improving the methods and procedures used by traditional residents by:

- strengthening the organization of production and of the community;
- developing technologies to produce subsistence goods and products for market;
- developing the economic and social infrastructure;
- maintaining stocks of natural resources; and
- preserving biodiversity.

Current projects also include:

- Support for community organization: organizing the extractive community was always a challenge, since the isolation of people in the forest and the lack of communication with urban centres are basic factors of life for extractive workers in the Amazon. Communities began to have a say in government policy-making in the 1970s and this participation has increased ever since. In the specific case of extractive reserves, their viability must depend upon sound organization, since a condition of establishing these areas is joint management between the government and an organized civil body.
- Training to improve rubber quality: in order to increase the rubber tappers' income, different kinds of training are being offered to improve rubber quality. The aim of the training is to introduce technology for producing smoked raw-sheet rubber instead of the traditional system of producing rubber in balls.
- Training for assistant supervisors: because the extractive reserve is a direct-use conservation area, which means that the community is involved in its management, training is now being offered on technical, legal and administrative aspects of supervising the area.
- Support for the improved use of cleared land: in forest areas affected by man's activities, measures are being introduced to improve the use of cleared lands, such as model fruit and vegetable gardens.
- Support for research projects: a technical and scientific cooperation agreement was recently signed between IBAMA and the University of São Paulo (USP) for the purpose of developing studies, research, the exchange of information and mutual advice for implementing activities in support of the extractive reserve.

Main problems

The reserve's main problems at present are connected with health and education. In the health area, despite an official agreement with Health Unlimited to develop a series of projects, there has been a lack of either preventive or remedial action on the part of the public health services against the most common illnesses in the area, such as yellow fever, malaria, hepatitis, worms and leprosy.

In the education sector, problems begin at the school planning stage, since there is no school programme which is adapted to the seasonal nature of local productive activities, and especially not to the peak periods of planting (August and September) and the fortnightly preparation of meal. Apart from this problem, a lot of basic equipment is lacking, such as desks, slates, water filters, toilets, and teaching material such as books, textbooks and pencils.

The teachers are all women, young and with only basic training. There is no inspection within the reserve area. There is a shortage of schools and teachers in places in the interior of the reserve to cater for some 1500 children who live outside the attendance radius of the main schools. In the primary sector, there is no real credit and incentive policy to improve and increase the production of natural rubber from native trees, or any incentive to develop other extractive activities.

24 COLLABORATIVE MANAGEMENT OF PROTECTED AREAS*

Grazia Borrini-Feyerabend

INTRODUCTION

Protected areas span an immense variety of ecological habitats and social contexts, from some of the least explored areas in the world to densely populated territories highly affected by human presence. It is estimated, for example, that about half of existing protected areas and possibly 80 per cent of the ones in Latin America have people living in them (Amend and Amend, 1995). Throughout Europe, protected areas are commonly inhabited by legal residents.

Most protected territories are under common property regimes (they are state property or communal property). In some cases disputes exist between the state and local communities (often indigenous) for the control of the protected territory (Lynch and Talbott, 1995). In particular, this is true for territories officially owned by the state but de facto controlled by local residents, who exploit their natural resources in a more or less organized way. Besides common property, protected territories can also be found under private ownership or mixed ownership status. In fact, the concept of protected area blurs into the concept of productive reserve for privately owned territories where biodiversity is economically exploited (such as for wildlife ranching or tourism).

What many protected areas have in common, however, is that the responsibility for their management is assigned to a single agency, which is often a public body, such as a state national park agency, a ministerial department, an ad hoc authority or a parastatal institution. At times the agency put in charge by the government is a non-governmental organization (NGO). In general, this agency has the mandate of conserving the area for its own intrinsic value

* This chapter is extracted from a longer paper, *Collaborative Management of Protected Areas: Tailoring the approach to the context*, by Grazia Borrini-Feyerabend, published by IUCN in 1996 and reproduced here with the kind permission of IUCN. In the full paper several concrete collaborative management (CM) examples are discussed with reference to their place in Figure 24.1 and the process by which CM is usually developed is discussed in some detail. Figure 24.2 summarizes this discussion.

(habitat, species and genetic diversity). Increasingly, this mandate also includes benefiting present and future human generations, especially those living within or close to the protected area.

Two main strategic models for approaches to protected area management emerged in the 1960s and 1970s (West and Brechin, 1991): 'exclusive' management and 'inclusive' management. In the first – largely adopted in the US – management plans were developed with the intention of de-coupling the interests of local people from protected areas, with options ranging from an open antiparticipatory attitude to the outright resettlement of the resident communities. This stance was common to both state-owned and privately owned reserves. In the second model – more frequently adopted in Western Europe – the interests of local societies were central to the protected area, private ownership of land within protected areas was common, and local administrators were largely involved in management planning.

STAKEHOLDERS

Regardless of whether the responsibility for managing a protected area is assigned to a specific agency, its management – or mismanagement – affects various groups in society. Above all, these groups include the communities who live within or close to protected areas and, in particular, the people who use or derive an income from their natural resources, the people who possess knowledge, capacities and aspirations that are relevant for their management, and the people who recognize in the protected area a unique cultural, religious or recreational value. Many such communities possess customary rights over the protected territories and resources, although official recognition of those rights may be uncertain or nil.

In addition to local residents and resource users, other social actors may have an interest in protected area management. In particular, these include the governmental agencies dealing with various resource sectors and the administrative authorities (district or municipal councils) dealing with natural resources as part of their broader mandate. They include the local businesses and industries (for example, tourist operators and water users) who can be significantly affected by the status of natural resources in the protected areas. They include research institutions and non-governmental organizations which find the relevant territories and resources at the heart of their professional concerns. Last, but not least, they include – as individuals – local staff of the public management agency and the staff of environment and development projects established to support the protected area.

In this chapter, the various institutions, social groups and individuals who possess a direct, significant and specific stake in the protected area will be referred to as *stakeholders*. Their stakes may originate from institutional mandate, geographic proximity, historical association, dependence for livelihood, economic interest, and from a variety of other capacities and concerns. In general, stakeholders:

- are *aware of their interests* in managing the protected area (although they may not be aware of all its management issues and problems);

- possess *specific capacities* (knowledge, skills) *and/or comparative advantage* (proximity, mandate) for such management; and
- are usually *willing to invest* specific resources (time, money, political authority) in such management.

Not all stakeholders are equally interested in conserving a resource, nor are they equally entitled to have a role in resource management. For the sake of effectiveness and equity, it is necessary to distinguish amongst them on the basis of some agreed criteria, such as relating to existing rights (for example, property), continuity of relationship, or unique knowledge, and skills in resource management.

Social actors who score high on several accounts may be considered primary stakeholders, versus secondary stakeholders who may score high only in one or two areas. In collaborative management processes, primary stakeholders assume an active role, possibly involving decision-making (for instance, they could hold a seat on a management board). Secondary stakeholders are involved in a less important way (they could hold a seat in a consultative body).

The relationship between the agency in charge of the protected area and its other stakeholders is often not as good as is desirable. It is not uncommon, for instance, that the agency in charge sees the local community primarily as a potential threat to the protected area (Adams and McShane, 1992), that the indigenous inhabitants of the area are not recognized in their role of maintaining biodiversity, or that local residents see the creation of a protected area as an oppressive development, bringing in foreign values and depriving them of wealth and culture (Ghimire and Pimbert, 1996). Conflicts between agencies and local residents are the cause of some of the most serious failures in managing protected areas. Conflicts may also arise between the agency in charge of the protected area and various public authorities (such as national, district or municipal governments).

At times, conflicts are 'resolved' by violent means: the residents are forced to resettle a territory or are kept out of it by armed guards. Wars of attrition can continue for years, with protected area managers spending considerable resources in enforcing rules against a tide of 'encroachers' and 'poachers'. Useful knowledge and skills are wasted and problems go unrecognized until it is too late to prevent serious damage. Worst of all, the great potential for cooperation between agencies and other stakeholders to fend off external threats of mutual concern – such as urban expansion or large-scale timber extraction – are never realized.

COLLABORATIVE MANAGEMENT

The term collaborative management – (also referred to as comanagement, participatory management, joint management, shared management, multi-stakeholder management or round-table agreement) is used to describe a situation in which *some or all of the relevant stakeholders in a protected area are involved in a substantial way in management activities*. Specifically, in a collaborative management process, the agency with jurisdiction over the protected area (usually a state agency) develops a *partnership* with other relevant stakeholders (primarily including local residents and resource users) which specifies and guarantees their *respective functions, rights and responsibilities* with regard to the area.

In general, the partnership identifies:

- a protected territory (or set of resources) and its boundaries;
- the range of functions and sustainable uses it can provide;
- the recognized stakeholders in the protected area;
- the functions and responsibilities assumed by each stakeholder;
- the specific benefits and rights granted to each stakeholder;
- an agreed set of management priorities and a management plan;
- procedures for dealing with conflicts and negotiating collective decisions about all of the above;
- procedures for enforcing such decisions; and
- specific rules for monitoring, evaluating and reviewing the partnership agreement, and the relative management plan, as appropriate.

Collaborative management regimes and other similar arrangements can and do also operate in territories that do not have a protected area status, and can apply to virtually all types of natural resources (Metcalfe, 1994). Collaborative management, on the other hand, is not an approach that is applicable and effective in all cases. In situations that require rapid decisions and actions – for example, to block the rapid ecological deterioration of an area – it is better to act than to wait for a general consensus on what to do about a devastated territory. On the other hand, practical experience has shown that it is especially advisable to pursue a management partnership when the active commitment and collaboration of stakeholders are essential for managing the protected area (for instance, when the protected area's territory is inhabited or privately owned); and when access to the natural resources included in the protected areas is essential for local livelihood security and cultural survival.

In addition, it is particularly appropriate to pursue partnership agreements when one or more of the following conditions apply:

- The local stakeholders have historically enjoyed customary/legal rights over the territory at stake.
- Local interests are strongly affected by the way in which the protected area is managed.
- The decisions to be taken are complex and highly controversial.
- The agency's previous management has clearly failed to produce the expected results.
- The various stakeholders are ready to collaborate and request to do so.
- There is ample time to negotiate.

Some specialists believe that at least a 'mild' version of collaborative management – consultation and the seeking of stakeholder consensus – is essential *in all cases* (Renard, 1998). A 'strong' version of collaborate management – the inclusion of stakeholders in a management board or outright devolution of specific authority and responsibility – may or may not be appropriate according to the specific conditions at stake (see Figure 24.1).

TAILORING COLLABORATIVE MANAGEMENT

How could a collaborative management partnership develop? In an ideal case, all the major stakeholders – including the agency in charge of protected areas in the country – would together review relevant background data and issues, consult with various institutions and individuals, agree on declaring a specific territory under protected status and negotiate a share of management rights and responsibilities that reconcile the interests and capacities of all parties. The parties would then develop a permanent or semipermanent body – in which each of them would be fairly and equitably represented – to remain in charge of implementing, monitoring and reviewing the agreement. Unfortunately, even in relatively favourable circumstances, this is rarely the case.

For most protected areas, 'site identification' is done by national decree and one (usually state) agency has full discretion to decide if and how to involve other stakeholders. According to its perceptions of what is possible and desirable in legal, political, financial and social terms, the agency may:

- ignore the interests and capacities of other stakeholders and minimize their relationship with the protected area;
- inform the stakeholders about relevant issues and decisions;
- actively consult stakeholders about such issues and decisions;
- seek their consensus on those;
- negotiate with them on an open basis and develop a specific agreement;
- share authority and responsibilities in a formal way (for example, by asking them to join a management board); and
- transfer some or all authority and responsibility to one or more stakeholders.

If we choose to interpret the term partnership in a broad and encompassing sense, we could picture the area of collaborative management as in between the extremes of full control by the agency in charge and full control by other stakeholders. In Figure 24.1 a portion of the continuum between 'actively consulting' and 'transferring authority and responsibility' is identified as such.

Some maintain that it is not appropriate to use the term collaborative management for a situation in which stakeholders are merely consulted and not given a share of authority in management (Franks, 1995). It is difficult, however, to identify a sharp demarcation between various levels of participation in management activities. For instance, a process of active consultation with local stakeholders may result in the full incorporation of their concerns within a protected area's management plan. Conversely, a lengthy negotiation in which various stakeholders hold seats in a decision-making body may leave many local demands unmet. Is the second necessarily more collaborative management than the first?

The term collaborative management is used here as a broad concept spanning a variety of ways by which the agency in charge and other stakeholders develop and implement a management partnership. Collaborative processes and partnerships are also clearly strengthened by supportive tenurial rights, policies and legislation. Yet, more often than one may think, there is a schism between policy and practice.

Full control by the agency in charge	Shared control by the agency in charge and other stakeholders	Full control by other stakeholders

Collaborative management of a protected area

actively .... seeking .... negotiating ......sharing authority..... transferring
consulting   consensus   (involving in   and responsibility   authority and
                                     decision-making) in a formal way   responsibility
                                     and developing   (eg via seats in
                                     specific   a management
                                     agreements   body)

No interference or
contribution from
other stakeholders

No interference or
contribution from the
agency in charge

increasing expectations of stakeholders ⟶

increasing contributions, commitment and accountability of stakeholders ⟶

Note: A schematic representation of participation in PA management (sharing of influence and control), seen from the perspective of the agency in charge. The representation refers to de facto situations, regardless of underlying tenure rights, policies and legislation. Obviously, if supportive policy and legislation exist, they strengthen a management partnership.

Figure 24.1 *Participation in protected area management – a continuum*

MAIN ASSUMPTION AND CONSEQUENCES

A few basic principles and assumptions appear common to most collaborative management cases, including the following:

- Collaborative management stands on the virtues of multiplicity and diversity in management: different stakeholders possess different capacities and a management partnership stresses and builds upon the *complementarity* of their distinctive roles. The challenge is to create a situation in which the pay-offs are greater for collaboration than for competition.
- Collaborative management stands on the concept of *common good*: in particular, collaborative management assumes that it is possible to manage protected areas in an effective way while treating the relevant people with respect and equity.
- Collaborative management stands on the principle of *linking* management rights and responsibilities.
- Collaborative management regimes in protected areas are part of a broad social development towards more direct and participatory democracy. Moreover, as an equitable CM agreement provides a guarantee for the interests and rights of stakeholders – in particular the least powerful among them – it thereby fosters social justice.
- Collaborative management is a process *requiring ongoing review and improvement*, rather than the strict application of a set of established rules. Its most important result is not a management plan but a management partnership, capable of responding to varying needs in an effective way.

Moving from the left to the right of the participation continuum sketched in Figure 24.1, what accompanying phenomena can be expected? First of all, stakeholders are likely to increasingly contribute to management – for instance, by providing knowledge, skills, time, labour and various resources in cash and kind. Some may contribute by foregoing benefits and sustaining opportunity costs. Others may take on the responsibility of daily surveillance of the protected areas (for example, for early warning of fire and natural disasters, and to watch over illegal trespassing and extraction of resources), or the responsibility of monitoring biodiversity and social indicators. Secondly, the agency and other stakeholders are likely to increase their capacities in various areas related to management as a consequence of their enhanced communication, dialogue and common work. In other words, the accountability of stakeholders is likely to increase.

When stakeholders get more involved in management, their expectations are likely to rise, and this needs to be taken into serious consideration. For instance, the agency in charge needs to make sure that the agreement can be respected through time. It would be detrimental to craft difficult compromises just to see them nullified by a lack of means to implement them or by a judicial dispute that could have been foreseen well in advance. Yet, this does not mean that policy and laws must always precede practice. In several countries, pilot collaborative management initiatives that were conceived to experiment beyond existing policies have opened the way to substantial policy and legal change. In fact, examples of collaborative management cases exist all along the participation continuum of Figure 24.1.

Importantly, many collaborative management agreements depend upon the good work, energy and commitment of one or more individuals and/or on the presence of dedicated projects. If the individual(s) are transferred or stop contributing, or if the project ceases to function, the process may be blocked, derailed and/or simply fail. These risks point to the need for institutionalizing the process, making it, as soon as possible, as independent as possible from individuals and outside inputs.

POTENTIAL BENEFITS, COSTS AND OBSTACLES

By examining and comparing numerous field-based experiences it is possible to derive a series of key potential benefits, costs and obstacles in collaborative management processes. Potential benefits are likely to include:

- alliances between state agencies and local stakeholders to fend off resource exploitation from non-local interests which often represent the main threat to conservation;
- effective sharing of management responsibilities among all the parties involved in the agreement;
- negotiated specific benefits for all parties involved in the agreement (this has major ethical implications as negotiated benefits may be crucial for the survival of some local communities);
- increased effectiveness of management as a consequence of harnessing the stakeholders' knowledge and skills and comparative advantages;

- enhanced capacities in resource management for both the agency in charge and the other stakeholders (as a consequence of enhanced communication and dialogue);
- increased trust between state agencies and stakeholders, shared ownership of the conservation process and greater commitment to implement decisions taken together;
- reduction in enforcement expenditures because of voluntary compliance;
- increased sense of security and stability (of policies, priorities, tenure) leading to increased confidence in investments and a long-term perspective;
- increased understanding and knowledge among all concerned of the views and positions of others and thus prevention of problems and disputes;
- increased public awareness of conservation issues;
- more integration of conservation efforts into social, economic and cultural issues and agendas; and
- contribution towards a more democratic and participatory society.

However, collaborative management is not a panacea and, in fact, a number of costs and potential obstacles need to be evaluated before embarking on specific processes. These include:

- early and substantial investments of time, financial resources and human resources in both the preparatory phase and the process of developing the agreement; the human resources need to include professionals with uncommon skills (for example, stakeholder analysis, mediation and facilitation skills, etc); the time requirement, in particular, may be unsustainable for conservation initiatives promoted by donor agencies following a short-term project approach;
- potential opposition by agencies or individuals unwilling to share authority with other stakeholders;
- potential opposition by local residents who see the very existence of the protected area as depriving them of a needed potential for jobs and economic development;
- a potential opposition by stakeholders who bank on people–park conflicts to pursue their own agendas (for example, businesses which use people as a front line to penetrate protected territories and eventually set up economic activities);
- chances that the collaborative management agreement cannot be achieved without compromising the conservation goals of the protected area; and
- chances that the agreement cannot be maintained because of underestimated problems or intervening factors (for example, changes in economic conditions or political administration, the emergence of new stakeholders, violent unrest, etc).

CONCLUSIONS

Professionals dealing with collaborative management processes often have the exciting and unsettling feeling of watching a phenomenon touching upon the most significant aspects of life – democracy, equity, development and cultural

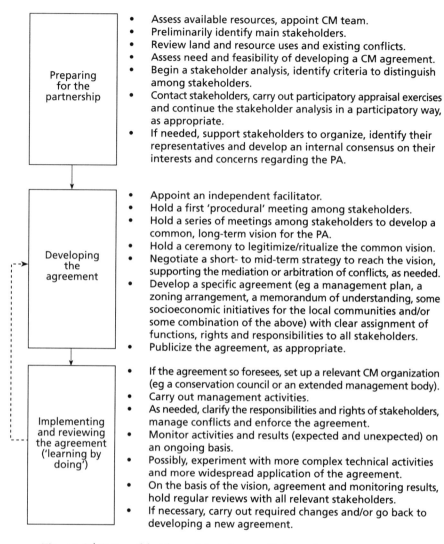

Figure 24.2 *Possible phases/steps in a collaborative management (CM) process*

survival – alongside the specific concerns of conservation and sound management of resources.

Experiences in partnership management in various locations allowed us to synthesize some general points for reflection. Among these are recommended conditions for developing collaborative management agreements, the basic principles, assumptions and consequences to be expected, and the potential benefits, costs and obstacles as listed and discussed above. The collaborative management process itself – preparing for a partnership, developing an agreement, implementing it and reviewing it – is complex and context dependent and cannot be in a rigid guideline. An outline of important steps, however, is provided in Figure 24.2.

If any conclusions can be drawn from the various considerations gathered in this chapter, they are perhaps most meaningful in terms of questions. Here are some examples.

- What is true collaborative management of a protected area? Some individuals speak about it in broad terms as a process that spans from active consultation of stakeholders on management decisions to full devolution of authority. Others would reserve the term for situations in which an effective sharing of decision-making power is achieved. This, however, is more easily said than done. Considering that collaborative management includes many aspects that are socioculturally specific, is it appropriate to carve a narrow definition for it?
- What are the essential feasibility conditions for collaborative management? For instance, are economic opportunities for local stakeholders a crucial requirement? Is meeting local needs the crucial factor that will make a difference for conservation? Should the management of protected areas involve partnerships among *all* the sectors of society that are – in one way or another – involved in meeting the needs of the relevant people?
- What obstacles are most likely to stand in the way of collaborative management agreements? Will government staff oppose or subvert a devolution of their power? Will rapid market forces undermine patiently crafted compromises? Will the communication and trust among different parties prove too difficult to achieve?
- What social phenomena are most likely to facilitate the spread of collaborative management agreements? Will democracy help? Will the privatization of the economy help? Will decentralization of governmental agencies help? Will the expanding media play a supportive role?
- What is the best course of action when indigenous inhabitants view themselves as the sole legitimate stakeholders in managing their territory and take a radical all or nothing stand with respect to their functions and rights? In these cases, is collaborative management a potential solution?
- Should local residents maintain their customary rights in protected area territories independently of their own behaviour, or should those rights be conditional in some way upon a 'traditional' or sustainable life style? On what legal and ethical basis could national resources be exploited by local residents but denied to migrants?
- What lessons have we learned in terms of best practices of collaborative management for conservation and the sustainable use of natural resources? For instance, is external facilitation always needed? What types of agreements work best – simple and well focused, or broad and encompassing? How often should reviews take place?
- Should well-respected international bodies advocate a set of best practices or even become promoters of a code of conduct for collaborative management processes?

The answers to the above questions are only likely be found as collaborative management agreements are further developed, meeting the specific conditions and needs of different protected areas and societies throughout the world.

REFERENCES

Adams, J and McShane, T (1992) *The Myth of Wild Africa*, Norton and Co, New York

Amend, S and Amend, T (1995) *National Parks Without People?*, IUCN, Quito

Franks, P (1995) *What role for communities in protected area management in Uganda*, CARE Uganda

Ghimire, K and Pimbert, M (eds) (1996) *Social Change and Conservation*, UNRISD, Geneva

Lynch, O J and Talbott, K (1995) *Balancing Acts: Community-based Forest Management and National Law in Asia and the Pacific*, World Resources Institute, Washington DC

Metcalfe, S (1994) 'The Zimbabwe Communal Areas Management Programme for Indigenous Resources (CAMPFIRE)', in Western, D and Wright, R M (eds), *Natural Connections*, Island Press, Washington DC

Renard, Y (1996) *Pers comm*

West, P C and Brechin, S R (eds) (1991) *Resident Peoples and National Parks*, University of Arizona Press, Tucson

25 A NETWORK OF SMALL COMMUNITY-OWNED VILLAGE FISH RESERVES IN SAMOA*

Michael King and Ueta Fa'asili

INTRODUCTION

Under a community-based fisheries extension programme in Samoa, 44 coastal villages have developed their own village fisheries management plans. Each plan sets out the resource management and conservation undertakings of the community, and the servicing and technical support required from the government fisheries division. Community undertakings range from enforcing laws banning destructive fishing methods to protecting critical habitats such as mangrove areas. An unexpectedly large number of villages (38) chose to establish small village fish reserves in part of their traditional fishing areas. Although by social necessity many of the community-owned reserves are small, their large number, often with small separating distances, forms a network of fish refuges. Such a network may maximize linking of larval sources and suitable settlement areas and provide the means by which adjacent fishing areas are eventually replenished with marine species through reproduction and migration. As the fish reserves are managed by communities which have a direct interest in their continuation and success, prospects for continuing compliance and commitment appear high. Results confirm our belief that the responsible management of marine resources will be achieved only when fishing communities themselves accept it as their responsibility.

* The authors wish to thank AusAID (the Australian Agency for International Development) for its support for a project which resulted in community-owned fish reserves in Samoa. They also received valuable contributions from Neil O'Sullivan, Marc Wilson, Siamupini Iosefa, Etuati Ropeti, Apulu Fonoti, Nichole Horsman, Peter Matthew, Lyn Lambeth and a team of enthusiastic young extension staff members, all of whom had considerable input into the success of the fisheries extension programme. They are grateful to Cheri Recchia and Graeme Kelleher for comments on the manuscript. This article was first published in *PARKS*, 8(2) June 1998, and is reproduced with permission.

DECLINING STOCKS

In many countries in the tropics, inshore catches of fish and shellfish are in decline. In the Pacific Island of Samoa, catches of seafood from lagoons and inshore reefs have been decreasing for over ten years (Horsman and Mulipola, 1995). Reasons for this decline include overexploitation, the use of destructive fishing methods (including explosives, chemicals and traditional plant-derived poisons) and environmental disturbances.

Despite concerns over declining fish stocks, government actions and national laws to protect fish stocks are rarely successful. This is due to many factors, including poor enforcement regimes and particularly the lack of community involvement. Fishing communities are often repositories of valuable traditional knowledge concerning fish stocks, and have a high level of awareness of the marine environment (Johannes, 1982). In addition, many subsistence fishers in tropical regions live in discrete communities that have some degree of control, either legal or traditional, of adjacent waters. Together, these factors provide an ideal basis on which communities can be encouraged and motivated to manage their own marine resources.

THE EXTENSION PROJECT

The community-based fisheries extension project began in 1995. After staff training, a culturally acceptable extension process was developed which recognized the village *fono* (council) as the prime instigator of change, while still allowing ample opportunities for the wider community to participate (see Figure 25.1; see also King and Faasili, in press). Full field operations began in 1996.

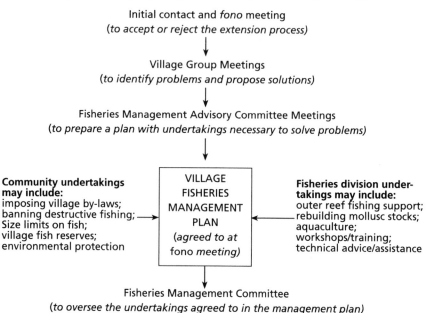

Figure 25.1 *The community-based fisheries extension project in Samoan villages*

Following an indication of interest, a village *fono* meeting was arranged to provide the community with information to allow either acceptance or refusal of the extension programme. If the *fono* accepted, it was then asked to arrange for meetings of several village groups, including women and untitled men (*aumaga*).

Over a series of meetings, each group held separate meetings to discuss their marine environment and fish stocks, decide on key problems, determine causes, propose solutions, and plan remedial actions. Problem and solution trees were recorded on a portable whiteboard by a trained facilitator. Finally, a village fisheries management advisory committee was formed, with three people nominated from each group, to prepare a draft village fisheries management plan (assisted by extension officers) for discussion and approval by the village *fono*. One third of all village group meetings were for women only, and approximately one third of members of the management committees were women. The proportions for untitled village men were similar.

Each village fisheries management plan listed the resource management and conservation undertakings of the community, and the servicing and technical support required from the fisheries division. If the plan was accepted, the *fono* then appointed a fisheries management committee to oversee the working of the plan.

RESULTS OF THE EXTENSION PROJECT

Within almost two years of full operation, fisheries extension staff attempted to introduce the extension programme in 65 villages. The extension process was rejected by nine villages and discontinued in a further four villages when extension staff noted a lack of community commitment (King and Faasili, in press). Forty-four of the remaining villages have produced village fisheries management plans so far. The time taken from initial contact to approval of the plan by each village community averaged 13.4 weeks.

In their plans, communities included undertakings to support and enforce government laws banning the use of chemicals and explosives to kill fish. Traditional destructive fishing methods such as the use of plant-derived fish poisons (*ava niukini*) and the smashing of coral to catch sheltering fish (*fa'amo'a* and *tuiga*) were also banned. Most villages made their own rules to enforce national laws banning the capture of fish less than a minimum size, and some set their own (larger) minimum size limits. Some villages placed controls on the use of nets and the use of underwater torches for spearfishing at night. Community conservation measures included collecting crown-of-thorns starfish, *Acanthaster planci* (L) and banning the removal of beach sand and dumping of rubbish in lagoon waters. An unexpectedly large number of villages (38) chose to establish their own small village fish reserves, closed to all fishing, in part of their traditional fishing area. The size of reserves ranged from 5000 to 175,000 metres^2 (see Figure 25.2).

Fisheries division actions to support community undertakings included the provision of assistance with the farming of tilapia, *Oreochromis niloticus*, in freshwater (in 16 per cent of villages), in facilitating the purchase of medium-sized boats to allow community members to fish outside the lagoons

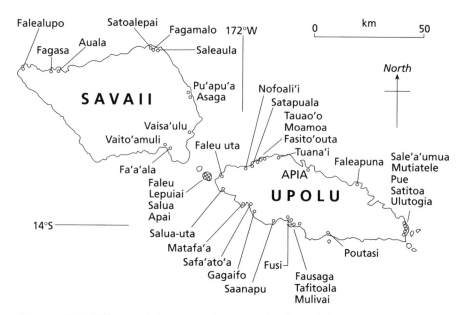

Figure 25.2 *Villages with community-owned village fish reserves in Samoa*

(39 per cent), and the restocking of giant clams, *Tridacna derasa*, in village fish reserves (82 per cent).

Giant clams have been heavily depleted in Samoa and ongoing attempts to breed from native species (*Tridacna squamosa* and *T maxima*) have been hampered by the difficulty of finding sufficient numbers of large animals in the wild. Large numbers of a related species (*T derasa*) were imported from American Samoa to fill the vacant ecological niche (for a photosynthesizing filter-feeder). After a quarantine period, these were placed in village reserves to be monitored and cared for by communities. These translocations were regarded as low risk, involving hatchery-raised clams from an adjacent island, which is geographically, if not politically, the same country.

A quantitative assessment of villages with fisheries management plans in place for over six months revealed that all but eight were still actively pursuing undertakings and enforcing conservation rules included in their plans. Villages received low scores for various reasons, including holding few village fisheries management committee meetings, not enforcing village rules, failing to care for restocked clams and poorly maintaining their reserve signs and markers.

DISCUSSION

Community-owned fish reserves may be discussed in terms of expected benefits to both villages and government. The community expectation is that, by banning fishing in part of its traditional fishing area, fish catches in adjacent areas will eventually improve. Although government authorities may share this expectation, there are additional public benefits relating to management, compliance, and sustainability and conservation of biodiversity.

As the Samoan village fish reserves are being managed by communities with a direct interest in their success, compliance with bans on fishing is high and there are not the enforcement costs associated with national reserves. Most villages with reserves have actively enforced their own rules and applied often severe penalties, including traditional fines of pigs or canned goods for infringements. Some villages have made their village rules into fisheries by-laws in order that these can be applied to people from other villages (Faasili, 1997). Community enthusiasm and commitment suggests that the prospects for continuity of the reserves are high.

The fisheries management benefits of marine protected areas are usually stated in terms of providing refuges in which invertebrate and fish stocks can grow and reproduce without interference. There is evidence that fish biomass increases rapidly for some species in areas where fishing is excluded (see Roberts, 1995), and some evidence that this increase will result in higher catches in adjacent fishing areas (Roberts and Polunin, 1991; Alcala and Russ, 1990). Fish larvae, previously thought of as passive drifters, may be able to detect the presence of, and swim towards, reefs several kilometres away (Wolanski et al, 1997). This suggests that refuge-derived larvae may actively move to, and repopulate, nearby reefs. Alternatively, if larvae settle in the same area in which they were spawned, juvenile or adult fish may eventually move out of refuges in response to increased crowding and competition. Tagging studies in South Africa suggest that excess stocks of fish in reserves move to adjacent exploited areas (Attwood and Bennett, 1994).

Ideally, a reserve should be located in such a position, and be of sufficient size, to encourage a significant increase in the numbers of sedentary species (including corals) and fish stocks, thus also contributing to conserving biodiversity. However, in the case of village ownership, there are often constraints on both position and size.

In Samoa, when a village had proposed a reserve in an unsuitable position (for example, an area of bare sand or coral rubble), additional scientific information was provided to encourage the community to select a more appropriate site. Some villages initially elected to have very large reserves and a few wanted to ban fishing in their entire lagoon area. In such cases, extension staff were obliged to curb overenthusiasm and ask the community to balance the perceived fish production advantages of a large reserve against the sociological disadvantages of banning fishing in a large proportion of the village's fishing area. In the latter case, although young men would still be able to go fishing beyond the reef, women (who traditionally collect echinoderms and molluscs in subtidal areas) and the elderly would be particularly disadvantaged in losing access to shallow-water fishing areas. A large reserve may also force people to fish in the waters of neighbouring villages, thereby increasing the potential for intervillage conflict.

In terms of total fisheries production (and conservation of biodiversity), a small reserve is unlikely to be as effective as a large one. Larger reserves are more likely to provide suitable breeding areas for small inshore pelagic fish, such as mullets and scads, but studies in South Africa (Buxton, 1996) suggest that even small reserves are beneficial for non-migratory species. Indeed, it could be argued that, for non-migratory species, the combined larval production from many small reserves is likely to be greater than that from a smaller number of large ones. However, as the interconnections between larval sources and settlement areas are poorly understood, this remains an hypothesis which is not easy to test.

There is currently a proposal to subsume several existing small single-village village fish reserves within two larger marine protected areas (MPAs) which would be managed by districts rather than single villages (Kelleher, pers comm, 1998). If these larger MPAs contain some no-fishing areas, as is proposed, it is possible that two large reserves connected via a broken chain of smaller village fish reserves may confer the dual benefits of linking larval sources with settlement areas and providing larger breeding areas for inshore migratory species.

In addition to the availability of people-motivating skills, the success or otherwise of community-based fisheries management depends on the availability of professional technical support for the communities involved. Scientific input is required to assist communities with alternative sources of seafood and to advise on and monitor community actions.

Whether community-based or not, most fisheries conservation measures, including the prevention of destructive fishing and the imposition of fish size limits, will cause a short-term decrease in catches. The same is so for village fish reserves because they reduce the area available for fishing. As most subsistence fishers require seafood for their families on a daily basis, it is unreasonable to expect fishing communities to adopt conservation measures which will initially reduce present catches of seafood even further without offering alternatives. Accordingly, the Samoan extension programme included the promotion and development of alternative sources of seafood to those resulting from the present heavy and destructive exploitation of near-shore reefs and lagoons. These alternatives included the introduction of medium-sized, low-cost boats (to divert fishing pressure to areas immediately beyond the reefs), the promotion of village-level aquaculture, and the restocking of depleted species of molluscs in village areas. It is doubtful that community-based fisheries management would continue on a sustainable basis without such ongoing support.

Scientific input is also required to advise on, and monitor, the effects of village actions. For the community-owned village fish reserves, this included providing advice on the placement of reserves, monitoring biological changes within the reserves, and collecting data on fish catches in adjacent areas. An additional benefit of fisheries staff working closely with communities is that the collection of scientific data on subsistence fisheries is greatly facilitated by community involvement. A large amount of information, and even estimates of sustainable yield by area, may be gained from such extensive surveys on subsistence fisheries. Where data are collected from different areas with similar ecological characteristics, it may be possible to apply a surplus yield model (over area rather than time) to estimate not only the average sustainable catch, but also to highlight villages where resources are presently under pressure (King, 1995).

CONCLUSIONS

The Samoan model appears applicable to other countries in which fishing communities have either traditional, defacto or legal control over their adjacent waters. In countries where this is not the case, it may be necessary to grant such rights (territorial use rights in fisheries, or TURFs) as proposed in The Philippines (Agbayani and Siar, 1994) to facilitate community management and the establishment of village fish reserves. Indeed, results in Samoa have confirmed our belief that, regardless of legislation or enforcement, the responsible management of marine resources will be achieved only when fishing communities themselves see it as their responsibility. If community actions include the declaration of even small fish reserves, this is likely to contribute to fisheries and biodiversity conservation.

Finally, it should be noted that the small community-owned village fish reserves in Samoa are not easy to classify under existing IUCN categories for MPAs. Category IV (habitat/species management area) appears to provide the best fit, although the category guidelines refer to national rather than community ownership. Given the increasing trend towards community-based management, the popularity of reserves as a fisheries conservation tool, and the necessarily small size of village MPAs, there may be a need for another IUCN category for 'networks of small, highly protected, community-owned MPAs'.

REFERENCES

Agbayani, R F, and Siar, S V (1994) 'Problems encountered in the implementation of a community-based fishery resource management project', in Pomeroy, R S (ed) *Community management and common property of coastal fisheries in Asia and the Pacific: concepts, methods and experiences*, ICLARM Conference Proceedings 45, 149–160

Alcala, A C, and Russ, G R (1990) 'A direct test of the effects of protective management on abundance and yield of tropical marine resources', *Journal du Conseil International pour l'Exploration de la Mer* 46, 40–47

Attwood, C A, and Bennett, B A (1994) 'Variation in dispersal of galjjoen (Coracinus capensis) (Teleostei: Coracinidae) from a marine reserve', *Canadian Journal of Fisheries and Aquatic Sciences* 51, 1247–1257

Buxton, C (1996) 'The role of Marine Protected Areas in the management of reef fish: a South African example', in *Developing Australia's Representative System of Marine Protected Areas*, Ocean Rescue 2000 Workshop Series, 114–124

Fa'asili, U (1997) *The use of village by-laws in marine conservation and fisheries management*, Pacific Science Association Intercongress, July, Fiji

Horsman, N, and Mulipola, A (1995) *Catch data and collection from market surveys in Western Samoa. South Pacific Commission and Forum Fisheries Agency Workshop on the management of South Pacific Inshore Fisheries*, Integrated Coastal Fisheries Management Project Technical Document, South Pacific Commission, New Caledonia

Johannes, R E (1982) 'Traditional conservation methods and protected marine areas in Oceania', *Ambio* 11(5): 258–261

Kelleher, G (1998) *pers comm*, Vice Chair, Marine, IUCN – the World Conservation Union

King, M (1995) *Fisheries biology, assessment, and management*, Fishing News
    Books/Blackwell Scientific Books, Oxford
King, M, and Fa'asili, U (in press) 'Community-based management of subsistence
    fisheries in tropical regions', *Fisheries Ecology and Management*
Roberts, C M (1995) 'Rapid build-up of fish biomass in a Caribbean marine reserve',
    Conservation Biology 91(4): 815–826
Roberts, C M, and Polunin, N V C (1991) 'Are marine reserves effective in management
    of reef fisheries?', *Reviews in Fish Biology and Fisheries*, 1, 65–91
Wolanski, E, Doherty, P, and Carleton, J (1997) 'Directional swimming of fish larvae
    determines connectivity of fish populations on the Great Barrier Reef',
    Naturwissenschaften, 84, 262–268

26 THE CENTRAL AFRICAN EXPERIENCE IN TRANSFRONTIER PROTECTED AREAS

*Steve Gartlan**

INTRODUCTION

The following chapter discusses the case of transboundary protected areas, with particular reference to their possible role in resolving local and regional conflicts and in improving relationships between countries. A very high proportion of protected areas in Africa abut or adjoin national boundaries, and regional, transnational and internal civil conflicts seem endemic in much of sub-Saharan Africa. The causes are various; interethnic rivalry, disputes over resources, and the existence of artificial national boundaries inherited from the colonial era but vigorously defended by present nation states. It should be noted in passing that the existence of conflict per se is not necessarily incompatible with habitat conservation. There is much evidence to show (Richards, 1966) that large areas of West African forests have retained their ecological integrity because of the existence of disputes in which neither side was able to achieve hegemony over the resource base. There is no doubt, however, that for rational management of transboundary protected areas, a non-conflict context is desirable. However, in much of sub-Saharan Africa the impediments to this are considerable. This case study raises some of these issues and attempts to establish some criteria that should be in place before such transboundary management is attempted.

The Republic of Cameroon covers almost 475,000 square kilometres. It is located in Central Africa and is exceptionally diverse biologically, partly because of the existence of Pleistocene refugia and partly because of an exceptionally varied landscape, including the highest mountain in West Africa (and only active volcano), Mount Cameroon, which exceeds 4000 metres in height. Cameroon has a human population of about 15 million and a growth rate of some 3 per cent. The human population density of the country is very unevenly distributed; some agricultural areas (near Waza National Park, for example) have populations exceeding 100 persons per square kilometre. In contrast in

* The views expressed here are those of the author and not necessarily of WWF.

much of the south-east, the human population density is below one person per square kilometre.

Cameroon provides a valuable case study because of experiences gained during the creation of a protected area system, and also because of actual armed conflict in the immediate vicinity of a transboundary protected area. In the south-east of the country three new protected areas are in the process of creation: Boumba-Bek – 249,920 hectares; Nki – 181,568 hectares; and Lake Lobeke – 206,528 hectares. The proposed protected area of Lake Lobeke has a common boundary of circa 27 kilometres with the Dzangha-Sangha dense forest reserve of the Central African Republic, and (depending on the ultimate size and limits of the Lac Lobeke Reserve) a similar boundary with the Nouabale-Ndoki National Park of the Congo. In addition, the Korup National Park (125,900 hectares) lies against the south-western boundary of Cameroon with Nigeria, and opposite the Cross River National Park, and shares a joint boundary of some 14 kilometres with it. Two other Cameroon savanna national parks lie very close to international boundaries: Faro (less than eight kilometres from the Nigerian border) and Waza (less than five kilometres). Furthermore, two other parks have boundaries with Tchad; Boubanjidah has a 34-kilometre boundary with the Tchad Republic, and Kalamaloue lies on the western bank of the Chari River, separating Cameroon and Tchad, with Tchad on the eastern bank.

Cameroon is bordered to the west by Nigeria, a country with twice the land area and a human population of over 100 million. Relations between Cameroon and Nigeria are tense, partly because of the continued impasse over the Bakassi Peninsula where Cameroonian and Nigerian troops are engaged in a protracted and ongoing armed conflict. The Bakassi Peninsula lies less than 40 kilometres south of the southern boundary of Korup National Park. To the east, Cameroon is bordered by Chad, the Central African Republic (CAR) and Congo. All these are Francophone countries and all are members of the same customs and economic union (UDEAC) and share a common currency, the CFA Franc. These countries have relatively low human populations and relations between them and Cameroon have been generally friendly over the past few years. However, civil disturbance in neighbouring countries over the last decade has had consequences in Cameroon with influxes of refugees. Also, as in all civil conflicts, firearms become readily available and are then used in poaching wildlife. The north-east sector of the Boubanjidah National Park in Cameroon has for several years been occupied by armed Tchandian factions, with significant negative effects on the wildlife of the park. The continued civil unrest in the Central African Republic (mainly confined to the capital, Bangui) has had little discernible effect on Cameroon. To the south, Cameroon is bordered by Equatorial Guinea, Gabon and Congo. These are all members of the CFA Franc zone and are Francophone apart from Equatorial Guinea, where Spanish is the official language. Relations with these countries are generally good, apart from occasional problems with Gabon. The countries bordering Cameroon to the east and south are ethnically similar, with people of similar tribal affinities both sides of the border. However, in the case of Nigeria there is a clear ethnic difference with the Nigerian/Cameroonian border essentially dividing Bantu and semi-Bantu ethnic affiliations; furthermore, there is also a clear linguistic and cultural divide.

THE PRE-CONFLICT SITUATION

The Korup National Park was created by presidential decree on 30 October 1986. Much of the land had previously been occupied by the Korup Forest Reserve, which was established by the British colonial administration in the early 1930s. The process of negotiation and gazettement was a lengthy one. However, it was evident from the outset that the former president of the Republic, Ahmadou Ahidjo, was taking a keen personal interest. No questions were asked about the security aspects of a national park on the boundary with Nigeria. The president's concerns were institutional, and his approval was finally given in principle for the park to be created as long as the then Federal University was involved, and that it was used for field studies.

The judicial process for setting up a protected area is set out clearly in the legislation. Official notice must be posted on the doors of local government premises, and public meetings must be held. At this early stage, private opposition to the idea of creating a protected area in the Korup region was frequently expressed by officials of the security forces and by special branch agents who attended public meetings and who reported back through the hierarchy to the minister in charge of security. The security forces did not wish to see the creation of a people-free area, which they saw as a vacuum, right against the boundary with their populous neighbour, Nigeria. Part of the reason for slowness in the process of the gazettement was opposition from the security services. Things came to a head in 1986 when the British Overseas Development Administration (ODA) offered funding as long as the park was officially gazetted. With the active assistance of influential people from the area who were close to the centre of government, and after apparently detailed scrutiny of the texts by the new president, Paul Biya, the park was created in the same year.

The prime mover in creating the Korup National Park was WWF-UK through its partnership with the ODA. Both WWF-UK and ODA had significant interests in Nigeria, and after the successful gazettement of Korup in Cameroon, moves soon began to create a similar project Nigeria. By June 1988, WWF had finished its preliminary survey of the Oban Group Forest Reserve in Cross River State of Nigeria and concluded that setting up a national park there, adjacent to Korup, would be both desirable and feasible. The initiative stemmed partly from a wish to increase the size of the conservation unit in an area of high biodiversity, partly to access European Community (EC) funds available for transfrontier projects, and partly because of an affinity for Nigeria on the part of a key individual within WWF-UK. Funding was located and the Cross River National Park was established in 1991 by Federal Decree 36. It should be emphasized that while there were extensive interactions with the governments of both Cameroon and Nigeria during the period prior to the gazettement, there was no attempt to promote the idea of a transnational park to either government. Although within WWF there was a feeling that this was an important step, this was largely because it had secured a large block of forest for conservation purposes. The projects had different managers, and although there were occasional meetings between Nigerian and Cameroonian project staff, they operated and continue to operate as independent, separate projects.

The situation regarding the proposed trinational parks of Cameroon, the Central African Republic (CAR) and Congo was rather different. During the early and mid 1980s, field studies were carried out in the region and the biological value began to become apparent. A proposal for creating the trinational protected area in the CAR, Cameroon and Congo was drawn up by WWF-US and the New York Zoological Society and submitted to US-AID in 1991. Funding failed to materialize, but extensive contacts were made with the various governments. In CAR and Congo the idea of a trinational park was welcomed and steps begun towards gazettement of the areas. In Cameroon, however, the situation was different. There was opposition from the outset to the idea of a trinational park. The opposition stemmed from the fact that the process was seen to be flawed. To begin to create a trinational area would have required, so it was thought, extensive international lobbying and agreements. It was thought more practical to start with the gazettement of the individual units within the respective countries and then, at a later stage, to discuss joint management strategies and collaboration. Because of this opposition, the movement towards creating the protected areas was much slower in Cameroon. Both Dzanga-Sangha and Nouabale-Ndoki have been officially gazetted – the former in 1990 and the latter in 1994. Lake Lobeke and the other proposed protected areas still have to be officially gazetted.

It is useful here to examine the demographic context. Nigeria, the most populous nation in Africa with a population of over 100 million, is also one of the most densely populated, particularly along the coast and in the south-east of the country. The town of Calabar is an ancient and major trading post and was an important embarkation point for the slave trade. The adjacent area of Cameroon, in contrast, is remote (there was at the time no road connecting it to the rest of Cameroon) and with a very low human population density. The Nigerians are also great traders. All along the western border of Nigeria, there is a network of paths where traders head-load all manner of goods: illicit gin, bushmeat, dried fish, medicines, gasoline, radios, television sets and, recently, illegal drugs. The villages on the border have a strong strategic position and smuggling is a lucrative way of life. While the people in the west of the park have strong ethnic ties with Nigeria (Korup people), the people in the east of the park have little (Bantu/semi-Bantu divide). The Cameroon side of the border is remote, with low human population density, and people make their money principally by trapping and farming. In Nigeria, the area is accessible, has high human population density and people make their money by trading; furthermore, the ethnic affinities are not close.

DURING CONFLICT

The Bakassi Peninsula lies some 40 kilometres south of the Korup National Park. During Christmas 1995, after a series of incidents involving Cameroonian gendarmes and Nigerian military, the Nigerian army invaded what had been, until that point, part of Cameroon. They are still there almost three years later and there are frequent skirmishes. The noise of shell-fire is clearly audible from Mundemba, the headquarters of the Korup National Park. When a military emergency was declared, the whole area of the Ndian division was affected by military actions. The military decided that the construction of a road to the village of Ikassa from Mundemba was important, and construction began without reference to the Cameroon Ministry of the Environment and Forests (MINEF), which has jurisdiction over the national park. Only when the Korup project brought this to the attention of MINEF were they aware of what was going on. This road cuts through the southern portion of the national park and isolates some nine square kilometres from the rest of the park. The military presence has resulted in an increase in hunting within the protected area. Park activities are also inhibited because of military rules that are in place. This case has been forwarded to the International Court of Justice in the Hague for jurisdiction; but, in the meantime, hostilities continue.

POST-CONFLICT PERIOD

There is little data on the post-conflict period. The Bakassi conflict continues. A major effect of armed conflict in the region is the persistence of firearms afterwards. The Korup National Park is close to the Ibo heartland of south-east Nigeria that comprised the break-away Republic of Biafra in 1965. Biafra has come and gone, but guns from this civil conflict were still being used for poaching in Korup almost 25 years later.

LESSONS TO BE LEARNED

The function of promoting peace by creating transfrontier protected areas is essentially an institutional one to be negotiated and agreed upon between the highest levels of government. This emergent function is *additional* to the functions of conservation and habitat protection and the interface will be at government rather than at grassroots level. It is therefore necessary that the institutional conservation measures (gazettement, management plans, staff and infrastructure, effective budgets) are in place on both sides of the border. The first priority is to ensure that there are efficiently managed protected areas both sides of the border; the emergent functions can be negotiated and implemented at a later stage.

Military and strategic considerations play an important role in determining the viability or otherwise of transborder protected areas. In many sub-Saharan African countries the military voice is exceptionally powerful and defense considerations outweigh other priorities. If national security is threatened, there is little doubt that, international agreements notwithstanding, the protected areas will be invaded if the military believes that access is necessary. Similarly, the military view is often opposed to creating no-go protected areas against national boundaries since these are seen as an invitation to invasion.

There should be homogeneity on both sides of the border. It is important that economic conditions on both sides are roughly similar (if there is economic imbalance, there will be infiltration from low to high). It is important that population pressures on both sides are roughly similar. If population pressure on one side of the border is high and on the other is low, there will be infiltration from high to low. Cameroon (13 million) feels very threatened by the size of Nigeria (100 million). Similarly, there should be comparability of way of life between the two sides. If one side of the border has producers (farmers, trappers) and the other has traders, the traders will invade and will become involved in commerce in the producing side. There should be ethnic and cultural homogeneity. French-speaking Cameroon distrusts English-speaking Nigeria; the semi-Bantus distrust the Bantus.

The protected areas must also provide approximately equal economic benefits to local populations on both sides of the border. Each individual unit of a transboundary protected area should meet the criteria for protected status without taking the other unit into account. Both units should have a similar conservation status (an ecologically rich zone adjacent to an ecologically impoverished zone should be avoided). Both units should have appropriate and approximately similar levels of institutional development (legal status, management plans, staff and infrastructure, budgets). Laws, regulations, charges and fines should be consistent on both sides of the border.

Lastly, transnational protected areas should not be created in regions where land-use conflicts are likely to develop (such as demographic trends or the presence of reserves of oil, gold or diamonds).

REFERENCES

Brandon, K E and Wells, M (1992) 'Planning for People and Parks: Design dilemmas', *World Development* 20(4): 557–570

Caldecott, J (1991) *The Cross River National Park Project, Nigeria: Operational Experience During the Start-up Phase*, Internal WWF Report

Carroll, R W and Weber, W (1991) *An integrated plan for regional forest conservation and management in Southeastern Cameroon, Southwestern Central African Republic and Northern Congo*, Proposal submitted to US-AID, Washington, DC

Harrison, M and Agland, P (1987) *Southeast Cameroon: A Proposal for Three New Rainforest Reserves*, Report for Secretary of State for Tourism, Yaoundé, Cameroon

Richards, P (1966) 'Forest indigenous peoples: concept, critique and cases', *Proceedings of the Royal Society of Edinburgh* 104B, 349–365

27 MEASURING THE EFFECTIVENESS OF PROTECTED AREAS MANAGEMENT

Nigel Dudley, Marc Hockings and Sue Stolton

INTRODUCTION: THE PROBLEM

Putting time and effort into selecting and designing protected areas only makes sense if there is a reasonable chance that the areas can be secured for the foreseeable future – indeed, this underpins the entire philosophy of protected area management. Unfortunately, this is often not the case today. Around the world, there is a growing recognition that many protected areas are being degraded and destroyed. A fair proportion of the national parks, wilderness areas and nature reserves that appear in global surveys of protected areas exist in name only – the so-called *paper-parks* phenomenon – and there has never been any real attempt to manage them for conservation. In these circumstances, degradation comes in many forms, including poaching (of wildlife, fish, timber and other resources), illegal mining, encroachment by settlers, overuse by tourists, and the development of infrastructure such as roads and dams. Sometimes local opposition to protected areas contributes to their loss. Even when protected areas are being actively managed, significant degradation may occur, especially when visitor pressure is high.

Threats to protected areas occur all over the world, although they are apparently most acute in the tropical countries of Asia, Africa and Latin America. For example, recent research by WWF and IUCN has found evidence of illegal logging in over 50 countries, much of which targets protected areas because they are relatively 'soft' targets for poachers (Dudley, in press). A report published by IUCN and WWF also identifies threats to protected areas from metal mining (Finger, 1999). Kelleher et al (1995), in a review of MPAs carried out by IUCN, the World Bank and the Great Barrier Reef Marine Park Authority, concluded that fewer than 50 per cent of marine protected areas are effectively managed.

Assessing Management Effectiveness

This book is concerned with how such losses can be avoided. However, one important element in addressing the problem of paper parks is identifying where there is a problem in the first place. But this is not as easy as it appears at first sight. Although gross damage to protected areas is usually fairly obvious, by the time such problems are noticed it is often too late to do much about it. There is, therefore, growing interest in finding ways to measure the *effectiveness of management* in protected areas. These could act both as an early warning system for problems and also to put managers and owners of protected areas under the spotlight, encouraging them to improve implementation of their own protected area strategies. An assessment of effectiveness of protected area management could be used to identify the *gaps* in a protected area network, to identify protected areas at *risk*, to *prioritize* conservation effort and funding, to improve management through *advocacy* and to put *pressure* on institutions that are degrading protected areas. Additionally, information on the effectiveness of efforts is essential for managers who want to take an adaptive approach to their work, where they strive to learn from their own and others' past successes and mistakes.

One option is to measure the effectiveness of management in a protected areas system through some kind of national evaluation framework. An alternative or additional system could be an international system, under the auspices of an existing vehicle such as the Convention on Biological Diversity, the World Commission on Protected Areas (WCPA) or the World Heritage Convention. Another possibility is to act through a new body that could set criteria and indicators for national or regional assessment systems. These options and progress to date are discussed below.

Measuring Effectiveness of Management in Protected Areas

Accountability of performance is increasingly being demanded across all sectors of society, and conservation management is no exception. Traditionally, concerns for accountability focused on issues of financial and managerial probity, but this has now expanded to include concerns for management effectiveness. Accountability viewed in this light is not so much about 'checking up' on managers to see where they are failing, but about developing a professional approach to management.

At present, the IUCN categories are assigned according to the *objectives* of management, but conservation organizations are equally concerned with the *effectiveness* of this management. The need for some systematic approach to evaluating the effectiveness of protected area management has therefore long been recognized – with those wishing to have information on effectiveness ranging from senior management, government and funding agencies through to NGOs, local communities and the wider community, both nationally and internationally.

Any assessment system must be democratic and fully participatory at a local level. It could work with an existing institution or through its own dedicated organization. Assessment is needed at varying levels, including:

- projects with protected areas;
- individual protected areas;
- national protected area systems;
- international protected area systems; and
- local, national and international institutions responsible for protected areas.

Any system of assessing or verifying protected areas, or their systems, should include analysis of, at least: institutional capacity; biological effectiveness; social effectiveness (benefits obtained or social systems involved); financial sustainability; and legal status. Any assessment system should be sensitive to issues of national sovereignty and the rights of local and indigenous peoples, and is only likely to be effective if it has the support *and involvement* of local and indigenous peoples and local protected-area officials. Local knowledge and perceptions should be incorporated within the assessment systems. Assessment of a protected area can only be effective if it is accepted and welcomed by the organizations and individuals involved.

A number of different options are available, varying in both the level of detail and the extent to which local partners are involved in the assessment. Quick survey methods, relying mainly upon, for example, published information and GIS systems, can be used to assess whether biodiversity needs are being met and protected areas are really being safeguarded. Such schemes may be useful to international and national organizations to give an approximate picture of national or regional progress. Rapid ground survey methods could allow protected area managers, governments, funding agencies, aid organizations and local NGOs to carry out an assessment of protected areas from ecological, social and economic perspectives. Indepth, participatory methods can provide a detailed assessment of the environmental and social aspects of a protected area for use in management planning, targeting aid projects and assessing progress.

WCPA FRAMEWORK

A World Commission on Protected Areas task force has been investigating the evaluation of management effectiveness of protected areas. The group highlighted the two primary questions that arise concerning the effectiveness of protected areas in meeting conservation objectives. These relate to the adequacy of:

- the design of the protected area system (does the protected area network include adequate and appropriate areas of land or sea?); and
- the management of the system (are areas effectively managed?).

Management of protected areas can be monitored through a process of observation and can be evaluated by assessing achievement against some predetermined criteria. Performance monitoring is concerned with the routine collection of data by an organization to assess its management programmes and the achievement of associated goals and objectives. Programme evaluations are periodic or one-off exercises aimed as drawing conclusions about some aspects of the worth of a management programme or activity.

The WCPA working group proposed a framework for evaluation, which draws on elements from the various approaches to evaluating conservation management, and seeks to combine these elements to produce an integrated approach that can be flexibly applied to meet the needs of protected areas in different circumstances (Hocking, 1997). The framework aims to be strongly linked to the concerns and interests of managers so that it will provide a basis for management improvement while also providing for the accountability needs of other stakeholders.

The framework suggests the division of evaluation into five areas: design, input/process and output/outcome.

Design evaluation

Design evaluations assess the likely effectiveness of a project or programme based on an assessment of the details of the proposal for the project/programme. In the context of protected areas, an important element of assessing effectiveness is the question of the network's adequacy.

Input evaluation

Input evaluation seeks to answer the questions: are sufficient resources being devoted to managing the protected area/system; and how are resources being applied across the various areas of management? The key resources to be assessed are funds, staff, equipment and infrastructure.

Process evaluation

The assessment of management processes focuses on the way in which management of a protected area or system is conducted. The objective of process evaluation is to assess the standards of the management system and the processes and functions used in administering the area. This is a largely qualitative rather than quantitative process. The starting point for process evaluation is to establish standards for the conduct of management that can be used as a basis for assessing performance.

Output evaluation

One way of assessing management effectiveness is to look at the outputs derived from management activity. This type of evaluation is most useful where pre-existing plans, targets or standards have been established against which achievements can be measured. Two principal questions are involved: firstly, what products and services have been delivered and, secondly, have the managers carried out their planned work programme?

Outcome evaluation

Outcome indicators are important because they measure the real impacts of management action by assessing the extent to which management objectives are being achieved. As such they need to be based upon a clear understanding of what it is that managers want to accomplish. The process of establishing an outcome-based monitoring and evaluation programme is likely to highlight areas where objectives are unclear and/or lack specificity.

Since it is not possible to measure directly all the attributes that relate to protected area management (either the condition of the environment itself or aspects of management action), it is necessary to use a limited number of indicators that are representative or indicative of the system under consideration. For example, the management of large protected areas with multiple objectives, and usually with limited resources, means that monitoring efforts must be targeted at high priority areas, using a limited number of indicators in each case.

Because indicators are selected to reflect the achievement of management objectives, the extent to which a common set of indicators can be developed depends upon the level of commonality amongst objectives. One task to be undertaken in preparing guidelines on assessing management effectiveness is to develop a set of indicators that reflect protected area objectives which can be fine tuned to match the particular environmental, social and managerial characteristics of a protected area or system.

The framework suggested above could be applied at different scales from an individual protected area to an agency and even national scale. At an agency or national scale, the assessment of management effectiveness should focus on both the effectiveness with which sites within the system are being managed and also on agency or systemwide issues that affect the overall operation of the protected area network.

REGIONAL ASSESSMENTS

The WCPA proposals are a first attempt to provide an international framework for evaluating effectiveness. However, there are also other several similar systems devised by different organizations, some of which have already been field tested. Some examples are given below.

- *Assessment of protected areas:* WWF Central America, in association with the research centre CATIE, has devised and tested assessment guidelines for protected areas over the past eight years, including field tests in Costa Rica, Mexico and the Galapagos Islands (Valery). Researchers in Mexico have developed a protected area assessment system in connection with Mexico's national biodiversity strategy (Salicido, pers comm). IUCN has also collaborated on a project to look at management effectiveness in UNESCO biosphere reserves (Corbett, 1995).
- *Rapid assessment of management effectiveness:* WWF has produced a short study on rapid assessment methods for the WWF/World Bank Alliance, which is being used in assessing the effectiveness of the protected

area management in projects supported by the bank (Dudley, 1998).

- *A database of effectiveness:* the World Conservation Monitoring Centre (WCMC) is developing a monitoring system for use with its protected area data base.
- *Scorecard systems:* the Nature Conservancy, an NGO in the US with a large international conservation programme, has a scorecard system for testing management effectiveness in protected areas that it is using with its own projects (Brandon et al, 1998). WWF-Canada's Endangered Spaces Campaign has a system of annual support cards that assess government progress in completing the national system. WWF-Australia and other national and state environment groups have a similar annual report card which assesses the performance of government in five key areas. WWF-Brazil also has a scorecard system in operation.
- *Rating systems:* the WWF European Forest Team is developing criteria for rating the quality of protected areas in association with its Pan Parks project, which aims to link protected areas in different countries. Several IUCN offices use their own system of rating protected areas.
- *Criteria and guidelines:* private protected areas are increasingly establishing networks with agreed criteria for membership (see Chapter 19), and extractive reserves in Brazil have guidelines for their creation and legalization, from the government agency IBAMA, that are, in effect, a set of criteria for the reserve (Murrieta and Rueda, 1995).

VERIFICATION OF PROTECTED AREA MANAGEMENT[*]

A further mechanism for improving management effectiveness would be the development of a system to assess and verify management of protected areas both terrestrial and marine at the global level. This would require the development of a globally recognized system of international standards or range of standards (Dudley and Stolton, 1998). Individual governments or protected area agencies could be responsible for assessments; they would be carried out as part of an international system under an existing convention. Or a new body could be established to undertake evaluations. This issue is currently being addressed in international fora, and the CBD could provide one tool for taking it further.

RELATED CRITERIA AND INDICATOR GUIDELINES

In addition to systems being developed specifically for protected areas, several other guidelines, principles and criteria and certification systems have relevance to protected area management, particularly with respect to IUCN Categories IV to VI. While schemes such as these are not suitable for evaluating a protected area on their own, they suggest techniques which verification systems might draw upon for evaluating specific issues within or close to a protected area. Some examples are given here:

---

[*] In this chapter, the word *verification* is used to imply a system of assessment and/or certification without specifying the exact form that this will take. See Box 27.1.

- forest management: principles and criteria for sustainable forest management, such as those of the Forest Stewardship Council, including certification for non-timber forest products (Viana et al, 1996);
- sustainable agriculture: such as organic farming schemes which meet national standards under the auspices of the International Federation of Organic Agriculture Movements (IFOAM, 1996a);
- sustainable use of marine resources: including the Marine Stewardship Council and the Marine Aquarium Council;
- fair trade: such as the guidelines for coffee, tea, etc;
- mining: guidelines for mining in protected areas, currently drawn up by the World Commission on Protected Areas;
- social rights: a range of guidelines and charters relating to the treatment of people, including those of the International Labour Organization, UN Human Rights Commission and WWF principles for working with indigenous peoples in protected areas;
- tourism: guidelines for ecotourism developments – there are currently many national and regional examples of ecotourism guidelines; and
- climate change mitigation: various guidelines (apparently at least ten are under development) for application of joint implementation or clean development mechanism payments to forest management, under the Kyoto Protocol of the Framework Convention on Climate Change; whilst this could, in theory, benefit conservation in the future, this is not possible under current proposals. Some environmental NGOs also reject this option because, to some extent, it replaces reduction of pollutants at source.

There is, therefore, already considerable work in progress. However, many of these schemes are new, relatively untested and, crucially, have little incentive for them to be used. There is also the question of to what level the assessments are made. Methods that just measure biological integrity are perhaps the easiest to implement; but without some understanding of human interactions, opinions and problems, they can give little indication of likely developments in the future.

WOULD CERTIFICATION PROVIDE A USEFUL OPTION?

During discussions about the paper-parks problem, the question of certification has been raised several times by environmental NGOs who support other certification systems, such as those covering forests and agriculture. Development of independent certification of forest management has played a key role in the debate on forest conservation over the past few years. Under this system, forest owners or managers can agree to meet a set of management criteria that are supposed to ensure social and environmental guidelines and can require areas of the forest estate to be protected from commercial activity (see Chapter 20). All such certification schemes should meet the *principles and criteria* of the Forest Stewardship Council and should be inspected by accredited personnel. The wood products from certified forests gain market access and, sometimes, a price premium.

There is a growing, grassroots consensus amongst many environmental NGOs that some kind of official verification or certification system for protected areas is also needed. However, the parallels with forest management are not exact. Whereas a forest owner can expect to get some commercial return from the costs incurred in certification, governments may have little incentive to open their protected areas up for criticism. There have been considerable problems in promoting forest certification to forest companies and these could expect to be magnified in the case of protected areas. This is not to argue that such a system is impossible, but that considerable care and some ingenuity will be needed to introduce and promote such an option.

Indeed, it already seems clear that organizations are acting unilaterally to measure effectiveness in protected areas that they manage, own or fund. Non-governmental organizations are also beginning to do the same from the perspective of putting pressure on governments to improve systems of protected areas. Whether such schemes can eventually be combined into a global system, or whether a proliferation of assessment systems will eventually be in existence, is open to question.

CONCLUSIONS

At present, many protected areas are protected in name only. There seems to be little point in spending time expanding a protected area network without first addressing questions of implementation. Indeed, in some cases, there may be opportunity costs in expanding the size or number of protected areas because conservation resources will have to be spread more thinly, with a consequent decline in the intensity and quality of management. There may be cases where it is more important to *optimize* the location and size of components of the protected areas system rather than automatically trying to *maximize* the network.

Policy-makers charged with decisions about designating and managing protected areas need reliable information about their effectiveness. Local

---

BOX 27.1 SOME DEFINITIONS

Accreditation: 'a procedure by which an authoritative body gives a formal recognition that a body of person is competent to carry out specific tasks' (ISO, 1996; IFOAM, 1996b).

Assessment: 'the combination of monitoring, evaluation and diagnosis' (IUCN,1997).

Certification: 'procedure by which a third party gives written assurance that a product, process or service conforms to specified requirements' (ISO, 1996). In relation to forestry: 'a process which results in a written certification being produced by an independent third party attesting to the location and management structure of the forest in which the timber originated' (Elliott, 1997).

Evaluation: 'ascertain amount of; appraise; assess' (*The Concise Oxford English Dictionary*)

Inspection: 'conformity evaluation by observation and judgement, accompanied as appropriate by measurement, testing or gauging' (ISO, 1996).

Verification: 'establishment of the truth or correctness of, by examination or demonstration' (*The Concise Oxford English Dictionary*).

communities, NGOs and others with an interest in individual protected areas or systems also require this information if they are to contribute meaningfully in the management process.

In this chapter, the first moves in this direction have been outlined; further work is now needed. To provide background information relevant to assessment and verification, several studies are required: an assessment of the effectiveness of existing protected areas in terms of meeting stated objectives of biodiversity conservation, cultural heritage, etc; the further development of methodologies for assessment and verification; the identification of the most suitable institutional arrangements to carry out or coordinate assessment; and the development of case studies detailing current active evaluation projects. There are major opportunities for WWF, IUCN and the World Conservation Monitoring Centre to work together in further developing these ideas.

REFERENCES

Brandon, K, Redford, K H and Sanderson, S E (eds) (1998) *Parks in Peril: People, Politics and Protected Areas*, The Nature Conservancy, Island Press, Washington DC

Corbett, M R (1995) *An Evaluation of the Coverage and Management Effectiveness of Biosphere Reserves*, prepared for the International Conference on Biospehere Reserves, Sevilla, Spain, March 1995, IUCN, Gland

Dudley, N (in press) *The Illegal Timber Trade and Global Forest Conservation*, WWF and IUCN, Gland

Dudley, N (1998) *Rapid Assessment of Protected Area Status*, Draft proposals for the World Bank and WWF International, WWF, Gland

Elliott, C A (1997) *WWF Guide to Forest Certification 1997*, WWF International, Gland

Finger, A (1999) *Metals from the forests: Mining and forest degradation*, IUCN and WWF, Gland

Hockings, M (1997) *Evaluating Management Effectiveness: A Framework for Evaluating Management of Protected Areas*, Draft discussion paper, IUCN/WCPA

IFOAM (1996a) *Basic Standards for Organic Agriculture and Processing and Guidelines for Coffee, Cocoa and Tea; Evaluation of Inputs*, International Federation of Organic Agriculture Movements, Tholey-Theley, Germany

IFOAM (1996b) *Operating Manual: IFOAM Accreditation Programme*, Tholey-Theley, Germany

ISO (1996) *ISO/IEC Guide 2: 1996, Standardisation and Related Activities – General Vocabulary*, International Organisation for Standardisation, Geneva

IUCN (1997) 'Overview: Approach, Methods, Tools and Field Experience', in *An Approach to Assessing Progress Towards Sustainability: Tools and Training Series*, IUCN–IDRC International Assessment Team, Gland

Kelleher, G, Bleakley, C and Wells, S (eds) (1995) *A Global Representative System of Marine Protected Areas*, vols 1 to 4, the World Bank, IUCN and the Great Barrier Reef Marine Park Authority, IUCN, Gland

Murrieta, J R and Pinzón Rueda, R (1995) *Extractive Reserves*, IUCN Forest Conservation Programme, IUCN, Gland

Salcido, R P G (1998) *pers comm*

Valery, A I (undated) *Manual para la medición de la Eficiencia de Manejo de un Sistema de Areas Protegidas y sus Zonas de Influencia, aplicado a una Area de Conservación en Costa Rica*, WWF and CATIE, Costa Rica

Viana, V M, Ervin, J, Donovan, R Z, Elliott, C and Gholz, H (1996) *Certification of Forest Products: Issues and Perspectives*, Island Press, Washington DC

28 CONCLUSIONS

*Nigel Dudley, Biksham Gujja, Bill Jackson,
Jean-Paul Jeanrenaud, Gonzalo Oviedo, Adrian
Phillips, Pedro Rosabel, Sue Stolton and Sue Wells*

INTRODUCTION

The preceding chapters have highlighted a range of new directions and opportunities in protected area management and planning. They show a world in
which protected areas are becoming more diverse, more flexible and increasingly being recognized as an essential element in the wider landscape or
seascape. The most important of these changing attitudes are summarized
below. However, although much has changed in the last few years, many
challenges remain. This section therefore ends with some unresolved questions
which everyone involved in protected areas – from organizations promoting
protection to managers on the ground – should be trying to address.

EMERGING STRATEGIC DIRECTIONS IN PROTECTED AREA
PLANNING AND MANAGEMENT

There has been a broadening of perspectives with regard to protected areas
planning and management over the last 20 years. Some key indicators of what
may accurately be discussed as a paradigm shift include the following:

- *A change in emphasis from government to civil society, with protected
  area planning and management moving from centralized to decentralized models:* this has resulted in an increasing number of innovative
  approaches to protected area management. Many of these are more
  responsive to people's own initiatives for caring for their lands and involve
  a wider range of partners than was the case in the past, including NGOs,
  local communities and indigenous people, the private sector, religious
  institutions and local government.
- *Recognition of the importance of the connections between protected
  areas:* as a result, protected area planning systems are moving away from

a site-based approach to a *bioregional* level – from protected areas as islands to protected area networks which are integrated with other land uses. Individual protected areas are also expanding beyond country boundaries, with *transnational* protected areas being agreed jointly by two or more neighbouring countries.

- *An increase in the range of values that protected areas are expected to fulfil:* this is most apparent in the adoption of a wider range of protected area models (as represented by the IUCN categories) and the new directions for protected area management that this encourages. Along with biodiversity, many protected areas are now also expected to fulfil environmental, social and cultural needs.

- *A growth in availability of expertise and methodologies to improve selection and management:* a range of different science-based selection methods for protected areas is emerging that allow the development of a more efficient and logical protected area network.

- *Development of a more dynamic approach to protected area planning:* protected areas need to be resilient enough to take account of rapidly changing conditions, brought about by, for example, climate change and rapid social and political upheavals.

- *Greater emphasis on bottom-up approaches:* a new phenomenon is emerging, where local communities are creating their own protected areas, often in cooperation with NGOs or governments. Such protected areas are usually part of a broader approach to protection, which includes sustainable use.

- *The emergence of social science as an important contributor to protected area planning and management:* it is clear that more than just knowledge of ecology is needed to create an effective protected area. Anthropologists, social scientists, managers, educationalists and other disciplines all have a part to play.

- *A changing role for protected area managers, with the emphasis shifting from direction to facilitation:* professionals are now increasingly encouraged to be more holistic and multidisciplinary, and to set priorities *with* local people rathen than imposing ideas from above.

- *A rapid growth in knowledge about and interest in restoration within protected area networks:* as more protected areas are set up in degraded areas, the need for recreating habitat is being increasingly recognized.

SOME UNRESOLVED QUESTIONS

Approaches to protected areas are still developing very quickly. Many questions remain unresolved. A few of the key issues to be addressed are outlined below.

Systems

- *How broadly should the concept of protected areas be interpreted?* This question ranges from a discussion on the boundaries between IUCN categories (and multiple classification), to questions of access and the issue of total protection versus multiple use.

- *How much is enough?* This question includes, in particular, a debate on the role of 'targets' for particular areas to be placed under protection.

Assessment

- *How effective are protected areas (both in location and management)?* This includes the question of *quality* versus *quantity* of protection. Measurement of management effectiveness, and options for some form of 'certification' of protected areas, are issues of increasing concern.

Planning

- *Do different biomes require different approaches to protected area planning?* In particular, the challenges facing marine protected areas are often very different from those in forests or freshwaters, and the extent to which experience can be transferred from one biome to another still remains unclear.
- *How much adaptability is needed in designing a protected area network?* Protected areas need to be secure in order to provide real security for the values they have been established to protect. But, at the same time, future climate and other environmental change may alter the location of habitats and this has yet to be seriously addressed by protected area planners.
- *To what extent should the location and management of protected areas be biologically or socially driven?* In places where high biodiversity areas coincide with high human use, or high political tension, trade-offs between human and other biological values are inevitable. There is still a great deal to be learned about how these tensions can be minimized.

NEW OPPORTUNITIES FOR PROTECTED AREAS

Every ten years the World Commission on Protected Areas convenes the World Congress on National Parks and Protected Areas. The next congress is due to be held in Africa in 2002. The main objective of this, the fifth World Congress, will be to set a 100-year vision for protected areas and to address the basic question: 'where are protected areas going in the 21st century?' We hope that this book has provided some initial ideas to feed this vision. The congress will aim to ensure that protected areas regain their place as the integral tool to achieve biodiversity conservation and ecologically sustainable development at national levels. This can be achieved through implementing the Caracas Action Plan, which was adopted at the Fourth World Parks Congress. The four objects outlined in the plan are to:

- integrate protected areas into a larger planning framework;
- expand support for protected areas;
- strengthen the capacity to manage protected areas; and
- expand international cooperation in the finance, development and management of protected areas.

The aim of this book has been to highlight the many exciting new ideas and directions which are available to all those involved in protected areas and to create new Partnerships for Protection.

CATEGORIES OF PROTECTED AREAS

Adrian Phillips and Jeremy Harrison

Each of the categories defined by IUCN (1994) are listed below with key guidance on the application of the category, and some examples of sites which demonstrate each category's principal aspects.

CATEGORY I

Category I is used when the purpose of management is strict protection for areas of land or sea for science or wilderness preservation. The areas are expected to include some outstanding ecosystems or species of flora and fauna. They may be important centres of biological diversity or habitats of endangered species or have special geological or physiographic features. The category is subdivided:

- Category Ia is for *science*, implying research as well as protection, and the educational function of the site is to serve as a resource for studying and obtaining scientific knowledge.
- Category Ib is for *wilderness protection*, which imports a different aim. Wilderness – if there is any left on Earth – is wild land, bearing only a slight human footprint. It does not have to support outstanding ecosystems or species of particular conservation importance, and protecting wilderness may mean avoiding intrusive science or educational use.

Therefore, Category I may contain a rather wide spectrum of sites, managed for different purposes. What unites them is that human uses, other than for science and education which maintain the features for which the areas were designated, are virtually excluded, although the management guidelines of IUCN do recognize that there may be a limited, low-impact use made of some wilderness areas by indigenous peoples.

CATEGORY IA – PROTECTED AREAS MANAGED MAINLY FOR SCIENCE

Guidance for selection

- The area should be large enough to ensure the integrity of its ecosystems and to accomplish the management objectives for which it is protected.
- The area should be significantly free of direct human intervention and capable of so remaining.
- The conservation of the area's biodiversity should be achieved through protection and not require substantial active management or habitat manipulation. Sites might vary widely in size.

Examples

The Sunderbans National Park in India is strictly protected from human access, acting as the core zone of the Sunderbans Tiger Reserve. Most Indian national parks are oriented towards tourism, but the Sunderbans National Park and the Nanda Devi National Park in the Himalayas, have strict protection. The Svalbard Islands in the far north of Norway also demonstrate this category; the islands are large and significantly free of human intervention, and have scientific research as the main use of the reserved areas.

CATEGORY IB – PROTECTED AREAS MANAGED MAINLY FOR WILDERNESS PROTECTION

Guidance for selection

- The area should posses high natural quality, be governed primarily by the forces of nature, with human disturbance substantially absent, and be likely to continue to display these attributes if managed as proposed.
- The area should contain significant ecological, geological, physiogeographic or other features of scientific, educational, scenic or historic value.
- The area should offer outstanding opportunities for solitude, to be enjoyed, once the area has been reached, by simple, quiet, non-polluting and non-intrusive means of travel.
- The area should be of sufficient size to make practical such preservation and use.

Examples

The wilderness concept originated in the US and is demonstrated by the chain of wilderness areas located along the Rocky Mountains. These have high natural quality, are significantly free of human intervention and offer outstanding opportunities for solitude.

CATEGORY II – PROTECTED AREAS MANAGED MAINLY FOR ECOSYSTEM PROTECTION AND RECREATION

The genesis of Category II is also to be found in the US, traceable to the Yellowstone National Park, established in 1872. Since then, the term national park has been used in different senses around the world. In 1969 the IUCN General Assembly, meeting in New Delhi, urged governments to reserve the term for relatively large areas where:

- There were ecosystems little altered by human use.
- There were species or landscape features of special scientific, educational or recreational value, and landscapes of great natural beauty.
- The exploitation or occupation of the areas had been prevented or elimi-nated by action of the highest competent authority in the country.
- There was effective action to safeguard its special features.
- Visitors were permitted 'for inspirational, educative, cultural and recre-ative purposes'.

Few would try to uphold such a definition today. In particular, since 1969 there has been a major reassessment of the wisdom of seeking to exclude people entirely from Category II parks. Of course, large-scale occupation and resource use has no place in such areas, but there are, in fact, few parts of the world that have not been shaped by interaction with humanity to some extent. Moreover, the presence of indigenous peoples, living sustainably in a tradi-tional mode, may be a positive asset to conservation. It has also become evident that excluding people creates antagonism and can undermine conser-vation effort, especially if it stimulates poaching of wildlife or repeated efforts to encroach. This has been a problem, for example, in the Ngorongoro caldera and Serengeti plains in East Africa. Moreover, the unreal nature of policies designed to exclude all people from park areas was illustrated in recent research, which revealed that 86 per cent of national parks in South America had a resident human population (Amend and Amend, 1992).

For these reasons, the definition of a Category II national park was adjusted by the Fourth World Congress on National Parks and Protected Areas, held in Caracas, Venezuela, in February 1992 (McNeely, 1993). A Category II area is now intended:

> ...to protect the ecological integrity of one or more ecosystems for future generations, to exclude exploitation or occupation inimical to the purposes of designation of the area *and to provide a foundation for spiritual, scientific, recreational and visitor opportunities, all of which must be environmentally compatible (authors' emphasis).*

In other words, occupation is now acceptable so long as it is compatible with the objectives of the park's management – as it is, for example, where indige-nous peoples occupy forest areas in Venezuela or Brazil.

Guidance for selection

- The area should contain a representative sample of major natural regions, features or scenery, where plant and animal species, habitats and geomorphological sites are of special spiritual, scientific, educational, recreational and tourist significance.
- The area should be large enough to contain one or more entire ecosystem not materially altered by current human occupation or exploitation.

Examples

National parks are now found in all parts of the world. For example, the Nahuel Huapi National Park in Argentina was declared for the protection of large ecosystems and the provision of recreation. The Grand Canyon National Park in the US was established for the same reasons, as well as for the spectacular canyon scenery. Rocky Mountain National Park, also in the US, is large enough to protect natural regions and is oriented towards visitor use, with an extensive system of roads and interpretation.

The provision of public access for recreation may be a key factor in the development of Category II areas. For example, Canada's Banff and Waterton Lakes national parks were established during the last century to attract customers to the newly installed railways. Wildlife viewing may also be a key aspect of national parks, as in the Nairobi and Zambezi national parks in Africa, Corbett National Park in India, and Royal Chitwan National Park in Nepal. In Chitwan National Park villagers are also allowed seasonal access to retrieve thatching grass. Such access is in keeping with the provision for subsistence resource use where it does not affect the primary management objective for a Category II area.

CATEGORY III – PROTECTED AREAS MANAGED MAINLY FOR CONSERVATION OF SPECIFIC NATURAL FEATURES

Category III is for natural monuments – that is, areas with specific natural or natural and cultural features of outstanding value. The category includes physical features – like a great waterfall or a rock formation. A natural monument is often too small to merit designation as a Category II area (because it is focused on a feature rather than an ecosystem), but may need safeguarding in the same way – for example, by preserving a forest or wetland setting, and preventing intrusive hydropower or other developments.

Guidance for selection

- The area should contain one or more features of outstanding significance (appropriate natural features include waterfalls, caves, craters, fossil beds, sand dunes and marine features, along with unique or representative fauna and flora; associated cultural features might include cave dwellings,

cliff-top forts, archaeological sites, or natural sites which have heritage significance to indigenous peoples).
- The area should be large enough to protect the integrity of the feature and its immediately related surroundings.

Examples

The Victoria Falls national monument in Zimbabwe protects the area of the falls, and is clearly a national monument. There might be concern, however, that the area protected is not, and could not be, adequate to ensure the integrity of the feature – probably a common problem with water features. Dinosaur National Monument in the US protects a palaeontological site, and interpretation for public education is provided as well as protection of the fossil record of the site.

CATEGORY IV – PROTECTED AREAS MANAGED MAINLY FOR CONSERVATION THROUGH MANAGEMENT INTERVENTION

Category IV recognizes that many areas are specifically managed for the purposes of wildlife conservation. And, unlike Category I areas, this may require active management, including the maintenance of traditional farming practices, such as mowing of reeds or sedge fens, heath burning and regulated grazing. In areas where the landscape has been greatly altered by human action over the centuries and wildlife has adapted to human pressures, as is the case in much of Europe, it is the category into which most nature reserves fall.

Guidance for selection

- The area should play an important role in the protection of nature and the survival of species.
- The area should be one where the protection of habitat is essential to the well-being of nationally or locally important fauna, or to resident or migratory fauna.
- Conservation of these habitats and species should depend upon active intervention by the management authority, if necessary through habitat manipulation.
- The size of the area should depend upon the habitat requirements of the species to be protected and may range from relatively small to very extensive.

Examples

Examples of areas in Category IV include Luneburger Heide Nature Reserve in Germany, which was established to protect heathlands which are currently maintained through grazing, and the North Norfolk coast bird reserves in England, which contain human-made ponds in salt marsh areas, specifically designed to attract birds. Outside Europe, the Halegi Lake in Pakistan is an example of a Category IV site, where the waterways are cleared for waterfowl.

Category V – Protected areas managed mainly for landscape/seascape conservation and recreation

Category V is the variety commonest in Europe (where it accounts for two-thirds of the land within protected areas) and other long-settled and densely populated regions. A Category V protected area is: 'an area of land, with coast and sea as appropriate, where the interaction of people and nature over time has produced an area of distinct character'.

The point about its protection is that it restricts the range of activities that may be carried out there, but also recognizes that the continuance of human management and use is often essential to the conservation of the features for which the area was designated.

Guidance for selection

- The area should possess a landscape and/or coastal and island seascape of high scenic quality, with diverse associated habitats, flora and fauna, along with manifestations of unique or traditional land-use patterns and social organizations, as evidenced by human settlements and local customs, livelihoods and beliefs.
- The area should provide opportunities for public enjoyment through recreation and tourism within its normal life style and economic activities.

Examples

Examples include the landscapes of the Pembroke Coast and North York Moors national parks of the UK, areas with high scenic quality, diverse habitats, and traditional land-use patterns.

Category VI – Protected areas managed mainly for sustainable use of natural ecosystems

Finally, Category VI includes areas where ecosystems or species of wildlife are conserved in order that they may be used sustainably. In many such areas, control has been devolved to local communities; these areas should qualify in this category and may, indeed, be better safeguarded by this process so long as economic benefits flow to the local community so that they have an interest in maintaining the site.

Guidance for selection

- The area should be at least two-thirds in a natural condition, although it may also contain limited areas of modified ecosystems; large commercial plantations would not be appropriate for inclusion.
- The area should be large enough to absorb sustainable resource uses without detriment to its overall long-term natural values.

Examples

As this is a 'new' category, examples selected are indicative of the potential of the category – it is possible that some of these sites may not, on reflection, be classified as Category VI. Likewise, it is also important to stress that Category VI areas must fall within the definition of a protected area.

Examples might include the safari areas surrounding the Mana Pools National Park in Zimbabwe, which are managed to maintain the natural habitat and allow sustainable hunting, or the areas outside the core zones of the Sunderbans National Park in India, where quota-operated fishing allows sustained use by locals. Watershed areas such as the Matopos Hills in Zimbabwe, the Flathead National Forest in the US, and Sinharaja in Sri Lanka may also qualify in the future if management is adapted to maximize the conservation potential of these areas. Other examples include mangrove areas along the Central American coast and the Caribbean such as the Kuûa Yala area in Panama, where Kuûa Indians approached the government to establish a protected area which allows local traditional use but excludes outside exploitation. All these are large, substantially natural areas which can absorb sustainable resource use.

REFERENCES

Amend, S and Amend, T (ed) (1992) ¿Espacios sin Habitantes? Parques Nacionales de America del Sur, Editorial Nueve Sociedad, IUCN – the World Conservation Union, Caracas

IUCN (1994) Guidelines for Protected Area Management Categories, CNPPA with the assistance of WCMC, IUCN, Gland and Cambridge

McNeely, J A (1993) 'A Summary Report of the Fourth World Congress on National Parks and Protected Areas', in McNeely, J A (ed) Parks for Life. Report of the Fourth World Congress on National Parks and Protected Areas, Gland, IUCN – the World Conservation Union, Gland

APPENDIX 2
WCMC Protected Areas Data Base

The World Conservation Monitoring Centre (WCMC) protected areas data base holds the following forms of information:

- text describing the protected areas system of each country, together with definitions of protected area designations based on the national legislation;
- budget and staffing levels of some protected area agencies;
- records of individual protected areas (and other designated areas); and
- text describing some individual protected areas (information sheets).

The WCMC protected areas data base is linked to the WCMC Biodiversity Map Library, a geographic information system (GIS) which includes a spatial layer for protected areas based on their digitized boundaries. This layer is incomplete due to the lack of available maps of national protected area systems showing the boundaries of individual protected areas. In such cases, it is possible to map the approximate location of protected areas if geographical coordinates are known.

United Nations List of Protected Areas

The UN *list of protected areas* provides a single definitive list of the world's protected areas, classified according to IUCN's system of management categories. Many countries attach considerable political importance to the UN list. Thus, it is in the interests of the respective management agencies to ensure that their protected areas are listed. In order to be listed, a site must meet IUCN's definition of a protected area. For practical reasons alone, only those protected areas larger than 1000 hectares are actually listed, as well as offshore or oceanic islands of at least 100 hectares where the entire island is protected.

APPENDIX 3

IMPERATIVES FOR PROTECTED AREAS

Below is the statement adopted by the IUCN/World Commission on Protected Areas (WCPA) Symposium on Protected Areas in the 21st Century: From Islands to Networks, 24 to 29 November 1997 in Albany, Western Australia:

> *A new alliance is sought among all stakeholders at the local, national, regional and global levels to pool their talents and capacities to realize a new vision for protected areas in the bioregional context.*

Protected areas are special places on land and sea which are managed for conservation purposes. The current global system comprises some 30,000 sites, covering about 13.2 million square kilometres (larger than India and China combined). They are of various kinds. Many have cultural components and support appropriate sustainable use. They play a key role in conserving natural ecosystems and, where managed effectively, contribute substantially to sustainable development.

Protected areas provide options for humanity in a rapidly changing world. They ensure the continuing flow of ecosystems services, including maintaining water and air quality and the availability of soil nutrients, and act as carbon sinks. They provide economic benefits and contribute to spiritual, mental and physical well-being. Protected areas also help to fulfil our ethical responsibility to respect nature.

This role is challenged by various factors such as macroeconomic policies, rural poverty, land tenure issues, habitat fragmentation, climate change, inadequate funding, inadequate management capacity and lack of political commitment. There is insufficient appreciation of the linkage between protected areas and the realization of human expectations.

If in the 21st century, humanity is to have:

- security for habitats and species;
- an environment which is productive, healthy and harmonious;
- restored productivity of soils, forests, water, air and seas; and
- sustainable use of the biosphere and natural resources for food security;

then we call on all members of the protected areas community to:

Rethink: we need to place protected areas in their broader context so as to demonstrate that they contribute to local economies and human welfare as integral components of a productive and secure environment. We need to ensure that our sites are selected and managed primarily for their biodiversity and ecosystem service values, while considering the livelihoods of the communities dependent upon them. We need to develop ways of working with land managers in areas surrounding protected areas. Our communication strategies need to convey this new image.

Reorient: we need to expand on our principal role of establishing and managing protected areas by emphasizing the bioregional approach and working for the compatible management of surrounding areas. We need to connect them with nature-friendly corridors to form a conservation matrix using a range of protected area types.

Respond: we need to respond to global concerns about issues such as biodiversity, climate change, desertification, international waters and peace, and emphasize the role protected areas can play in addressing these.

Reach out: we need to establish partnerships and encourage cooperation with neighbours and other stakeholders, promote stewardship, enhance the use of relevant information, and strengthen the policies and other instruments which support protected areas objectives.

Our efforts need to be complemented by those of other public and private organizations and interests that have the required skills and capabilities, and especially by those with authority and responsibility over natural resources as to realize this vision.

Acronyms and Abbreviations

ANCA	Australian Nature Conservation Authority
APECO	Peruvian Association for the Conservation of Nature
AUSAID	Australian Agency for International Development
AUSLIG	Australian Surveying and Land Information Group
C	Celsius
CAMPFIRE	Zimbabwe Communal Areas Management Programme for Indigenous Resources
CAPC	Conservation Projects Support Committees, Peru
CAR	Central African Republic
CBD	Convention on Biological Diversity
CDC	Peruvian Conservation Data Centre
CEO	chief executive officer
CITES	Convention on International Trade in Endangered Species
CM	collaborative management
CNPPA	Commission on Natural Parks and Protected Areas
CNPT	National Centre for the Sustained Development of Traditional Communities, Brazil
CNS	National Council of Rubber Tappers, Brazil
CODEFF	National Committee for the Defence of Fauna and Flora, Chile
COP	Conference of the Parties
CPR	common property regime
DEM	Digital Elevation Model
DGAPFS	General Directorate of Protected Areas and Wild Fauna, Peru
DGFF	General Directorate of Forestry and Fauna, Peru
EC	European Community
ECONET	ecological network
EEA	European Environment Agency
EEZ	exclusive economic zone
EU	European Union
EMBRAPA	Brazilian Farm Research Enterprise
FAO	Food and Agriculture Organization
FONANPE	National Protected Area Fund, Peru
FPCN	Peruvian Foundation for the Conservation of Nature
FRI	Forest Resource Inventory
FSC	Forest Stewardship Council
GEF	Global Environmental Facility
GIS	geographic information system
GPS	global positioning system
ha	hectare

IBAMA	Brazilian Institute for the Environment and Natural Resources
IBRA	Interim Biogeographic Regionalization for Australia
ICDP	integrated conservation and development project
IFOAM	International Federation of Organic Agriculture Movements
IIED	International Institute for Environment and Development
INCRA	Instituto Nacional de Colonização e Reforma Agrária, Brazil
INRENA	National Institute of Natural Resources, Peru
IPA	indigenous protected area
ISO	International Organization of Standards
IUCN	International Union for Conservation of Nature and Natural Resources (The World Conservation Union)
IWC	International Whaling Commission
km	kilometre
LAC	limits of acceptable change
MHT	major habitat type
MINEF	Cameroon Ministry of the Environment and Forests
MPA	marine protected area
NFZ	no-fishing zone
NGO	non-governmental organization
NTFP	non-timber forest products
ODA	Overseas Development Administration
ODI	Overseas Development Institute
PA	protected area
PAE	extractivist settlement policy, Brazil
PARC	Protected Area Resource Centre
PRA	participatory rural appraisal
RAPP	network of protected areas, Chile
RPPN	Private Reserves of Natural Heritage, Brazil
RRNSC	Civil Society Natural Reserves Network, Colombia
SCA	Svenska Cellulosa AB, Sweden
SDR	sustainable development reserve
SINANPE	Peruvian National System of Protected Areas
SINUC	National System of Conservation Units, Peru
SLC	Soil Landscapes of Canada
SNASPE	National Protected Areas System, Chile
SPREP	South Pacific Regional Environmental Programme
STINAPA	Netherlands Antilles National Park Foundation
TIDE	Toledo Institute for Development and Environment
TIPNIS	Subcentral Indigenous Territory and National Park Isiboro Secure, Bolivia
TNC	the Nature Conservancy
TURFS	territorial use rights in fisheries
UNCED	United Nations Conference on Environment and Development
UNCLOS	United Nations Convention on the Law of the Sea
UNEP	United Nations Environment Programme
UNESCO	United Nations Educational, Scientific and Cultural Organization
US-AID	US Agency for International Development
USP	University of São Paulo
WCC	World Conservation Congress
WCPA	World Commission on Protected Areas

WCMC	World Conservation Monitoring Centre
WRI	World Resources Institute
WWF	World Wide Fund For Nature (UK)
	World Wildlife Fund (US and Canada)

INDEX